ECONOMY, CRIME AND WRONG
IN A NEOLIBERAL ERA

EASA Series

Published in association with the European Association of Social Anthropologists (EASA)

Series Editor: Aleksandar Bošković, University of Belgrade

Social anthropology in Europe is growing, and the variety of work being done is expanding. This series is intended to present the best of the work produced by members of the EASA, both in monographs and in edited collections. The studies in this series describe societies, processes and institutions around the world, and are intended for both scholarly and student readership.

For a full volume listing, please see back matter.

ECONOMY, CRIME AND WRONG IN A NEOLIBERAL ERA

Edited by
James G. Carrier

berghahn
NEW YORK · OXFORD
www.berghahnbooks.com

First published in 2018 by
Berghahn Books
www.berghahnbooks.com

© 2018 James G. Carrier

Library of Congress Cataloging-in-Publication Data
A C.I.P. cataloging record is available from the Library of Congress

British Library Cataloguing in Publication Data
A catalogue record for this book is available from the British Library

ISBN 978-1-78920-044-7 hardback
ISBN 978-1-78920-045-4 ebook

Contents

Preface

For years I have been a regular reader of the business pages of *The New York Times* and *The Guardian*. Around 2008 the stories that I was reading began to change; it was the beginning of the bursting of the credit bubble that had been so important in the American and British economies that I know best, as well as elsewhere.

The change in what I was reading was as much a matter of tone as anything else. Previously, those pages mostly contained fairly straightforward reporting of business and economic news – what was going up or down, who was buying or selling what, what the Federal Reserve Board or the Bank of England had to say. The emerging new tone took business much less at face value, and increasingly resembled something else I had been reading regularly for years, namely the Slicker column in *Private Eye*, which was probably the best source of investigative business journalism I knew of, though Gretchen Morgenson's work in *The New York Times* came close. That tone was adversarial; not because it reflected an opposition to business per se, but because it was based on an awareness that sharp dealing, sleight of hand and trickery can exist in even the most staid corporate offices.

As my invocation of the bursting of the credit bubble suggests, much of this new tone appeared in reporting about financial institutions, some of which I invoke in the Introduction to this volume. However, and perhaps because of what was revealed about institutions in one commercial sector, more and more such stories appeared about more and more firms in more and more commercial sectors, some of which I also invoke in the Introduction. Commercial wrongdoing, it seemed, had become news.

How might I make sense of this change? One obvious answer was that it was something relatively new. It was a consequence of the extension and deregulation of markets that was part of economic reform that began around 1980, commonly seen as a sign of the growing influence of neoliberalism and commonly associated with the slogan Greed is Good. The desire to investigate the adequacy of that answer led me to undertake the reading and thinking that, in turn, led to this volume. As is clear in the pages that follow, that obvious answer is valid only in part.

A volume on economic wrongdoing could take many forms. Given that most of the people who have contributed to this one are anthropologists, it could easily have been dominated by a concern with individuals, their perceptions and agency, especially marginal individuals. Instead, and reflecting my argument that such a concern is an inadequate basis for the discipline (see Carrier 2016), I sought contributors who would take a more systemic approach. With such an approach, we can begin to make sense of the forces, structures and relationships at work in economy and society that make it more or less likely that some people will do things that others would call economic wrongdoing, and also make it more or less likely that they would see the things that they do as unexceptional and even laudable. And that is the foundation for understanding the sorts of activities that are the concern of this volume.

A Note on Usage

As material is quoted accurately, no emphasis has been added or removed unless otherwise noted.

James G. Carrier

References

Carrier, James G. (ed.). 2016. *After the Crisis: Anthropological Thought, Neoliberalism and the Aftermath*. London: Routledge.

Introduction

Economy, Crime and Wrong in a Neoliberal Era

James G. Carrier

Economic wrongdoing has been around since people have possessed objects worth having and fellows who want them. Also, and for just about as long, some people have complained about these activities and those who undertake them, and other people have defended them. Although the activities, complaints and defences are ancient, they are likely to take on different forms and raise different questions in different eras.

The era at issue in this volume is commonly called the era of neo-liberalism, which began in earnest in the 1970s. Our purpose is to consider whether there are forms of economic activity, expectations of the normal and the abnormal, and understandings of the proper and the improper that are distinctive to that era. Such consideration is appropriate because neoliberalism includes a set of assertions about what proper economic behaviour is, part of a view of what economic activity and economy more generally are and ought to be. Inevitably, then, the rise of neoliberalism has made the question of proper and improper economic activity more visible than usual.

Neoliberalism is a slippery concept, even suspect (e.g. Venkatesan 2015). So, it is useful to explain what it is taken to mean in this volume. It means three things: a historical period, an economics and a political economy. The historical period began roughly in the middle of the 1970s and, in many places, continues in the present, though the rise of more clearly nationalist parties in several countries indicates that it may be weakening. The middle of the 1970s also is when economics and political economy changed in important ways. In economics, the older, more systemic Keynesian macroeconomics declined in the face of a rising individualist and market-oriented microeconomics that commonly is called neoclassical economics.

Around that time the political economy began to change as well. For one thing, this period saw the increasing salience of the economy, illustrated by the increasing concern in public debate about the economic effects of government policy (e.g. MacLennan 1997). As well, there was an increasing value placed on market activity, commercial success and the innovation that was taken to produce it. Running a profitable business, and the individuals who were seen to be the basis of such businesses, were increasingly celebrated, while the older social and systemic concerns that were part of Keynesianism and its associated Fordism became less appealing. This strengthened the political position of businesses, especially as they sought to encourage government policies that would benefit them. Also, the individualist orientation meant that people were increasingly encouraged to see themselves as entrepreneurs, self-reliant gain-seeking market actors, exemplified by seeing themselves as a brand (Williams 2018). Conversely, those who were not successful were increasingly seen to bear the blame for their lack of success. As this suggests, whatever the origins of neoliberalism as a form of economics and of government policy, it has had the tendency to become an aspect of class politics.

The economics and political economy emerged gradually, drawing on a variety of sources (Cockett 1994; Mirowski and Plehwe 2009; Turner 2011) and, to a degree, coexisted with other forms, though this is more so for the political economy than for the economics. As well, they changed over the past forty years or so, occasionally in ways that can be called neoliberal primarily because they were the result of neoliberal policies and programmes. Equally, as the prefix in 'neoliberal' and 'neoclassical' attests, they were not wholly new. They had existed previously in recognizable forms in different places and at different times.

I said that this volume is concerned not just with economic acts, relationships and systems, but also with how people think about them and how those thoughts may find expression and perhaps moral and legal authority. In view of those concerns, I will use 'deviance' to denote unusual economic activity. Deviance does not, then, speak of wrong (or right), but only of whether people conform to or deviate from expectations that may or may not have moral or legal force. The term also suggests that expectations are situated, that different people in different situations are likely to have different expectations about how others will behave, and perhaps how they should behave. This means that what is deviant or even wrong for some people can be unexceptional or even laudable for others.

In this Introduction I lay out an analytical framework that allows us to consider the possible relationship between neoliberal political economy, particular sorts of economic activity, the perception of that activity as conventional or deviant and the evaluation of it as proper or improper. I present it in fairly broad terms, leaving more detailed considerations of that relationship to the chapters that follow. After indicating some of the economic activity that has become visible since the financial crisis of 2007 and that many consider deviant and improper, I use the conventional, popular account of such activity as wrongdoing as a foil to lay out how we might fruitfully approach it. Then, before describing the chapters in this volume, I consider some of the aspects of neoliberal thought and practice that might lead to changes in people's economic practices and to changing ethical perceptions of economic right and wrong.

Disruption and Crisis

The neoliberal stress on the free market implies the assumption that when people are free to transact as they choose, they will be fairly straightforward and predictable in their economic activities, if only because it is in their own interest to be so. This assumption was undercut by the disruption of the financial sector that began in 2007 and that turned into the Great Recession. As I shall explain, that disruption revealed significant deviant economic activity in the sector that many thought was wrong, though as I also shall explain, such activity turned out to be widespread elsewhere as well. I start with a description of that financial disruption and what it, and the ensuing economic crisis, showed us about one sort of economic activity in a neoliberal era.

A key event in that disruption was the decline of the investment bank Lehman Brothers, which began in August 2007 and ended when the firm filed for bankruptcy in September 2008. At that point, many financial firms lost confidence in each other and became reluctant to trade. The financial system began to freeze up, and financial disruption started to become economic crisis. Describing the nature of some of Lehman Brothers' operations helps us to understand their collapse and the sort of practices that the crisis revealed (a detailed description of Lehman Brothers and its fate is in McDonald 2016).

Many of Lehman Brothers' assets were collateralized debt obligations (CDOs). These are the final stage in a process that begins when a person goes to a bank or other financial firm and takes out a mortgage in order to buy property, commonly a house. Since the 1980s, firms that issued mortgages have increasingly been likely to sell them on to other firms, which would then receive the mortgage payments (see Mizruchi 2010: 107–9). Some firms bought lots of mortgages in order to put them together in pools or bundles and sell these to investors. These pools or bundles were the basis of CDOs, and their price depended on the income that they were expected to produce as the people who took out the mortgages repaid them. People's ability to repay looked increasingly dubious as 2006 turned into 2007, which meant that the market price of CDOs fell. Because Lehman Brothers held lots of CDOs, that fall in market price meant that the value of Lehman Brothers' assets also fell; other financial firms began to doubt the bank's ability to meet its obligations and thus became reluctant to trade with the company.

The crisis has been linked to a variety of causes (some are described in Bandelj et al. 2016: 448–49; a more expansive view of its cause is in Appadurai 2015). At first, though, many people thought that it was simply the result of a bubble in the American housing market. A decade earlier, during a different bubble, Alan Greenspan (1996), then the head of the Federal Reserve in the United States, had warned us about them and their associated deviance, 'irrational exuberance'. Many held that the housing bubble demonstrated such exuberance, as people bought more expensive property and took out larger loans than they would normally, confident that the rising price of their property would cover their debt. When the bubble burst and prices began to return to conventional levels, many of those borrowers were in trouble and could not make their mortgage payments.

A bubble in the housing market is not a good thing, but economic history is littered with bubbles of different sorts. So, at least in general terms, this one looked like something that people understand and know how to deal with, and that heads of the Federal Reserve know enough to warn us against. However, as the analyses and newspaper stories increasingly showed, more had been going on than just irrational exuberance. There were widespread practices in the housing market that many people would see as deviant and wrong (Silver-Greenberg and Eavis 2014; for an extended description, see Lewis 2011).

We were told that companies had issued mortgages intended to become part of CDOs without doing what most people would probably think normal and prudent, verifying the income of the people applying for the loans (i.e. do they look like they can repay?) and the value of the houses that they want to buy (i.e. what asset can we seize if they do not?). The fact that many people thought that this was wrong is indicated by a common name for those mortgages, 'liar loans'. Countrywide Financial was the firm best known for making them (Morgenson 2012a, 2016b; Protess, Silver-Greenberg and Corkery 2014), but hardly the only one (Corkery and Protess 2014; Morgenson 2014a). We were told of CDOs being produced that were so complicated that the firms selling them could not understand them (Antilla 2013). We were told that the agencies that assessed the credit-worthiness of those CDOs were paid by the companies that issued them and, often enough, seemed happy to do what those companies wanted – make assumptions that would justify rating them highly (Krugman 2010; Lattman 2013; Norris 2014b). At the other end of the mortgage process, we were told that some of the firms going to court seeking to evict people for failure to make their mortgage payments presented documents that had forged signatures or that were simply lies (Henning 2010; Associated Press 2012). We were told that other firms tried to evict people who had been making their payments, who had no mortgage with the evicting firm or even who had no mortgage at all (Morgenson 2012b).

It might be, of course, that this sort of thing was only a side effect of the bubble. After all, in extraordinary circumstances people might behave in extraordinary ways and things might get out of hand. If this were the case, then we could remain confident that in more ordinary circumstances, and in sectors of the economy not affected by the bubble, the firms that people dealt with were basically trustworthy and predictable. Things might not, in other words, have been so unsettling as they seemed.

However, such a comforting conclusion seemed unjustified. Newspaper stories told us of things like a large American company that makes artificial hip joints and kept selling them long after they knew that they were faulty and could harm those who got them (Meier 2013), like another large American company that sold automobiles that they knew were dangerously faulty and denied that they knew (Ruiz and Ivory 2014; Stout et al. 2014); and, of course, of how Volkswagen developed cars to cheat on emissions tests (Ewing 2018; Parloff 2018). They told us of a large drug company that paid doctors to prescribe their products (Reuters 2013) and of drug manufacturers who published the results of trials that showed that their products were safe and effective, while suppressing the results of trials that showed that they were no more effective than a sugar pill, and a lot less safe (Sample 2013). We also learned of drug companies that simply bought the rights to existing drugs and raised the price: Turing bought the rights to a drug called Daraprim and raised the price from $13.50 a tablet to $750; Rodelis bought Cycloserine and raised the price for thirty pills from $500 to $10,800 (Pollack 2015; see also Editorial Board 2015). They told us as well of a British security firm that charged the government for work that they did not do, to the tune of £24 million (Travis 2013), and of an American firm that did the same, to the tune of 650,000 security checks billed to the government but not completed (Apuzzo 2014). And, of course, they told us of the electronics firm Apple, renowned for its innovations that boost the company's profits. We learned that one of these innovations was the creation of a set of company divisions that are effectively nowhere, located in no tax or regulatory jurisdiction whatsoever (Schwartz and Duhigg 2013; Drucker and Bowers 2017).

It appears, then, that economic behaviour that many would see as deviant and as imprudent or wrong was not restricted to the housing sector, the financial sector or sectors that were experiencing a bubble. Rather, it was widespread. Moreover, it was different from what many had thought to be the most important form of economic deviance seen as wrongdoing, bribery and corruption (Wedel 2012: 460). That usually was seen as 'a Third World disorder; a pathology endemic to "backward" developing countries' (Shore 2004: 36; see also Shore and Haller 2005: 3–6) and to the former Second World of post-socialist countries (see Wedel 2012: 454–55). Those people appeared to think that firms and individuals in the First World were fundamentally trustworthy and predictable. Like the advocates of market deregulation, it seems that they need to think again.

Accounting for Wrong

There has long been a common view that accounts for wrongful economic activity: it is the violation of a clear rule by a person who is deficient in some way. A story about a famous American, Willie Sutton, illustrates this. He robbed banks, which violates a clear rule. Also, he was deficient. It is said that when asked why he robbed banks, he replied 'Because that's where the money is', an answer that shows an inadequate moral compass.

This view has much to recommend it. For one thing, its individualist orientation reflects common Western, and especially

Anglo-American, thought. As well, there really are people who are immoral, heedless individuals. For instance, there is Nick Leeson, whose deceptions about his failed transactions with other people's money brought down the British merchant bank Barings in the 1990s (Stevenson 1995). Less spectacular is Mathew Martoma, a hedge-fund manager convicted in 2014 of insider trading. While at Harvard Law School he altered his university transcript to raise his grades and used the faked transcript when he applied for a clerkship with a federal judge (Stevenson and Goldstein 2014). Also, this view of wrongdoing is reassuring because it points to ways that we can deal with the problem. We can raise our children to have an adequate moral compass (Sullivan 2014) and set up programmes to encourage people to think and act in terms of it (Tugend 2014).

Whatever its attractions, this common view is limited, even misleading, as the events of the years following the crisis have made apparent. I turn now to those limitations, by considering the ideas that there are defective individuals and that they break clear rules.

Defective Individuals

> Poirot nodded his head slowly. 'Love of excitement,' he murmured, 'and a little kink in the brain somewhere.'
> —Agatha Christie, *The Mystery of the Blue Train* (1928)

Individuals break rules, but this common view ignores the fact that individuals live in a social world, one that can make it more or less likely that they will act in ways that others see as wrong. This is so in two ways. Firstly, people's values and orientations are shaped by their socialization and situation, what they see around them. As a result, they will vary in what they value and what they see as reasonable behaviour. Secondly, social situations will vary in the degree to which they make it likely that people will act reasonably and properly. So, in some situations it will be relatively easy to do so, while in others it will require substantial strength of will. Because people vary in their strength of will, we can expect more unreasonable and improper behaviour in the latter situations than in the former.

This indicates that we need a view of economic deviance and wrong that does not focus purely on individuals. In addition, we need a view that attends to the social world in which people live. We have long had the intellectual tools that allow such a view. For instance, over a century ago Durkheim ([1897] 1951) considered another deviant act that most people thought was wrong, *Suicide*. He argued that different sorts of social situations make it more or less likely that people will take their own lives, and he described the relationship between the likelihood that people will kill themselves and the sorts of situations in which they live.

Some eighty years ago, Robert Merton (1938) took Durkheim's approach and applied it to economic deviance. He focused on two American values. One is oriented towards the self: it is good to make money through one's efforts. The other is oriented towards the group: it is good to play by society's rules in those efforts. Merton's more self-oriented and more group-oriented values resemble what Maurice Bloch and Jonathan Parry (1989) described, half a century later, as the values of two different spheres of economic circulation, one oriented towards the satisfaction of short-term, personal desires and the other oriented towards the maintenance of long-term, social values and institutions.

Merton said that there are social situations in which the relative strength of these values differs from what is conventional. This could be because of changes that affect large parts of society, or because what people in some groups experience means that these two values have strengths that are different from what is found more generally. This differing will be reflected in the way that people think about and act in their economic lives, and this can affect the likelihood that they will act in ways that would be considered deviant by more conventional people in more conventional times. To speak of likelihoods and influences is to say that not everyone reacts to the same circumstances in the same way. However, as the following paragraphs make clear, it is to say that the chances of people reacting in certain sorts of ways will increase, and the contributors to this volume consider in more detail the processes that lead to those reactions.

The tools that Durkheim and Merton offer allow us to make sense of what happened in the housing bubble. It was an extraordinary time when, it seems, lots of people in the housing sector told themselves that the old rules no longer made sense. After all, people were doing extraordinary things that made them richer and richer and everything was turning out well. This is illustrated by praise of Angelo Mozilo, the head of Countrywide Financial, before the bubble burst (Bailey 2005). He was portrayed as deviant, an innovator in the housing market, one who was laudable, not imprudent or a wrongdoer. Because no one was hurt, the old rules seemed increasingly irrelevant, no longer guides to sensible behaviour but barriers to innovation and progress. Of course this view, that this time is different, is not restricted to the financial sector. When the Provincial Transport Minister of Quebec said that the firm Uber needed to conform to government regulations if it wanted its licence extended for twelve months, Jean-Nicolas Guillemette, the general manager of Uber Montreal, complained that '[t]he minister is attempting to impose old rules on a new model' (Austin 2017)

This being a social phenomenon, it had social corollaries. One was pressure to go along with what was happening. Something Charles O. Prince said shortly before the bubble burst expressed this. He was the head of Citigroup, which owned Citibank, which was deeply involved in CDOs and other financial instruments that were looking increasingly doubtful. He said, 'As long as the music is playing, you've got to get up and dance' (Dealbook 2007). Put differently, if your reputation and income arise from making deals, you are prone to keep making them as long as there are any left on offer and any competitors willing to make them if you do not. Not everyone responded to this situation in the same way, but enough did so that trouble followed.

Another social corollary is the spread of beliefs that justify those activities and the rewards that they bring, and many in the financial sector came to believe that they were extraordinarily intelligent (Ho 2009: Chaps 1, 2). So, they were better able than ordinary people to see when the rules should be applied, when they need not and when they should not; as Karen Ho (2012: 423) summarized it, 'bankers are allowed to break the rules because they're superior beings'. In words used to describe an earlier elite group, they saw themselves as *The Best and the Brightest* (Halberstam 1972). As well, those people could argue, and believe, that their activities were more important and beneficial than ordinary people understood. The financial sector is, they said, the mechanism for the rational allocation of capital and the benefits that it would bring. So, they were, in the somewhat ironic words of Lloyd Blankfein, the head of Goldman Sachs, 'doing God's work' (Dealbook 2009).

These sorts of self-conceptions and justifications combined to make it more likely that people would, like those working at Countrywide, engage in deviant economic activities that would, in more normal times, look like wrongdoing (for what Countrywide was doing at the time, see Morgenson 2014b).

What Merton had to say suggests that we can approach economic deviance in terms of what will be important in the paragraphs that follow, the relationship between the economic and social realms of life. The economic realm resembles what, I said, Bloch and Parry

(1989) called the realm of short-term economic circulation, for it is commonly seen as one of self-serving individualism and impersonal calculation. The social realm resembles Bloch and Parry's realm of long-term circulation, for it is commonly seen as one of social relationships and obligations. Also, Merton reminds us that people's moral values and their relationship to economic activity vary over time and across groups, as I have described for the financial sector before the collapse.

E.P. Thompson (1971) addressed these moral values in what he wrote of English peasants in the second half of the eighteenth century. As he described it, they had expectations about proper effort and behaviour and a reasonable livelihood, manifest in a set of understandings of how people ought to act in their economic relationships. This is the sort of thing that Julia Elyachar (2005: 65) calls a market of practice or habitus, which appears also to motivate some of the far Right in the United States (Hochschild 2016). In terms of common values, if not of invariable practice, this meant that people who behaved in the appropriate way in their dealings with others in those relationships (playing by the rules) could expect to receive what they needed for that reasonable livelihood (acquiring wealth).

Changes that were taking place in England in the period that concerned Thompson meant that those expectations were decreasingly met and those understandings were increasingly challenged. Playing by the rules was less and less likely to lead to the wealth needed for a reasonable livelihood. In parallel with this, institutions and practices that encouraged playing by rules of the sort that those peasants recognized were falling into disuse (Carrier 1995: 64–66). Important among these was the open market, visible to all and regulated to assure fairly honest dealings: 'With its cross, weighing beams, booths, pillories, and tumbrils, the market made of its publicity the basis of its claim to utility, security, and equity' (Agnew 1986: 31). Moreover, the adherents of the emerging economic order denied the morality of the old. As Adam Smith argued at the time, we do not get our supper because we behave properly in our relationships with our fellows. Rather, we eat only because we can give them what they want: 'Give me that which I want, and you shall have this which you want' (Smith [1776] 1976: 18).

Not surprisingly, Thompson's peasantry saw those who adopted the new forms of economic practice as seeking to impose an impersonal economic logic of price and profit on areas where it should not be important, people's relationships with their fellows and the livelihood that these generated. The peasants and their allies tried to impose their own rough justice to force those people to behave properly. From the perspective of the adherents of the emerging liberal economic order, on the other hand, those peasants and their allies were wrong. What the crowd saw as rough justice, those adherents saw as crime that denied people's right to enter into legal contracts, and they demanded that the crowd be stopped (these sorts of assumptions and tensions, in a very different time and place, are described in Elyachar 2005).

Thompson's work illustrates how there can be changes in the ways that different sets of people see the relationship between the economic acquiring of wealth and the social rules and expectations to which people should conform, and that these can affect the likelihood that people will engage in activities that other people see as wrong. It also illustrates how these changes affect what it is that people see as deviant, wrong or even criminal.

I have considered one element of the common understanding of economic wrong, that it is done by defective individuals. I turn now to the second element, that it involves the violation of clear rules.

Clear Rules

> I don't think he really meant to be dishonest. He just thought it was the sort of thing people did in the City.
> —*Agatha Christie, Death on the Nile (1937)*

There are such rules. Willie Sutton robbed banks and lived in a place where that is a crime; Nick Leeson lied about his speculative trades and lived in a place where that is a crime; Matthew Martoma forged his transcript and studied at a university where that is an offence. Sutton and Leeson went to prison and Martoma was thrown out of law school. Those people, like the people who are likely to read these words, live under the rule of law, the impersonal, routinized law of the statute book, the public prosecutor and the independent judiciary.

However, just as seeing economic wrongdoing only as a fact about individuals simplifies a more complex world, so too does the assumption that it always involves breaking clear rules. The sheer complexity of regulatory systems has implications for the idea of clear rules (McBarnet 2010; Williams 2012: Chap. 3), but here I want to illustrate this simplification in terms of what I call legal procedure and legal substance. I begin with procedure, common legal practices.

Under the rule of law, a person is innocent until shown to be guilty and an act is innocent until shown to be wrong in an administrative, civil or criminal proceeding. However, both the US Attorney General and the future head of the UK's Prudential Regulation Authority said that some financial institutions are too big to prosecute (Scott 2012; Sorkin 2013; see also Eisinger 2014a; for a later example, see Morgenson 2016a). They are so important for their countries' economies that prosecution, let alone successful prosecution, would cause real trouble. Not subject to legal proceedings, these institutions and their acts are innocent. So, in principle the rule may be clear, but its application may not, which means that our assessment of rights and wrongs may be difficult.

Bringing a case to court is not, of course, the only way that governments can apply the rules to identify wrongful acts and, perhaps, deter people from doing them. There are, for instance, non-prosecution and deferred-prosecution agreements (see Giudice 2011). These became common in the US government's dealings with companies after the prosecution of the accounting firm Arthur Andersen, following the collapse of Enron in 2001. That prosecution led in turn to the collapse of Arthur Andersen, and the Department of Justice decided that this harmed so many innocent bystanders that such prosecution should be avoided if possible (Guidice 2011: 358; see also Henning 2014). Appropriately, in the twelve years between 1992 and 2004, three years after the collapse of Enron, the Department of Justice reached 26 such agreements with corporations, while in the next eight years they reached 242 (Eisinger 2014b).

Non-prosecution and deferred-prosecution agreements differ in some ways, but their pertinent features are similar. In them, a government body, perhaps the Securities and Exchange Commission of the United States (the SEC) has evidence that some entity over which it has jurisdiction, perhaps Citibank, has broken the rules. The SEC then approaches Citibank and comes to an agreement. The bank hands over money and is not prosecuted, and according to the type of agreement it may or may not admit to any wrong act. Further, it agrees not to commit such an act for a specified number of years and institutes procedures to help to assure that it does not do so.

No one is prosecuted, and often a company can say that they were never shown to have broken the law. However, these agreements follow the rule of law, for they are produced under legal regulation (see Giudice 2011: 362–65). As well, a type of act is identified as wrong and the errant entity will, doubtless, be encouraged not to commit such acts in the future, especially as they know that the government has an eye on them. Not perfect, but people would probably agree that in a world of complex regulation and large, diverse organizations, this is fairly close.

However, in practice things may not be this simple. In 2011, Jed Rakoff was a judge of the US District Court for the Southern District of New York, which includes Wall Street. He asked the SEC whether it had ever brought legal proceedings against companies that had violated their agreements. The SEC told the judge that they had brought none in the previous ten years (for this and the remainder of this paragraph, see Wyatt 2011). The judge put his question to the SEC because they had presented to him for approval an agreement with Citibank in which the company agreed to pay $285 million in settlement for defrauding customers in violation of a part of a US securities law and promised never to violate it again. It seems, though, that Citibank or one of its divisions had reached an agreement concerning a previous violation of that same part of the law in 2010, as they had in 2006, 2005 and 2000. Rather than starting legal proceedings for breaking those previous agreements, the SEC negotiated new ones. Citibank, moreover, was not alone in this. In the fifteen years before 2011, it seems that there were fifty-one instances of fraud, involving nineteen financial firms, in which an agreement was violated, apparently without resulting in legal proceedings (see also Eisinger 2014a).

It appears, moreover, that even if those companies had been brought to court and convicted of a crime, their suffering would be limited. For example, firms convicted of violating a law covering stock underwriting are barred from underwriting for some years in the future, unless, of course, an exemption were granted by the pertinent government body. Such exemptions are granted routinely, it seems (Norris 2014a), as happened with Credit Suisse when it pleaded guilty in the United States to conspiring to aid tax evasion and was fined $2.6 billion (Protess and Silver-Greenberg 2014).

What I have said of procedure, of common legal practice, illustrates the simplification that comes with the idea that economic wrongdoing involves breaking clear rules: even if rules are clear in theory, they may not be so in practice. Considering the substance of law and regulation raises further questions about that idea. I turn to that now, starting with the question of whether legal penalties make a difference. If they do not, if the penalty for stealing a car were only to remain silent for 60 seconds, we would find it hard to argue that the rules are clear in a substantial rather than trivial way.

One could argue that Citibank agreeing to pay all that money suggests that there are clear rules. However, it may only show that

Citibank officers decided that it was cheaper and less disruptive to pay $285 million than it would be to fight the SEC. Further, $285 million is not that much money; Citibank are so large that it is not clear that it is really a penalty. In 2011, the year that they paid that money, Citibank's parent company, Citigroup, declared net revenues of $78.4 billion, net income of $11.1 billion and total assets of $1,874 billion (Citigroup 2012). So, the payment was 0.36 per cent of their net revenues, 2.57 per cent of their net income and 0.02 per cent of their total assets. For them, in other words, it was not a lot of money. Even a lot more money need not, in fact, be a lot of money. In 2013, JPMorgan Chase reached settlements with the US Department of Justice in which they paid about $20 billion, and they incurred legal costs of roughly the same amount. The result was to reduce their profit for that year to only $18 billion (Treanor 2014).

Nick Leeson and Willie Sutton served time. It is unlikely that Citibank's $285 million or JPMorgan Chase's $20 billion is a penalty in the way that time in jail is, and this, I have argued, is a matter of substance rather than a matter of procedure. So is the orientation of the law, and Anatole France pointed to that a century ago, when he said: 'In its majestic equality, the law forbids rich and poor alike to sleep under bridges, beg in the streets and steal loaves of bread'.

In representative systems, politics is the way that people are all supposed to try to shape law and policies in ways that they think best. People, groups and institutions vary in what they think best and, of course, in how well they are equipped to do the shaping (see Confessore 2014; Lipton 2014a; Bohlen 2017). Those variations were manifest late in the nineteenth century in the US Senate, which was composed of 'Standard Oil Senators, sugar trust Senators, iron and steel Senators and railroad Senators, men known for their business affiliations rather than for their states' (Morison, Commager and Leuchtenburg 1980: 152). Equally, however, this came to be seen as a scandal, a violation of the common belief that Senators are supposed to represent the interests of the states that elect them, not of the firms that bribe them. The result was a wave of reform that included the Sherman Antitrust Act of 1890, intended to break up the large trusts that controlled industries and bought Senators, and the Seventeenth Amendment to the US Constitution, ratified in 1913, which made Senators be elected by the voters in a state, thought to be harder to buy than the state legislatures that had elected them previously.

It seems, however, that standards have been changing, apparently reflecting changing ideas about what is proper and improper economic behaviour and about the proper relationship between economic activity and rationality on the one hand, and government on the other. In the United States in the 1970s, this took the form of policies that required the federal government to become more businesslike. In practice, this meant cost–benefit analysis, the use of economic criteria to assess the desirability of different sorts of regulation, criteria that turned out to be largely commercial (MacLennan 1997). In Britain in the 1980s, this took the form of encouraging government ministries to seek advice from senior officials in large companies (for the more recent form of this, see Ball and Taylor 2013). In both countries, those decades saw efforts to curtail the power of labour unions, effectively assertions that, at least in the labour market, certain sorts of activities that had been proper were now seen as improper. As the 1980s turned into the 1990s this took the form of decreasing government regulation and oversight of many sorts of commercial activity, such as the deregulation of banking and stock exchanges in the United States and the United Kingdom. This was justified in part by the old argument that profitable companies are good for the country and in part by a new neoliberal argument, the rational market hypothesis, the idea that the market knows best (Fox 2009).

The result was that governments and large companies became harder to distinguish. One sign of this, foreshadowed by the introduction of cost–benefit analysis, was the demand that regulators be more sensitive to the needs of the industries that they regulated, which in practice meant approving their proposals quickly (Gabriel 2014; Wines 2014). Another sign was that governments were paying more and more private companies to carry out more and more state activities, which gave people in those companies greater access to and influence over government (Wedel 2012: 477–78). Yet another sign of this became especially visible at about the time governments began to sell off many public services, a common aspect of neoliberal reform. That is what is called 'the revolving door', whereby governments recruit senior executives from corporations and industry groups, and corporations and industry groups recruit senior government officials (for the US automobile industry, see Jensen and Wald 2014; for the UK government, see Brooks and Hughes 2016). This easily turned into what Janine Wedel (2012: 478–85) calls a shadow state, peopled by those who are ambiguously in government and the private sector, policy organizations and perhaps universities (e.g. Lipton 2014b; Lipton, Confessore and Williams 2016; McIntire 2016). The next step in the process was government departments hiring corporate and industry representatives to shape policy (Press Association 2014). The conclusion, at least thus far, is that corporations and their representatives occasionally draw up legislation, rather than leaving the job to legislators (Lipton and Protess 2013).

These changes in the relationship of government and powerful businesses suggest that commercial interests are able to shape the production and application of the rules in ways that allow them to carry out activities with little or no legal censure, even though many people would think that many of those activities are wrong (for reactions to the activities of financial firms, see Schmidt and Wyatt 2012; Kopicki 2013).

What I have said in the preceding paragraphs points to an apparent gap between common views of right and wrong on the one hand, and legality on the other. What Steven Sampson (2005: 105) said about efforts to eliminate corruption expresses concern for this gap: those efforts seek 'to restore standards that were lost, the standards of morality and responsibility which connote what we call "community"'. These resemble the sort of standards invoked by Mark Carney, Governor of the Bank of England. He said that, for the economic system to survive, 'individuals and their firms must have a sense of their responsibilities for the broader system' (Carney 2014). They resemble as well what Christine Lagarde (2014), the head of the International Monetary Fund, said needs to be protected and strengthened, 'the principles of solidarity and reciprocity that bind societies together'. What Sampson, Carney and Lagarde say about morality and community points to another aspect of neoliberal assumptions about the relationship between economy and society.

Economy and Society

Once again, Durkheim's work is helpful, in this case *The Division of Labour in Society* ([1893] 1984). If Sampson is right that people are unhappy about a loss of morality and standards, what Durkheim wrote means that they should not be surprised by it. He argued that when a society's division of labour increases, its legal system becomes oriented less towards expressing and enforcing a moral order, and more towards commercial interest, especially loss arising from the failure of people to fulfil their contracts.

The neoliberal ascendancy has been accompanied by arguments about the nature of economy, and indeed about the nature of people generally. These illustrate the declining concern with morality and community that Sampson decried and that Durkheim described. These arguments began to assume their modern form in the work of Adam Smith, and developed into the neoclassical economics that is their current form and that is an important part of the intellectual armoury of neoliberalism.

Smith had much to say about economy and society, but the adherents of neoliberalism generally draw on a position he laid out in *The Wealth of Nations*. There, espousing a view that was fairly common in the Scottish Enlightenment (Silver 1990), he asserted the separation of the economic and the social realms, each governed by its own logic. He did this when he said that the basis of people's economic activity did not lie in their relationships with others, whether it be their place in the social system and the rights and duties that went with it or it be the social relations in which they existed and the expectations that were part of them. Instead, he rooted it in their personal desires. As he put it, '[i]t is not from the benevolence of the butcher, the brewer, or the baker, that we expect our dinner, but from their regard to their own interest', so that, in our dealings with our fellows, '[w]e address ourselves, not to their humanity, but to their self-love, and never talk to them of our own necessities, but of their advantages' (Smith [1776] 1976: 18).

Smith, then, treats people as isolated individuals to be approached only in terms of their individual desires, in terms of 'that which I want'. Marx and Engels ([1848] 1948: 11) put the same point differently, when they said that the rise of capitalism 'has drowned the most heavenly ecstasies of religious fervour, of chivalrous enthusiasm, of philistine sentimentalism, in the icy water of egotistical calculation'. Thompson's crowd rejected this individualism and the way that the emerging economic order severed the link between fairness and wealth, between their fulfilling their obligations to their fellows and their securing of a livelihood, between society and economy. But, as Thompson observed, the crowd lost the war.

Intellectually, the thread of individualistic economism in Smith's work became powerful in the nineteenth century, especially with the marginalist revolution in its closing decades. Politically, as Polanyi ([1944] 1957) describes, it became powerful in the legislation of laissez-faire capitalism in Britain and elsewhere. It began to weaken around 1900 in Britain and the United States, as reform movements sought to ameliorate the ill effects of its rigorous application (Turner 2011: 35–43), and it was weakened still further by Western responses to the Great Depression and the needs of the Second World War. However, in the 1950s it slowly began to re-emerge (Cockett 1994;

Mirowski and Plehwe 2009), with 'neoclassical economics' being the common name for its re-emergence as economic thought, and 'neo-liberalism' the common name for its re-emergence as political programme. Their common prefix indicates that they are not the same as their forerunners. However, they share the old individualism, apparent in their focus on the moment of choice, when individuals satisfy their desires through their market transactions.

This individualism is not unprincipled. Initially it was presented in terms of one moral argument and subsequently it was defended in terms of others. The initial argument is that of douce commerce. As Albert Hirschman (1977) describes it, this held that the pursuit of economic interest has a pacifying and civilizing effect, especially in comparison with the passion and faction that, its advocates said, disfigured the old system. The arguments that were subsequently used to defend it assert that the free market that is taken to be the home of individual economic actors allows people to make their own decisions about what will make their lives better, rather than having those decisions made for them by others, and that the drive for increased profit that is part of such markets encourages the efficient use of resources, which means that people will generally have lives that are more comfortable (Fourcade and Healy 2007: 286–91).

However, these later arguments say nothing about who shares in the well-being that the free market is supposed to produce, why and to what end, a silence that points to a noteworthy feature of this justification. Unlike the crowd, which was concerned with people's relationships and the livelihoods associated with them, the argument about the rational allocation of capital speaks impersonally of the system as a whole. This concern with an impersonal system and the principles that govern it are not new, for it is linked to the rise of economics as a specialist body of thought in the first half of the nineteenth century in Britain, as it aspired to become a science (Poovey 2008: Chap. 4).

This concern with system rather than people and their livelihoods is expressed in Schumpeter's idea of creative destruction, that progress involves not just bringing in the new, but also throwing out the old. Put more simply, you can't make an omelette without breaking eggs. A man who works in investment banking put it this way: 'Inefficiency requires reallocation of assets. That includes people, and that can be painful, especially if you are one of the people. But society as a whole is still, without question, better off' (quoted in Ho 2012: 420). One could say that this is only an ideological justification for the accumulation of wealth, revealed to be hollow by the generous way that governments treated banks during the financial crisis. However, it remains a coherent and elaborated moral position that commands substantial public assent, including by those on the lower rungs of the economic ladder.

While the good it asserts may be collective, this approach continues Smith's assertion that the motor of economic activity and the ultimate cause of the wealth of nations is individual desire, which those who use the approach do not investigate but take as given, as something that people bring into the market from outside. These desires came to be called 'preferences' or 'utility functions', and they are seen to arise from outside the scope of neoclassical models and pro-market politics, and are to be neither explained nor evaluated. All that is important about those desires is that people satisfy them, and that they do so as cheaply as possible, for that allows them to satisfy more with the resources that they have at hand. Such satisfaction is good and, for the more thoroughgoing, it is the only good. From such a perspective, which includes only individual desire and the impersonal system, the effect of that satisfaction on others slips from view (e.g. Carrier 1997: 52).

With its attention restricted to people's desires and the market in which they are satisfied, this approach contains a view of economy and society that is reflected in many aspects of neoliberal thought. That view is radical, for it denies that there is any significant relationship between the two, or even that there is such a thing as society. All that exists is individuals and their desires, and all of economy is only the sum of their efforts to satisfy those desires in market transactions with other individuals. In contrast to Thompson's English crowd, neoliberal thought generally recognizes no social relationships and their rules or expectations, whether social or legal, or at least none beyond the sanctity of the private property that people transact in the market and the contracts people voluntarily sign. Also in contrast to that crowd, it entails no assumption that conformity to the rules gives anyone a claim to anything at all, much less a reasonable livelihood. Better said, the treatment of the financial sector during the financial crisis showed such claims are only for those who are seen to be important for that abstract, impersonal system, even if they have not conformed to the rules.

In this construction of the world there is, then, a system that must be protected, but other than that there is no basis of judgement beyond individuals, with their desires and resources (Carrier 2012: 117–18). That is, there are no criteria of good or bad, harm or benefit, beyond individual desire and, in moments of crisis, the imperatives of the system through which people satisfy that desire. There are no people who deserve one's consideration. There is no entity to whom one is beholden, beyond one's individual desire to be so. There is no group on which one can make claims. As André Iteanu puts it, in his description of the French intellectual heirs of the Events of 1968, 'nothing stands outside the self' (Iteanu 2005). For the more radical, even the claims of the system are denied, so that this world of neoliberalism is one of anarcho-capitalism (see Brown 1997), in which individuals are subject only to their own will and constrained only by their ability to persuade others to deal with them.

I said at the outset that in different eras we can expect that there will be different sorts of economic expectation, different sorts of economic deviance and different evaluations of it. In the case of this volume, the pertinent era is neoliberal, and in this Introduction I have begun the task that the contributors to this volume pursue: indicating how neoliberalism might be associated with distinctive economic expectations and practices, and distinctive evaluations of them.

I approached that task by considering two features of what I said was a common understanding of economic wrong: it is done by individuals who are defective and who violate clear rules. Through that consideration I suggested that we might expect to see different sorts of economic activity in different parts of society as neoliberal ideas are realized. These differences reflect the ways that neoliberal practice can have different sorts of effects on the lives of different sorts of people located in different places in the political-economic order.

To close this introductory framing of a consideration of economic deviance in a neoliberal era, I want to stress a point made already. Because this volume is about that era, I have attended especially to the ways that the spread of neoliberal thought and programmes might affect the likelihood of deviant economic activity of one sort or another. My concern, then, has been to suggest that we consider whether certain sorts of deviance become more likely with that spread, and whether they are lauded as innovation or condemned as wrongdoing. Equally, in other sorts of social, cultural and economic contexts it might be that other sorts of deviant economic activity would be more likely. So, for instance, in the context of Soviet economic planning and policy, there emerged a system of favours among enterprise managers that was part of what was known more generally as *blat* (Ledeneva 1998). Equally, American city government in the later part of the nineteenth century was characterized by the deviance associated with political machines. In these, people violated fairly common rules and expectations in order to achieve valued ends. Thus, in different contexts in different eras we can expect that there will be differences in the nature of pertinent expectations, rules and ends, in the sorts of people who are likely to espouse or oppose them, in the nature of the violation of them and in the evaluation of those violations.

About the Chapters

I have suggested that we approach economic activities in terms of their conformity to or deviation from people's expectations, and that we approach deviant activities and the evaluation of them in terms of their context. A corollary is that the assessment of those acts is a debate, however implicit, about what kinds of economic activities are right and what kinds are wrong. The neoliberal era encourages this sort of approach, for it emerged in a cloud of assertions about how people should think and act in their economic lives. Reflecting the neoclassical economics that underlay neoliberalism, those assertions pointed to the need to free economic activity from collective constraint.

Neoliberal policies were commonly wrapped in the rhetoric of consumer choice and lower prices, suggesting that the economic activity to be freed was individual transactions: getting our supper from the butcher, the brewer and the baker. However, neoliberal policies seem mostly to have liberated firms, presented as the drivers of growth in modern market economies. Appropriately, then, the first pair of chapters in this volume is concerned with firms, their practices and how these relate to economic deviance.

The first of these chapters is by Kalman Applbaum, 'Marketing Clientelism vs Corruption: Pharmaceutical Off-label Promotion on Trial', which describes some of the common commercial practices among drug manufacturers. They produce things that are presented as being based on scientific research and tested, regulated and assured by government agencies and that often are crucial to our physical survival. They are, then, things that people are likely to see as part of a realm that should be fairly free of the calculating self-interest that many associate with the economic realm. But as Applbaum shows, those manufacturers commonly act in ways that violate those expectations and hence are seen by many as both deviant and wrong.

This chapter shows, however, that such activities are so widespread among pharmaceutical firms that they are taken for granted in the sector, an unavoidable part of commercial practice and, indeed, of much medical research and education. Being routine, they are routinized, in the sense that they are part of the institutions of American medical practice and research, as well as of the sector itself. In illustrating this, Applbaum reinforces two of the points made in this Introduction. One is that particular circumstances and social settings can make it likely that people will act in ways that appear deviant, even criminal, to those in more ordinary circumstances. The other is that people in those particular circumstances and settings may well see their activities as normal, even proper, rather than deviant, much less criminal. In other words, if we are to take seriously the people Applbaum describes, the two different views of those activities amount to a debate about how those in the sector and in the field of medicine associated with it ought to carry out their activities.

I said that Applbaum's chapter shows how activities that many would consider dubious can become routine in a sector of the economy. The next chapter is Emil A. Røyrvik's 'The Measure of Sociality: Quantification, Control and Economic Deviance', and it looks at one sort of institutional practice in other sectors of the economy. That is the use of measures of performance, whether of individuals or of organizations. These are pertinent because the rise of neoliberalism is associated with the growing use of measures, rankings and the like (Shore and Wright 1999; Strathern 2000).

Measurement may seem fairly neutral, in the way that a stopwatch is neutral with regard to how long it takes to run 100 metres. However, in some circumstances the measuring can shape the thing being measured, and do so in ways that can increase the likelihood that people will act in ways that seem self-serving and wrong. One simple example of this is management by objectives, common in many enterprises. In this, employees are measured in terms of what are called key performance indicators and are assessed according to whether they meet the targets set for them. This encourages employees to focus on the targets, even if doing so means that they have to ignore what they see as other important parts of their work. A subtler example concerns a Norwegian aluminium company, Hydro. They used a measuring device to assess whether proposed projects should be approved. As Røyrvik explains, the result was to orient Hydro towards projects located in places with cheap energy. Those places tended to be developing countries with weak regulations and greater opportunities for activities that were suspect and, as it turned out, that violated the company's code of conduct, even if they were not illegal.

Røyrvik argues that this assessment and auditing shares with neo-classical economics the intent to reduce complex situations to a single measure. In the case of auditing, that might be an employee's score or the expected profit of a project; in the case of neoclassical economics, that might be the decision to buy the apples on offer at the price asked. Many forms of this sort of assessment share something else with neoclassical economics, the assumption that the pertinent public is rational and, in the aggregate, sees things clearly. In the case of economics, the pertinent public for the evaluation of the worth of, say, frozen pork bellies or bonds issued by Singapore is people in the market. In the case of assessments of employees, the pertinent public for the evaluation of, say, a store clerk often is the colleagues, customers and superiors whose opinions are solicited in ways that Røyrvik describes. In such situations, doing one's job well tends to be reduced to pleasing others. This in turn reduces the likelihood that people will maintain their own judgement of how to do their job and of whether what they are asked to do is right or wrong. In this way, it becomes relatively easy for economic activity that people may see as wrong to become routine.

In different ways, Applbaum and Røyrvik describe how economic practices that many people would consider dubious can become routine. Applbaum does so in terms of the organization and practices of an industry. Røyrvik does so in terms of the ways that employees and projects are seen and evaluated. Both show how at least some organizations and practices reflect a view of economic life in which activities that many might think are dubious are unexceptionable. This routinization does not affect only the firms and commercial practices that Applbaum and Rørvik describe. As well, it affects society at large. The next two chapters point to some of those effects, both for the governments and for the citizens. They also point to some of the ways that economic right and wrong are defined and redefined, and the ways that those definitions are embodied, debated and evaded.

In 'Under Pressure: Financial Supervision in the post-2008 European Union', Daniel Seabra Lopes describes financial reform in Europe following the financial crisis. Lopes observes that financial reform is becoming a permanent condition, as new problems have emerged with depressing regularity since 2007. However, as his chapter describes, regulators are pessimistic about their task. That is, they are aware of the intricacies of the system that they seek to regulate, the limitations on their knowledge, authority and foresight, the dilemmas that they face – all compounded by their awareness of the ingenuity of people in the financial sector. There is, then, something like a loss of faith among those who oversee that sector and seek to make it fairly safe for the rest of us. In spite of this, Lopes notes, regulators have continued to produce new regulations, new sets of rules that seem to differentiate proper and improper economic activity. It is as if regulators do not know what else to do.

This loss of faith is matched by a growing scepticism among significant numbers of the public. Most obviously, the failure of regulators to foresee, much less prevent, the financial crisis and its economic aftermath raises questions about the justification for regulation, though such questions ignore the influence of neoclassical economics and neoliberal political economy on regulators themselves, such as Alan Greenspan (Mallaby 2016). Public scepticism emerged as well with regard to the way that governments sought to contain the effects of that crisis. To recall a distinction made earlier, many saw governments as more concerned with supporting banks in order to protect the system than they were with assuring people's economic well-being. To compound this, the rise of neoliberalism entailed, as I noted at the outset, a growing rejection of the old Keynesianism, which saw economy as political. This meant, among other things, a growing tendency to see economic policy as a matter for the professionals, especially central bankers, and hence as free of ordinary political debate. This was fine only so long as people thought that things were going well. Taken together, Lopes argues, these factors have challenged the authority of regulators and their reforms, both among regulators themselves and among important sectors of the public.

While Lopes describes a loss of faith among regulators, the next chapter looks at loss of a different sort. In 'Of Taxation, Instability, Fraud and Calculation', Thomas Cantens notes a contradiction in neoliberal practice and rhetoric. On the one hand, neoliberalism speaks of freeing the individual from government control, and on the other hand, governments need money if they are to implement neoliberal reforms, and so need to raise taxes. Governments have always needed to justify taxation. In the eighteenth century and into the nineteenth, that justification related taxation to political and moral values about things like the polity, progress and the good life. In the twentieth century this was replaced by a different justification, one that presents taxation as based on the accurate measurement of income and wealth, and on the rule-bound calculation of tax based on that measurement.

In the face of that calculation, individuals and companies who want to pay little tax seek ways to make their income and wealth less visible. This can be done through simple fraud. Also, however, it can be done in ways that arguably are legal, for instance through structures of ownership and control so complex as to be incomprehensible and through what is called aggressive interpretations of the tax code (see, e.g., McBarnet 2006). The result is that tax authorities often find themselves unable to produce an accurate measurement of people's and companies' income and wealth, and are reduced to the negotiation of tax liabilities.

This may amount to no more than authorities recognizing the limitations that they confront and doing the best that they can in the circumstances, just as during the financial crisis the US government seemed to recognize the limitations that they confronted and decided that the best that they could do in the circumstances was to prop up banks that had been reckless. As the financial crisis showed, the activities of those individual banks had systemic consequences. The activities of the individuals and firms that tax authorities confront have systemic consequences as well, although of a different sort. Cantens suggests that an important one is making it apparent that tax regimes are not always based on accurate measurement and dispassionate calculation, which in turn threatens one of the pillars on which the justification of taxation rests.

The chapters by Applbaum and Røyrvik showed how practices in particular firms and sectors can increase the chance that those involved would see as normal activities that many would think deviant and even wrong. The chapters by Lopes and Cantens extend this point, by showing how such practices can have broader effects. Important among them is challenging the legitimacy of government efforts to oversee and shape economic activity. If that challenge is effective, then there seems little room for the idea of economic wrongdoing, at least in any practical sense and at least among large and influential companies and industries. As well, their chapters strengthen a point made by Applbaum and Røyrvik, that important aspects of the economy have become increasingly disembedded, decreasingly oriented towards and constrained by the societies in which they operate. This disembedding is in accord with the individualistic rhetoric of neoliberalism and the neoclassical economics on which it draws. However, as the chapters by Lopes and Cantens also show, it does not justify the argument that Friedrich von Hayek (1974) made in his Nobel prize address, which echoed an argument he had made thirty years previously (von Hayek 1944), that the economy is so complex that governments and the rest of us should give up trying to understand it, much less influence it. Rather, they show how the rise of neoliberalism has been important for promoting that failure to govern, and for the unfortunate consequences that result.

The next two chapters address a question that is only implicit in the chapters described thus far; that is, how changing circumstances affect both the sort of economic activities that people undertake and the ways that those activities are perceived and evaluated. The circumstance that is of concern in the first of these chapters is US federal and state policies concerning marijuana since the 1970s. That chapter is Michael Polson's 'Marketing Marijuana: Prohibition, Medicalization and the Commodity'.

While marijuana was long illegal in the United States, control efforts intensified under the War on Drugs, launched in 1971 by President Nixon and continuing through much of the rise of neoliberalism. At the time, marijuana was overwhelmingly imported from Central and South America, and US government policy sought to stop that by destroying plantations, increasing security at the border and raising the penalties for selling it. One consequence was that the price of marijuana rose sharply. This occurred in conjunction with another change in many people's lives, increasing poverty in rural areas brought about by the reorganization of American agriculture and the decline in extractive industries, especially logging and mining. For those confronted with that poverty, the rising price of marijuana made it an attractive cash crop, and the economic wrongdoing that was domestic production began to expand.

The War on Drugs met with increasing disaffection in different parts of the country, most notably in California. In 1996 voters there approved Proposition 215, which allowed the possession and the non-profit production and distribution of marijuana for specific medical purposes. This affected the way that marijuana was treated, especially once marijuana dispensaries appeared. These began to turn it from a forbidden substance into a medicine, and turn its production and distribution from criminal activity into something like normal commerce. Since then, and in spite of occasional objections from the federal government, marijuana has increasingly been treated as a normal commodity, not restricted to medical use. And thus, as Polson observes, the nature of economic deviance associated with it has also changed. Now, it is the merchant who is secretive, the crop that is not certified, the accounts that are not audited that are deviant.

Using changing government policies regarding marijuana, Polson shows how changing circumstances affect not just the likelihood that people will engage in economic activities that are seen as wrong, but also affect what counts as wrong. The second chapter of this pair also looks at the importance of changing circumstances, and again those circumstances are government policies. That chapter is Sabina Stan's 'Neoliberal Citizenship and the Politics of Corruption: Redefining Informal Exchange in Romanian Healthcare'.

In Romanian healthcare, informal exchange has long been normal rather than deviant, whether exchange between patients and medical staff or among medical staff. As Stan describes, the nature and understanding of that exchange has varied with changes in government policy and in the state of the Romanian economy, and she begins with the old Communist era. Then, healthcare was a part of socialist citizenship, officially the right of everyone. However, the medical services did not have the resources to meet the demand, so that healthcare became part of the economy of favours, a system of circulation that existed alongside the formal economy. That meant that people were prone to secure medical care by giving gifts to medical staff, just as staff secured supplies by giving gifts to those who had what they needed. Such gifts were illegal, but censure tended to be restricted to those who took more from their workplaces to use as gifts than was thought to be their due or who sought gifts larger than were thought appropriate.

Since the end of the Communist system, Romania has experienced a variety of economic circumstances and government policies. The overall effect, however, was the decline of industry and agriculture and the rise of low-skill, low-wage work, and government policies that increasingly restricted the power of organized labour and citizens' rights to services, including healthcare. Throughout these changes, informal exchange persisted in the medical services, and Stan describes how the changes affected what sort of things were given in exchange, the effect of these exchanges on the ability of different sets of people to secure healthcare, and how people thought about those exchanges.

The result of these changes, at least so far, has been a country with a government seeking to impose what Stan calls entrepreneurial citizenship. Increasingly, parts of the healthcare system are being run by private companies, funding of healthcare increasingly comes from an insurance system rather than the state, and people are increasingly expected to pay part of the costs themselves. While some in Romania welcome this change, many criticize the reforms and the system that produced it. The government responded to these criticisms by blaming the system of informal transfers, which it now called corruption, and launched an anti-corruption campaign that, some observers noted, seemed aimed primarily at those in the healthcare system who publicly criticized government policy.

Stan's chapter, like Polson's, looks at historical changes in people's circumstances and how they relate to the likelihood that people will engage in dubious economic activities, the effects of those activities and how people think about them. The War on Drugs made growing marijuana more profitable and increasing poverty in parts of rural America made the need for that profit more insistent. Socialist citizenship made healthcare a right while inadequate funding meant that the sector could not meet the demand, making informal transfers a reasonable way for people to get what they needed and to which they were entitled. Changing public attitudes and the decline of the War on Drugs resulted in increasing tolerance of marijuana and changing attitudes about which activities associated with it are wrong and which are not. The end of Communist government in Romania and the increasing orientation towards a market economy resulted in decreasing public money for healthcare and a government decreasingly tolerant of criticisms of its policies, which led in turn to a changing set of views about what is reasonable give-and-take in the face of an inadequate system and what is wrong and ought to be made criminal.

Stan's chapter illustrates how government policies undertaken in the name of the free market can produce victims, and how official concern about economic wrongdoing can serve, in an older terminology, to blame the victim. The final two chapters in this collection look at a different situation in which policies and practices lead to economic activity that is defined as wrong and the victims are blamed. That activity is illegal migration to the United States from Mexico and Central America.

The first of these chapters is Kathy Powell's 'Neoliberalism, Violent Crime and the Moral Economy of Migrants'. She says that circumstances in countries in Central America have long induced people there to migrate: scarce and uncertain work, low wages and public insecurity, manifest especially in the form of violent government policing and criminal gangs. The spread of neoliberal reforms has made these circumstances more insistent through their principled indifference to people's economic condition and claims upon government, and through their support of market economy and the powerful interests that dominate it. Moreover, as she notes, neoliberal impatience with rules and advocacy of entrepreneurial self-reliance tends to blur the distinction between legal and illegal market activities. All of these factors facilitate the growth of criminal organizations, which in turn make migration even more attractive to poor people.

With their condition at home increasingly fragile, many of the poor in Central America see migration north as the best, and perhaps the only, realistic way for them to pursue a moral life, through work that will allow them to support themselves and their families. For those who lack a visa, their hoped-for entry into the United States to work may be illegal, then, but it is not a wrong. That is because they need to support the families that they leave behind, because they are willing to work hard for their pay and because their needs are modest. However, as their journey north is illegal, those migrants find themselves confronting the sorts of criminal organizations that they condemn. Along their route they are exposed to gangs that engage extensively in robbery and kidnap. Furthermore, the final border that they confront increasingly looks like a military zone staffed with hostile and possibly corrupt officials. So, migrants find themselves dealing with those criminal organizations, in the form of people smugglers.

Thus, Powell argues, the rise of neoliberalism does not stand in opposition to rising criminality, except perhaps in the abstract. Rather, neoliberal reforms in Central America have made many people's lives fragile to the point that the dangerous journey to the United States looks like the only reasonable way to survive. Those reforms have also resulted in stronger criminal gangs in the region and along the migrant route. And finally, Powell argues, the rise of neoliberalism in the United States has increased the likelihood that many will see those migrants not as people seeking to support those left behind in appalling circumstances, but as self-serving opportunists who want access to services and benefits to which they are not entitled, threatening their availability to those people who are entitled.

While Powell's chapter describes illegal migration to the United States in terms of relatively recent political and economic changes in Central America, the final substantive chapter in this collection approaches that migration from a different perspective in order to consider the relationship between it and neoliberalism. It is 'How Does Neoliberalism Relate to Unauthorized Migration? The US–Mexico Case', by Josiah McC. Heyman. In it, he focuses on migration from Mexico to the United States, describing how different forms of capitalism, including neoliberalism, relate to migration and its legal status. He describes how those forms induce some people to migrate and others to employ those migrants as workers, and how they affect the political processes by which migration is made legal, illegal or some mixture of the two.

Neoliberal reform, especially in the shape of the North American Free Trade Agreement, led to increased pressure on the Mexican rural poor, and so increased the attraction of migration to the United States in order to work, which in practice commonly meant economic wrongdoing: working illegally. However, as Heyman describes, Mexico has a long history of capitalist developments that have made rural life more difficult and led to those same pressures. The US firms that employ those migrants are no exemplary neoliberal enterprises, but instead seek the conventional capitalist goal of cheap, docile workers, no matter whether they are illegal or legal. Further, while public concern in the United States about migration is influenced by the insecurity that has come with neoliberal reform, as Powell observed in her chapter, that concern builds on a history of attitudes that denigrate those seen as not White, and of policies and practices that enacted that denigration.

Given what Heyman describes, then, it is reasonable to say that neoliberal reforms can be important for inducing people to migrate, even migrate illegally, for shaping commercial demand for migrant labour and for influencing public perceptions of, and political responses to, that migration. However, it is also reasonable to say that analogous pressures and political movements existed before the rise of neoliberalism. So, what we see as the neoliberal present may contain elements of novelty, but much of it was anticipated by, just as it builds on, what went before.

Some of the implications of what this volume describes are drawn out in the Conclusion, Steven Sampson's 'All That Is Normal Melts into Air: Rethinking Neoliberal Rules and Deviance'. In it, Sampson argues that if this volume shows us anything, it is that the very notion of deviance needs to be scrutinized. If the deviant is the act that deviates from some sort of expectation, then to speak of deviance is to presuppose fairly stable expectations. The most obvious sort of expectations are formal rules, and as Sampson notes, anthropologists have long been interested in the difference between those rules and actual practices. Deviance of some sort, then, has long attracted those in the discipline. However, for Sampson the neoliberal era presents us with wholesale deviance of a different sort that raises fairly unfamiliar questions.

As the chapters in this volume show in different ways, the neoliberal era is noteworthy for the way it makes apparent two things. One is the contemporaneous existence of sharply different expectations, so that it becomes difficult to speak of deviance except at the fairly local level, perhaps reflecting the views of those in the American pharmaceutical industry or in parts of California's Emerald Triangle. The other is that many of the chapters describe settings in which sets of expectation create or enforce circumstances in which deviance is a reasonable, expected response by significant numbers of people.

In the face of this, Sampson suggests, it may be that we should treat the notion of deviance as problematic, and do so in a radical way. That is, we should ask not simply why some people deviate from expectations, but also where expectations come from. That means asking what positions, orientations and interests they reflect, what are the sources of authority on which they draw and how they might induce deviation. We need, that is, an anthropology of rules and regulations.

Conclusion

This Introduction started with a consideration of how we might approach economic wrongdoing in the era of neoliberal ascendancy. It argued that even though it is individuals who act wrongly, different social situations make it more or less likely that people will do so. It also argued that we should situate such acts in the broader category of deviance, activities that deviate from the conventional and expected. Doing so encourages us to ask two questions. One concerns just whose conventions and expectations are involved, the other concerns how that deviance is interpreted. The chapters by the contributors to this volume illustrate by way of specific cases the points made in fairly abstract terms in this Introduction.

The first four chapters show how acts that many would consider as deviant and wrong are common among individuals and firms, and how those who engage in them can see those acts as mundane rather than deviant and as necessary to survive and prosper rather than wrong. With the rise of neoliberalism, several things have changed that are important for making those acts more likely. These include changing views of the deviance that is commercial innovation and changes in the relationship of firms to the societies in which they operate. They also include responses by governments, as they confront the linked tasks of defining wrongdoing and regulating economic actors. And finally, they point to some of the costs to innocent bystanders of economic wrong, and the way that those costs can lead to renewed scrutiny of one of the central elements of neoliberalism, the assertion that the economy should be disembedded as much as possible from the surrounding society.

The four remaining substantive chapters are concerned with specific sorts of activity, the factors that encourage them and the ways that those activities are evaluated as normal or deviant, by whom and to what effect. Between them, these chapters illustrate the ways that government agencies and actions can shape the understanding of different economic activities as wrong or otherwise, as well as the understanding of those who undertake those actions. They also illustrate the ways that these understandings, whether promulgated by governments or presented in public debate, reflect the goals and experiences of those who produce them.

Taken together, the chapters in this volume show how the rise of neoliberal rhetoric and reform has been associated with an increasingly asocial orientation by many firms, as well as by the people who run them and even who regulate them. In the events that led to the financial crisis, this orientation appeared to reflect a decreasing desire by governments to regulate the financial sector, an increasing fascination by those in the sector with the deviance that is financial innovation and the profit that it was expected to bring, and the spread of that fascination to firms and individuals more broadly. As the chapters in this volume show, that orientation appeared among some firms as an increasing indifference to inducements other than the economic, and it appeared among some governments as an increasing indifference to the claims made by their citizens.

To this extent, much of what people see as economic wrong in a neoliberal era is activities that deny the validity of social obligations and norms that many people see as right. However, as made clear earlier in this Introduction, this may be just another appearance of the recurrent process that Polanyi called the disembedding of economy from society. That disembedding and its associated moral disputes take a particular form in this neoliberal era. However, we have been here before, and doubtless we shall come this way again.

James G. Carrier is presently Associate at the Max Planck Institute for Social Anthropology and Adjunct Professor of Anthropology at Indiana University. He has long been interested in aspects of economy and society: *Wage, Trade and Exchange in Melanesia* (California, 1989, with A.H. Carrier), *Gifts and Commodities: Exchange and Western Capitalism since 1700* (Routledge, 1995), *Meanings of the Market* (Berg, 1997, ed.), *Ethical Consumption: Social Value and Economic Practice* (Berghahn, 2012, ed. with P. Luetchford) and *Anthropologies of Class* (Cambridge, 2015, ed. with D. Kalb). He has also worked on projects concerned with anthropology as a whole, *The Handbook of Sociocultural Anthropology* (Bloomsbury, 2013, ed.

with D.B. Gewertz) and *After the Crisis: Anthropological Thought, Neoliberalism and the Aftermath* (Routledge, 2016, ed.).

Note

For their thoughtful comments about earlier versions of this Introduction, I thank Kalman Applbaum, Michael Blim, Thomas Cantens, Julia Elyachar, Joe Heyman, Lotta Larsen, Daniel Seabra Lopes, Patrick Neveling, Michael Polson, Andrew Sanchez, Sergio Sismondo and Sabina Stan. A version of this was presented at the Department of Anthropology at the University of Vienna, and I am grateful for comments and suggestions from the audience. On behalf of myself and all contributors, I also want to thank those who read the manuscript of this volume for the EASA book series, for their time and the useful comments and suggestions that they made.

Earlier versions of portions of this Introduction appeared in 'Economic Wrong and Economic Debate in the Neoliberal Era', in David Whyte and Jörg Wiegratz (eds), *Neoliberalism and the Moral Economy of Fraud* (Routledge, 2016), and in 'Economy and Society, Neoliberal Reform and Economic Deviance', in Manos Spyridakis (ed.), *Market versus Society: Anthropological Insights* (Palgrave Macmillan, 2018).

References

All articles from *The New York Times* and *The Guardian* can be found by searching their web sites (www.nytimes.com, www.theguardian.com).

Agnew, Jean-Christophe. 1986. *Worlds Apart: The Market and the Theater in Anglo-American Thought, 1550–1750*. New York: Cambridge University Press.

Antilla, Susan. 2013. 'In Soured Investments, Brokers Emerge as Culprits and Victims', *The New York Times* (23 December).

Appadurai, Arjun. 2015. *Banking on Words: The Failure of Language in the Age of Derivative Finance*. Chicago, IL: University of Chicago Press.

Apuzzo, Matt. 2014. 'Security Check Firm Said to Have Defrauded U.S.', *The New York Times* (23 January).

Associated Press. 2012. 'State Settles on Forgeries by Servicer of Mortgages', *The New York Times* (2 August).

Austin, Ian. 2017. 'Uber Says It Will Leave Quebec Rather Than Face New Rules', *The New York Times* (26 September).

Bailey, Jeff. 2005. 'The Mortgage Maker vs. The World', *The New York Times* (16 October).

Ball, James, and Henry Taylor. 2013. '"Buddy" Scheme to Give More Multinationals Access to Ministers', *The Guardian* (18 January).

Bandelj, Nina, Julia Elyachar, Gary Richardson and James Owen Weatherall. 2016. 'Comprehending and Regulating Financial Crises: An Interdisciplinary Approach', *Perspectives on Science* 24(4): 443–73.

Bloch, Maurice, and Jonathan Parry. 1989. 'Introduction: Money and the Morality of Exchange', in J. Parry and M. Bloch (eds), *Money and the Morality of Exchange*. Cambridge: Cambridge University Press, pp. 1–32.

Bohlen, Celestine. 2017. 'American Democracy is Drowning in Money', *The New York Times* (20 September).

Brooks, Richard, and Solomon Hughes. 2016. 'Public Servants, Private Paydays', *Private Eye* 1426 (2–15 September): 19–24.

Brown, Susan Love. 1997. 'The Free Market as Salvation from Government: The Anarcho-capitalist View', in James G. Carrier (ed.), *Meanings of the Market: The Free Market in Western Culture*. Oxford: Berg Publishing, pp. 99–128.

Carney, Mark. 2014. 'Inclusive Capitalism: Creating a Sense of the Systemic'. At the Conference on Inclusive Capitalism, London, 27 May. www.bankofengland.co.uk/publications/Documents/speeches/2014/speech731.pdf (accessed 6 May 2016).

Carrier, James G. 1995. *Gifts and Commodities: Exchange and Western Capitalism since 1700*. London: Routledge.

———. 1997. 'Introduction', in J.G. Carrier (ed.), *Meanings of the Market: The Free Market in Western Culture*. Oxford: Berg Publishing, pp. 1–67.

———. 2012. 'Anthropology after the Crisis', *Focaal* 64: 115–28.

Christie, Agatha. 1928. *The Mystery of the Blue Train*. London: William Collins & Sons.

———. 1937. *Death on the Nile*. London: Collins Crime Club.

Citigroup. 2012. *200 Years Citi*. (Annual report 2011.) New York: Citigroup Inc. www.citigroup.com/citi/investor/quarterly/2012/ar11c_en.pdf (accessed 6 May 2016).

Cockett, Richard. 1994. *Thinking the Unthinkable: Think-Tanks and the Economic Counter-revolution, 1931–83*. London: HarperCollins.

Confessore, Nicholas. 2014. 'Big-Money Donors Demand Larger Say in Party Strategy', *The New York Times* (1 March).

Corkery, Michael, and Ben Protess. 2014. 'Bank of America Papers Show Conflict and Trickery in Mortgages', *The New York Times* (21 August).

Dealbook. 2007. 'Citi Chief on Buyouts: "We're Still Dancing"', *The New York Times* (10 July).

———. 2009. 'Blankfein Says He's Just Doing "God's Work"', *The New York Times* (9 November).

Drucker, Jesse, and Simon Bowers. 2017. 'After a Tax Crackdown, Apple Found a New Shelter for its Profits', *The New York Times* (6 November).

Durkheim, Emile. (1897) 1951. *Suicide: A Study in Sociology*. New York: The Free Press.

———. (1893) 1984. *The Division of Labour in Society*. London: Routledge & Kegan Paul.

Editorial Board. 2015. 'No Justification for High Drug Prices', *The New York Times* (19 December).

Eisinger, Jesse. 2014a. 'Seeking Tough Justice, but Settling for Empty Promises', *The New York Times* (7 May).

———. 2014b. 'Why Only One Top Banker Went to Jail for the Financial Crisis', *The New York Times* (30 April).

Elyachar, Julia. 2005. *Markets of Dispossession: NGOs, Economic Development, and the State in Cairo*. Durham, NC: Duke University Press.

Ewing, Jack. 2018. '10 Monkeys and a Beetle: Inside VW's Campaign for "Clean Diesel"', *The New York Times* (25 January).

Fourcade, Marion, and Kieran Healy. 2007. 'Moral Views of Market Society', *Annual Review of Sociology* 33: 285–311.

Fox, Justin. 2009. *Myth of the Rational Market*. New York: Harper Business.

Gabriel, Trip. 2014. 'Ash Spill Shows How Watchdog Was Defanged', *The New York Times* (28 February).

Giudice, Lauren. 2011. 'Regulating Corruption: Analyzing Uncertainty in Current Foreign Corrupt Practices Act Enforcement', *Boston University Law Review* 91(1): 347–78.

Greenspan, Alan. 1996. 'The Challenge of Central Banking in a Democratic Society'. Presented to The American Enterprise Institute for Public Policy Research, Washington, DC, 5 December. Washington, DC: Board of Governors of the Federal Reserve System. www.federalreserve.gov/boarddocs/speeches/1996/19961205.htm (accessed 6 May 2016).

Halberstam, David. 1972. *The Best and the Brightest*. New York: Random House.

Hayek, Friedrich A. von. 1944. *The Road to Serfdom*. London: Routledge.

———. 1974. 'The Pretence of Knowledge'. Nobel prize lecture (11 December). Stockholm: Nobel Foundation. www.nobelprize.org/nobel_prizes/economics/laureates/1974/hayek-lecture.html (accessed 6 May 2016).

Henning, Peter J. 2010. 'The Gathering Storm over Foreclosures', *The New York Times* (4 October).

———. 2014. 'Seeking Guilty Pleas from Corporations While Limiting the Fallout', *The New York Times* (5 May).

Hirschman, Albert O. 1977. *The Passions and the Interests*. Princeton, NJ: Princeton University Press.

Ho, Karen. 2009. *Liquidated: An Ethnography of Wall Street*. Durham, NC: Duke University Press.

———. 2012. 'Finance', in Didier Fassin (ed.), *A Companion to Moral Anthropology*. Malden, MA: Wiley-Blackwell, pp. 413–31.

Hochschild, Arlie Russell. 2016. *Strangers in Their Own Land: Anger and Mourning on the American Right*. New York: New Press.

Iteanu, André. 2005. 'When Nothing Stands Outside the Self', in Bruce Kapferer (ed.), *The Retreat of the Social: The Rise and Rise of Reductionism*. Oxford: Berghahn Books, pp. 104–13.

Jensen, Christopher, and Matthew L. Wald. 2014. 'Carmakers' Close Ties to Regulator Scrutinized', *The New York Times* (30 March).

Kopicki, Allison. 2013. 'Five Years Later, Poll Finds Disapproval of Bailout', *The New York Times* (26 September).

Krugman, Paul. 2010. 'Berating the Raters', *The New York Times* (25 April).

Lagarde, Christine. 2014. 'Economic Inclusion and Financial Integrity – an Address to the Conference on Inclusive Capitalism'. Washington, DC: International Monetary Fund. https://www.imf.org/external/np/speeches/2014/052714.htm (accessed 6 May 2016).

Lattman, Peter. 2013. 'Suit Charges 3 Credit Ratings Agencies with Fraud in Bear Stearns Case', *The New York Times* (11 November).

Ledeneva, Alena V. 1998. *Russia's Economy of Favours*: Blat, *Networking and Informal Exchange*. Cambridge: Cambridge University Press.

Lewis, Michael. 2011. *The Big Short: Inside the Doomsday Machine*. London: Penguin.

Lipton, Eric. 2014a. 'Fight over Minimum Wage Illustrates Web of Industry Ties', *The New York Times* (9 February).

———. 2014b. 'Major Research Groups Are Given Low Marks on Disclosing Donors', *The New York Times* (6 May).

Lipton, Eric, and Ben Protess. 2013. 'Banks' Lobbyists Help in Drafting Financial Bills', *The New York Times* (23 May).

Lipton, Eric, Nicholas Confessore and Brooke Williams. 2016. 'Think Tank Scholar or Corporate Consultant? It Depends on the Day', *The New York Times* (8 August).

MacLennan, Carol A. 1997. 'Democracy under the Influence: Cost–Benefit Analysis in the United States', in James G. Carrier (ed.), *Meanings of the Market: The Free Market in Western Culture*. Oxford: Berg Publishing, pp. 195–224.

Mallaby, Sebastian. 2016. *The Man Who Knew: The Life and Times of Alan Greenspan*. London: Penguin.

Marx, Karl, and Frederick Engels. (1848) 1948. *Manifesto of the Communist Party*. New York: International Publishers.

McBarnet, Doreen. 2006. 'After Enron Will "Whiter Than White Collar Crime" Still Wash?' *British Journal of Criminology* 46(6): 1091–109.

———. 2010. 'Financial Engineering or Legal Engineering? Legal Work, Legal Integrity and the Banking Crisis', in Iain MacNeil and Justin

O'Brien (eds), *The Future of Financial Regulation*. Oxford: Hart, pp. 67–82.

McDonald, Oonagh. 2016. *Lehman Brothers: A Crisis of Value*. Manchester: Manchester University Press.

McIntire, Mike. 2016. 'Haiti and Africa Projects Shed Light on Clinton's Public–Private Web', *The New York Times* (16 October).

Meier, Barry. 2013. 'Johnson & Johnson in Deal to Settle Hip Implant Lawsuits', *The New York Times* (19 November).

Merton, Robert K. 1938. 'Social Structure and Anomie', *American Sociological Review* 3(5): 672–82.

Mirowski, Philip, and Dieter Plehwe (eds). 2009. *The Road from Mont Pèlerin*. Cambridge, MA: Harvard University Press.

Mizruchi, Mark S. 2010. 'The American Corporate Elite and the Historical Roots of the Financial Crisis of 2008', *Research in the Sociology of Organizations* 308: 103–39.

Morgenson, Gretchen. 2012a. 'Bank Settles over Loans in Nevada', *The New York Times* (23 October).

———. 2012b. 'From East and West, Foreclosure Horror Stories', *The New York Times* (7 January).

———. 2014a. 'Credit Suisse Documents Point to Mortgage Lapses', *The New York Times* (9 March).

———. 2014b. 'An Unfinished Chapter at Countrywide', *The New York Times* (23 August).

———. 2016a. 'A Bank Too Big to Jail', *The New York Times* (15 July).

———. 2016b. 'Countrywide Mortgage Devastation Lingers as Ex-chief Moves On', *The New York Times* (24 June).

Morison, Samuel, Henry Steele Commager and William Leuchtenburg. 1980. *The Growth of the American Republic, Volume II* (7th edition). New York: Oxford University Press.

Norris, Floyd. 2014a. 'Convicted of Felonies, Banks are Allowed to Stay in Business', *The New York Times* (15 May).

———. 2014b. 'Regulators Struggle with Conflicts in Credit Ratings and Audits', *The New York Times* (21 August).

Parloff, Roger. 2018. 'How VW Paid $25 Billion for Dieselgate – and Got Off Easy', *ProPublica* (6 February). https://drive.google.com/drive/folders/1G3hFkbycs3ZB_GTg2g85NfF5cQoxVPi3?usp=sharing (accessed 7 February 2018).

Polanyi, Karl. (1944) 1957. *The Great Transformation*. Boston: Beacon Press.

Pollack, Andrew. 2015. 'Drug Goes from $13.50 a Tablet to $750, Overnight', *The New York Times* (20 September).

Poovey, Mary. 2008. *Genres of the Credit Economy: Mediating Value in Eighteenth- and Nineteenth-Century Britain*. Chicago, IL: University of Chicago Press.

Press Association. 2014. 'NHS Hires Drugmaker-Funded Lobbyist', *The Guardian* (11 February).

Protess, Ben, and Jessica Silver-Greenberg. 2014. 'Credit Suisse Pleads Guilty in Felony Case', *The New York Times* (19 May).

Protess, Ben, Jessica Silver-Greenberg and Michael Corkery. 2014. 'Bank of America Expected to Settle Huge Mortgage Case for $16.65 Billion', *The New York Times* (20 August).

Reuters. 2013. 'Medical Device Maker to Settle S.E.C. Bribery Charges', *The New York Times* (24 October).

Ruiz, Rebecca R., and Danielle Ivory. 2014. 'Documents Show General Motors Kept Silent on Fatal Crashes', *The New York Times* (15 July).

Sample, Ian. 2013. 'Unfavourable Results from Medical Trials Are Being Withheld, MPs Warn', *The Guardian* (17 September).

Sampson, Steven. 2005. 'Integrity Warriors: Global Morality and the Anti-corruption Movement in the Balkans', in Dieter Haller and Cris Shore (eds), *Corruption: Anthropological Perspectives*. London: Pluto, pp. 103–30.

Schmidt, Michael S., and Edward Wyatt. 2012. 'Corporate Fraud Cases Often Spare Individuals', *The New York Times* (7 August).

Schwartz, Nelson D., and Charles Duhigg. 2013. 'Apple's Web of Tax Shelters Saved It Billions, Panel Finds', *The New York Times* (20 May).

Scott, Mark. 2012. 'British Regulator Says Banks "Too Big to Prosecute"', *The New York Times* (14 December).

Shore, Cris. 2004. 'Corruption Scandals in America and Europe: Enron and EU Fraud in Comparative Perspective', in John Gledhill (ed.), *Corporate Scandal: Global Corporatism against Society*. Oxford: Berghahn Books, pp. 29–39.

Shore, Cris, and Dieter Haller. 2005. 'Introduction. Sharp Practice: Anthropology and the Study of Corruption', in D. Haller and C. Shore (eds), *Corruption: Anthropological Perspectives*. London: Pluto, pp. 1–26.

Shore, Cris, and Susan Wright. 1999. 'Audit Culture and Anthropology: Neo-liberalism in British Higher Education', *Journal of the Royal Anthropological Institute* 5(4): 557–75.

Silver, Allan. 1990. 'Friendship in Commercial Society: Eighteenth-Century Social Theory and Modern Sociology', *American Journal of Sociology* 95(6): 1474–504.

Silver-Greenberg, Jessica, and Peter Eavis. 2014. 'Wall Street Predicts $50 Billion Bill to Settle U.S. Mortgage Suits', *The New York Times* (9 January).

Smith, Adam. (1776) 1976. *An Inquiry into the Nature and Causes of the Wealth of Nations*. Chicago, IL: University of Chicago Press.

Sorkin, Andrew Ross. 2013. 'Realities behind Prosecuting Big Banks', *The New York Times* (11 March).

Stevenson, Alexandra, and Matthew Goldstein. 2014. 'Ex-SAC Trader Convicted of Securities Fraud', *The New York Times* (6 February).

Stevenson, Richard W. 1995. 'Breaking the Bank – a Special Report. Big Gambles, Lost Bets Sank a Venerable Firm', *The New York Times* (3 March).

Stout, Hilary, Bill Vlasic, Danielle Ivory and Rebecca R. Ruiz. 2014. 'Carmaker Misled Grieving Families on a Lethal Flaw', *The New York Times* (24 March).

Strathern, Marilyn (ed.). 2000. *Audit Cultures*. London: Routledge.

Sullivan, Paul. 2014. 'Having Enough, But Hungry for More', *The New York Times* (17 January).

Thompson, E.P. 1971. 'The Moral Economy of the English Crowd in the Eighteenth Century', *Past and Present* 50: 76–136.

Travis, Alan. 2013. 'G4S Admits Overcharging MoJ £24m on Electronic Tagging Contract', *The Guardian* (19 November).

Treanor, Jill. 2014. 'Legal Costs and Fines Hit JP Morgan's Earnings', *The Guardian* (14 January).

Tugend, Alina. 2014. 'In Life and Business, Learning To Be Ethical', *The New York Times* (10 January).

Turner, Rachel S. 2011. *Neo-Liberal Ideology*. Edinburgh: Edinburgh University Press.

Venkatesan, Soumhya (ed.). 2015. Debate: 'The Concept of Neoliberalism Has Become an Obstacle to the Anthropological Understanding of the Twenty-First Century', *Journal of the Royal Anthropological Institute* 21(4): 911–23.

Wedel, Janine R. 2012. 'Rethinking Corruption in an Age of Ambiguity', *Annual Review of Law and Social Science* 8: 453–98.

Williams, Alex. 2018. 'Remembering that Moment We All Became a "Brand"', *The New York Times* (19 January).

Williams, James. 2012. *Policing the Markets: Inside the Black Box of Securities Enforcement*. New York: Routledge.

Wines, Michael. 2014. 'Emails Link Duke Energy and North Carolina', *The New York Times* (14 March).

Wyatt, Edward. 2011. 'Promises Made, and Remade, by Firms in S.E.C. Fraud Cases', *The New York Times* (7 November).

Marketing Clientelism vs Corruption
Pharmaceutical Off-label Promotion on Trial

Kalman Applbaum

In 2011, in the midst of working on a project aimed at countering the unresponsiveness of industry, regulators and physicians to adverse drug events (see www.rxrisk.org), I received a phone call from a New York law firm representing those seeking damages for the sudden decline in the value of their shares in Medtronic Corporation. Medtronic, a Minneapolis-based manufacturer of medical devices ranging from mechanical heart valves and heart-lung machines to surgical supplies, produced Infuse Bone Graft (hereafter Infuse), the brand name for bone morphogenetic protein-2, or BMP-2. They had been implicated in a scam to expand the sale of that product beyond the uses approved for it by the US Food and Drug Administration (FDA).

To gain approval by the FDA, new drugs must be demonstrated as safe and effective for each of their intended uses. Intended uses are the 'indications' for which a drug is tested, and if the drug is licensed, they are described on the label. Off-label prescribing means prescribing for uses other than those approved by the FDA. Physicians are permitted to prescribe for unapproved or off-label uses but, given the commercial motivation of manufacturers to encourage ever-expanding sales of their products, it is illegal for firms to promote such use.

Following reports of injured patients, unlawful kickbacks to doctors and allegations of falsified data published in scientific journals, Medtronic's share price fell. Inquiry into the matter revealed that in 2006–07 an astounding 85 per cent of Infuse sales were for off-label uses, a rate that experts felt could hardly be achieved without off-label promotion.

Licensed for use in 2002, Infuse had revolutionary potential for application in spinal fusion surgery. That surgery is performed to reduce back pain by eliminating or reducing friction between verte-brae, and about 450,000 spinal fusions are performed in the United States annually, despite evidence that, for most patients, physical therapy works just as well (Resnick and Bozic 2013). Surgery has conventionally entailed harvesting bone from the hip and grafting it between vertebrae in the back, a procedure that is time consuming and painful. BMP-2, the bone growth agent in Infuse, was designed to help bypass the conventional grafting procedure. Unfortunately, proteins like BMP-2 can easily stimulate dangerous bone growth outside of the fusion area.

When Infuse was licensed, the FDA limited its use to a narrow range of spinal surgeries performed under specified conditions: it could be applied only in a 'single-level infusion' in the L4-S1 region of the lumbar spine in surgery intended to remedy disc collapse; the spine could only be approached through an incision in the abdomen, rather than from the back; it had to be used in conjunction with a device called an LT-Cage. These restrictions were imposed after clini-cal trial data revealed frequent adverse events when Infuse was used in other ways. The causes of the adverse events remain undetermined, but their consequences could be dire because Infuse is inserted near the spinal cord.

The restrictions and precautions indicated on a drug's label, if heeded, clearly limit its market potential. It may be difficult to estimate what the sales potential of Infuse might have been without off-label promotion, but assuredly it was only a small fraction of the $800 million reported for several years in the mid-2000s.

In June 2011, in an unprecedented move, *The Spine Journal* devoted an entire issue to repudiating the company-sponsored studies that had encouraged extensive off-label use of Infuse. The issue revealed that doctors who appeared to be co-authors of studies supporting off-label use of Infuse frequently had only put their names to articles written by a publication firm hired by Medtronic, and had been paid to do so. The *Spine Journal* authors linked use of the product to a number of adverse consequences: 'Uncontrolled bone formation and the need for additional surgery; life-threatening inflammation; infections; implant movement; cancer risk; and effects on nerves leading to radiating leg pain, bladder retention and a com-plication that causes sterility in men' (Fauber 2011). Two years later,

Annals of Internal Medicine published a comprehensive study that found no advantage from using BMP-2, and many risks (Resnick and Bozic 2013).

The New York law firm that telephoned me in 2011 was involved in what turned out to be a consolidated class-action suit against Medtronic. The complaint in that suit stated:

> Although undisclosed to investors, the first-hand accounts from over a dozen former Medtronic employees demonstrate that this extraordinarily high off-label use was driven by the Company sales force, which would direct doctors to Medtronic-compensated consultants or 'Key Opinion Leaders' in the medical field who were surgeons paid by Medtronic to promote off-label use of INFUSE Bone Graft . . . [Medtronic] materially misled investors . . . [because it did not inform them] that INFUSE Bone Graft sales were primarily dependent on higher risk off-label use of [the] product. (US District Court 2009: 3–4)

In other words, Medtronic had deployed physicians who were not formally their employees as part of their off-label promotion scheme to expand the use of the product. In language I have developed elsewhere to describe this procedure (K. Applbaum 2006a, 2009a), Medtronic had incorporated physicians into the company's distribution channel for the drug (i.e. as sales staff), even though they were not overtly part of it.

In part due to the pressure exerted by the public rebuke, and in light of Medtronic having recently been censured by the FDA for making false claims about another product (FDA 2012) in March 2012, the company agreed to settle for $85 million (I was not involved in the suit) (Stempel 2012). The company continues to deny any wrongdoing.

The situation I have described concerning Infuse points to a state of affairs in the pharmaceutical industry that helps to illuminate the concern of this volume, which is the relationship between neoliberalism, economic activities and the perspectives from which those activities are seen as deviant and perhaps wrong. One of the central elements of neoliberalism is its stress on the free market. The Infuse case indicates that in the pharmaceutical industry this stress has a corollary that is touted less widely – namely, pressure to market freely, a pressure that can lead to questionable practices. The incorporation of influential physicians, with their advocacy of off-label use of Infuse, into the marketing activities intended to increase the sale of the drug is a sign of such pressure. The result, the apparent widespread use of Infuse in ways and for conditions that the FDA had not approved, would strike many people as the consequence of economic wrongdoing.

In this chapter I pursue the ways that pharmaceutical firms market their wares freely, not simply by catering to demand for their drugs, but by doing what they can to create that demand. I do so not only because it is revealing in its own right, but also because it helps to point to the difficulties we can confront when we try to distinguish routine practice from the deviant, the wrong and the criminal. I approach pharmaceutical marketing in terms of the difference between what I call 'marketing clientelism' and corruption.

Separating Clientelism from Corruption

The Medtronic case is but one among a spate of suits prosecuted since the early 2000s under the False Claims Act, a whistle-blower statute permitting private citizens to file suits on behalf of the federal government (see Lansdale 2006). These suits have alleged that the defendants have made false claims about drugs to promote off-label use, and have resulted in the recovery of over $15 billion from the world's most reputable drug companies (Herman 2014). Despite harsh penalties and the imposition of rigorous compliance stipulations, called 'corporate integrity agreements', which are expensive and laborious to implement, malfeasance in the industry appears to continue. A multidisciplinary subfield of the social science of medicine called critical pharmaceutical studies has emerged to report on the myriad manifestations and mechanisms of corruption in the industry, from rigging clinical trials and the ghostwriting of scientific publications to the outright purchase of influence. One of my purposes here is to consider how and why wrongdoing in the industry continues at such a pace despite the manifestly credible threats of prosecution and increased government vigilance.

In earlier research, I observed that there appears to be a misalignment, conflict and even competition between the values of medicine and public health on the one hand, and those of pharmaceutical marketing on the other.

> Medical, scientific value consists in a discovery's capacity to explain phenomena verifiably and then be applied to reduce human suffering from disease. Marketing value, by contrast, is fluid, relative, and contingent on perceived utility. Marketing value is measured in accordance with its ability to achieve product differentiation, which refers to the process of making one's product offering appear unique in the marketplace and

superior to those of one's competitors. . . . Pharmaceutical value has increasingly become a marketing proposition, not a scientific one. What is valuable to marketers can be meaningless, dangerous, and costly to everyone else. (K. Applbaum 2009b: 15–16)

Among the criticisms I received for that line of thinking, one reader questioned my contrast between private (drug company) and public (medicine) spheres, pointing out that the distinction was in actuality difficult to draw because the boundary between them is porous and because in its everyday practice there is no such thing as disinterested science. The interests are not always commercial, but they are always there (Robert Rosenheck, pers. comm., 2009–10).

Without quite abandoning the original duality of brand and medical value, which echoes the familiar duality of exchange and use value, one could propose a more inclusive approach by framing the discussion in terms of the normative social exchange mechanisms by which pharmaceutical companies seek to advance their interests. One could ask under what circumstances these might be seen as working for and against the public health interest, with that interest being seen as served by drugs and devices that do more good than harm in the population, as per FDA guidelines, and that do so in keeping with legal marketing practices. If a firm's activities fail these two criteria, most people would classify them as corrupt.

However, to say of an activity that most people would see it as corrupt is not the same as saying that it is illegal. For instance, what if that activity were so widespread that the industry could not function normally without it? In such a case, the activity that most people would condemn would not be deviant, but would be the norm within the industry, and it would be difficult to challenge legally. It is this ambiguity that I will explore below in the suit against the makers of the drug Risperdal for illegally promoting it. Risperdal was developed by Janssen Pharmaceutica, a division of Johnson & Johnson. For convenience sake, in what follows I shall refer to the defendants in the suit as J&J.

The type of activity that the suit illustrates, and that is perceived as normal by industry actors, is the system of social exchange that I call marketing clientelism. I offer a hypothetical example of this sort of clientelism, though it involves the editorial rather than the marketing sort. Some years back, a colleague of mine teaching at a prestigious university was appointed editor of a well-known academic journal. Like many others, I felt that, under his direction, the quality of the journal began to improve. It also came to be remarked that a disproportionate number of his friends and colleagues were showing up in the table of contents. Critics grumbled that the editor's apparent favouritism was a form of corruption and should be condemned. Fairness, they said, is imperative because junior faculty rely upon publications in leading journals, like the one he edited, for promotion and tenure. Others countered that the appropriate aspiration of every journal editor is to publish high-quality papers, and that the editor had mobilized his personal networks to solicit an improved pool of submissions. In my terms, this was editorial clientelism, and therefore its benefits might be tolerated or even encouraged.

The border between clientelism and corruption is fuzzy, and in academic journals efforts to police it include having editors hold the post for a limited time and having an editorial board that is strongly involved with editorial decisions. There is, however, no absolute solution to the problem of the messy overlap of the two. (In the end, people in my ken concluded that the only accusation that could properly be laid against the editor was that he was too obvious in his partialities.)

Among the academic disciplines, political scientists and development theorists often seem to see little difference between the two. They regard clientelism as a near synonym for corruption, in which formal institutional rules are bypassed in favour of a resort to 'personal, particularistic ties to obtain preferential access to goods and services' (Torsello 2012: 271). It is suggested that this is more observable in non-Western societies, either because corruption is held to be concomitant with 'poverty, ignorance, repression of women, fundamentalism, fanaticism and irrationality' or, conversely, because clientelism 'has a positive function in development because it "fills the gap" left by partial bureaucratization and the incomplete penetration by the state' (Halle and Shore 2005: 3).

On the other hand, sociologists and anthropologists have been more prone to treat clientelism as a thing on its own, rather than as a cousin of corruption. So, they have looked for characteristic features of clientelism, including dyadism, unequal power relations or verticality among transactors, informalism and conditions of scarcity (Scott 1972; Gellner 1977; Eisenstadt and Roniger 1984). A similar approach has been taken by many seeking to understand marketization in places like China, with scholars linking clientelism with markers of stability in investment, information flows, social trust and other lubricants of market transaction (Wank 1996).

In this chapter, I straddle these different approaches. Marketing clientelism may, as I show, be associated with corruption. However,

I also want to emphasize its *strategic* use by corporations to further their goal of having stable distribution channels for the sale of their products (K. Applbaum 2009b). There is also a more specific reason to stress the difference between clientelism and corruption. The case that I describe centres on a court proceeding, where an absolute rather than relative judgement had to be made as to whether the company in question was guilty of off-label promotion (corruption) or rather was engaged in just the normal dissemination of information about their product through expert channels (marketing clientelism).

That case was brought by Texas Medicaid, the state health insurer, against J&J over the marketing of the antipsychotic drug Risperdal. I had the opportunity to attend the trial in its entirety in January 2012, in Austin, Texas. All quotes in the text concerning the trial are taken from my notes.

Case Study in Real Time: Risperdal on Trial in Texas

Between 2009 and 2011, Johnson & Johnson and Janssen were sued successfully for fraudulent marketing practices. They had to pay $257.7 million in Louisiana, $327 million in South Carolina and $1.1 billion in Arkansas (an additional $2.2 billion was levied in criminal and civil fines in 2013) (Herman 2014). On 10 January 2012, Texas launched its suit against J&J, claiming that the company defrauded the state of $579 million.

The case involved the marketing of 'atypical' or second-generation antipsychotic (SGA) medicines, of which Risperdal is one. As I explain below, these were introduced in the 1990s and were said to be better than the older, first generation antipsychotic medicines (FGAs), which appeared in the 1950s. There is no easy synopsis of the combined commercial and medical history of this class of drugs, but as will become clear, it is reasonable to conclude that their success lies far more in the commercial than the medical realm. Apart from the body of medical research now testifying to this, common sense resists the idea that antipsychotic drugs merited becoming the best-selling class of pharmaceuticals in America. In 2010, a small number of SGAs (including principally Risperdal, Zyprexa, Seroquel, Abilify and Geodon) had sales of $14.6 billion in the United States alone; to put that in perspective, it is equivalent to 1.5 times the public expenditure for all healthcare in India.

Risperdal earned J&J $34 billion during its 17-year patent period. Those with no first-hand knowledge of how large corporations work cannot easily comprehend the size and complexity of the machinery necessary to generate revenues on that scale. Explaining this to a jury was the challenge facing the Texas Attorney General's office, which had gathered a massive amount of information but had only a handful of hours to make their case.

In the plaintiff's opening statement, their attorney, Tom Melsheimer, accused J&J of implementing a 'systematic scheme . . . not a one-time event, not an accident'. The purpose of that scheme was to turn a drug designated for narrow use in the treatment of schizophrenia into a $34 billion pill with a 97 per cent profit margin, thereby defrauding Texas taxpayers of $579 million.

How could the company have accomplished this feat? Melsheimer alleged that the company did so in four ways: they influenced usage guidelines by bribing Texas officials; they illegally promoted the drug for use in children (half the patient population for the drug is under the age of thirteen); they made false claims that Risperdal is safer than other antipsychotic drugs; they confabulated research to support the claim that it was cost-effective to the taxpayer, even though it cost forty-five times as much as generic competitors and was not shown to be superior to them. All of these were, or were facilitated by means of, off-label marketing.

Melsheimer referred to warning letters sent by the FDA challenging the company's marketing copy, which had claimed that its drug was superior in efficacy and safety to FGAs. He argued that the company 'seeded' the scientific literature with ghostwritten articles claiming the drug's superiority. Finally, he alleged that bribes, in the form of 'unrestricted educational grants' and honoraria, were given to Texas medical officials serving on the influential Texas Medicines Algorithm Project (TMAP).

TMAP was set up in 1994, one year after Risperdal was launched in the United States. Initially it was funded by J&J, but soon thereafter all of the other major pharmaceutical companies had signed on as well. TMAP started with a panel of experts convened to produce a consensus on the use of antipsychotics. The first set of TMAP guidelines concluded that the SGAs, including Risperdal, were the drugs of choice for the management of schizophrenia (Healy 2006).

The defence attorney, Steve McConnico, appealed to jurors' common sense, their trust in doctors' judgement and their faith in the American free-market system. McConnico listed the debilitating side effects of FGAs, arguing that Risperdal does not cause them: you 'wanna talk about cost effectiveness? Knock down some of these [side effects]'. He said that FGAs address only the positive symptoms of schizophrenia (psychosis, delusion, hearing voices), but Risperdal also helps with the negative symptoms (inexpressiveness, lack of interest in life, monosyllabic speech), and so makes it easier for people to go back to work and lead normal lives (see K. Applbaum 2006b). Independent research, including the famous CATIE study (Clinical Antipsychotic Trials of Intervention Effectiveness; see Stroup and Lieberman 2010) discussed below, has shown these claims to be false advertising – but that is precisely the point. The defence sought to redeploy J&J's Risperdal marketing messages that had worked so well on doctors and others, only this time on the jurors.

In contrast to the prosecution, the defence attorney delivered a folksy, down-home speech about 'the real world'.

> The idea that we're some kind of master puppeteer that can control all these doctors all over the world and the country and say you're going to give this drug is simply not common sense. . . . Their whole theory is we pulled some smoke screen off [*sic*] the whole medical community. . . . That doesn't make one bit of sense. The idea that a drug rep [i.e. representative, effectively in sales] is telling a doctor how to prescribe a drug doesn't work. These drugs are prescribed by doctors.

Finally, McConnico appealed to the jurors' presumed acceptance of the market doctrine of value and truth: 'Now, the reason Risperdal did well was because they were superior. It's that simple. The marketplace proved it'.

I have described the outlines of the position of the plaintiff and the defendant. Those positions refer to facts and to plausible inferences from them. I said that the difference between corruption and marketing clientelism is often fuzzy. Part of that fuzziness revolves around the meaning of what seems to be a fact, the measure that we should use to evaluate, and even identify, a fact. I turn to that now.

Establishing Not Just Facts, but the Measure of Facts

The first deposition presented in the trial was that of Thomas Anderson, who had been one of two managers responsible for launching Risperdal in 1993. The exhibits placed before the jury included a slide from the early planning days, entitled 'Building a Consensus'. The slide, presumably Anderson's handiwork, exhorted the marketing team to 'assemble an expert task force and body of knowledge . . . formulate guidelines: Key experts ⇒ Thought leaders ⇒ Rank and file'.

The expert task force that was assembled included three psychiatrists. One was Dr Allen Frances, Chairman of the Department of Psychiatry at Duke University and head of the group that assembled the fourth edition of the *Diagnostic and Statistical Manual for Mental Disorder* (DSM-IV). Another was Dr John P. Docherty, Professor and Vice Chairman of the Department of Psychiatry at Cornell University. The third was David A. Kahn, Associate Clinical Professor of Psychiatry at Columbia University. These men accepted a total of $942,669 from the drug company, mostly in the form of 'unrestricted educational grants' to their newly formed company, Expert Knowledge Systems (EKS), to prepare practice guidelines for the treatment of schizophrenia. The guidelines, which formed the basis for TMAP, endorsed the use of SGAs, including Risperdal, as the preferred treatment, dislodging the FGAs from that position.

The $942,669 given to the company that those three experts had formed needed to be measured in terms of the issues important in the court case. In the deposition, the attorney for the state, Tommy Jacks, asked Anderson: 'Did it ever occur to you that in authorizing substantial payments to their business, that their independence or objectivity might be compromised in any way?' No, Anderson replied. They were involved in *education*. Jacks then asked:

> When EKS said they would help you 'achieve more broad strategic objectives ... influence state government ... build brand loyalty and commitment with large groups of key providers around the country ... develop pharmaco-economic studies' and be in touch with NAMI [the National Alliance for the Mentally Ill] to develop educational materials for rapid implementation of guidelines. ... When they said, 'We want to ensure that all of Janssen's needs are addressed so that Janssen can succeed in its efforts to promote Risperdal throughout the country', are you making a distinction between promotion and education?

On the second day of the trial, Dr Alexander L. Miller was called to the stand. He was Professor of Psychiatry at the University of Texas Health Center at San Antonio and, according to the description of him on the University of Texas website, Director of the Schizophrenia Module of TMAP. Miller confirmed that J&J provided some of the funding for TMAP, but took umbrage at the suggestion that the consulting money he accepted from J&J, more than $70,000, might have affected his objectivity when he offered recommendations regarding the guidelines, which ultimately designated SGAs, including Risperdal, as the preferred treatment for schizophrenia.

The prosecutor challenged Miller's integrity and objectivity, and these were defended during cross-examination by the defence attorneys. They reviewed, in painstaking detail, Miller's gold-plated credentials: Yale, Washington University, the National Institute of Mental Health (NIMH), Massachusetts General Hospital, Harvard, Distinguished Life Fellow at the American Psychiatric Association and twenty years of service to the State of Texas, in addition to his full professorship at the University of Texas.

My initial assumption was that the extended review of Miller's credentials was to substantiate his credibility before the jury so that they would not think his judgement was corruptible by J&J money. I had a different thought when Miller listed among his accomplishments that he was on the advisory board of, and a Texas co-researcher for, CATIE, the selfsame drugs trial the plaintiff was using to establish that the SGAs are not superior to the FGAs. My new thought was that the defence was not seeking directly to exculpate Miller of any possible wrongdoing. Rather, Miller's positions and accomplishments were described in order to establish what it means to be trustworthy in a particular sphere of professional activity, a sphere that was central to the suit that the jury was hearing. That is, the case would turn on whether the jury would think that Miller and people like him were involved in corruption by illicitly taking money from the drug industry in return for favours, or whether they were engaged in marketing clientelism, the kind of relationship normal to the dissemination of new, vital information about medicines. If the latter, then common sense about conflicts of interest would not apply, and this was precisely what the defence was seeking to establish. As Tom Anderson, the product manager for Risperdal, had said when the prosecutor had interrogated him about giving money to key opinion leaders, funding speaker bureaus, making unrestricted grants and the like, 'I don't recall the specifics, but this is a usual and customary practice within the pharmaceutical industry'.

In other words, the defence was telling the court that, whatever may be the case elsewhere, in medicine the taking of company money while serving on guideline committees, being involved in the compilation of the DSM-IV or being a member of editorial boards is not regarded as a conflict of interest. On the contrary, it is difficult to rise to prominence in academic medicine without participating in give-and-take relationships with pharmaceutical companies. Indeed, not just academic status but the very science and policy of psychiatric medicine are co-constituted by drug companies and leading psychiatrists. Miller himself assumed this. Like a Shakespearean villain who feels completely justified in his actions, he responded to the defence attorney's question about how this charge to his reputation made him feel: 'I think it's grossly inaccurate and unfair and – and I feel like a pawn in somebody else's game'.

Miller shared the witness stand with Dr Steven Shon, the former Medical Director for Texas Mental Health and Mental Retardation (TMHMR). The prosecution systematically exposed Shon as having violated his contract with the State of Texas. They brought as a witness a fraud investigator for the state's Medicaid division who showed, among other things, that Shon did marketing work for J&J during working hours and that he accepted moneys that would not have been offered to him had he not occupied the position he did at TMHMR, which was illegal. Like the expert task force described above, Shon had helped J&J to figure out how to make Risperdal sell so well.[1]

Other individuals, including Dr John Rush, Dr Lynn Crismon and Dr John Chiles, were also identified as having received money from J&J while serving on the TMAP panel. The Texas director for NAMI, Joe Lovelace, also took money from J&J, some of which was deposited in an account under the name of his wife's law firm. J&J referred to these relationships as 'strategic alliances', a term borrowed from the management literature, where it refers to a relationship between two companies, often competitors to each other, that seek to cut costs or expand capabilities by joining forces (K. Applbaum 1999).

For a researcher like myself interested in the rationality (and irrationality) of medication prescription practices in psychiatry, the first point brought out in the cross-examination of Steven Shon struck a chord. Shon said that the reason TMAP came about was because prescription practices across the state were erratic. He said that if a person visited six psychiatrists, he might receive the same diagnosis from all six but could still be prescribed different medications by each one.

The revolutionary DSM-III was constructed, among other reasons, to standardize diagnostic criteria (Kleinman 1988). Why should there not be another undertaking, such as TMAP, to standardize treatment programmes? The failure of this logic does not lie in the aspiration to rationalize treatment, but in the current scientific limits of psychopharmacology, particularly in the non-specificity of the drugs and the variability of patient response, beneficial or adverse, to different drugs. The effort to establish a fairly strict algorithm (the 'A' in TMAP) for treatment in psychiatry is to impose pharmacological progress where it has not yet been achieved.

For J&J and the other firms that sold SGAs, the key implicit messages they wished to convey about their drugs were that this progress had in fact been achieved and that psychiatrists should espouse treatment standardization. In their optimism, many psychiatric researchers may have embraced the vision of progress that the drug companies were touting with the SGAs.[2]

A Matter of Trust: Clinical Trial Evidence vs Physician Judgement

The system of influence described above is part of the operation of a reliable machine for creating blockbuster demand, as readily for unworthy as for worthy drugs. A key source of the influence wielded by pharmaceutical companies lies in the design, reporting, publication and dissemination of data from clinical trials. Those trials are used to evaluate the efficacy and safety of newly devised medicines, and to investigate new uses for existing ones. In the past few decades, the standard form has become large-scale randomized controlled trials (RCTs). These produce the large volume of data that allows statistical analysis of the results, which is taken to be the most reliable way to demonstrate true drug effects. The movement advocating RCTs is called evidence-based medicine.

Much of the Risperdal court case turned on the presentation and interpretation of clinical trial data associated with the drug. The plaintiff had already made several references to CATIE, a trial of the effectiveness of antipsychotics drugs carried out in the United States, and to CUtLASS (Cost Utility of the Latest Antipsychotic drugs in Schizophrenia Study), a similar trial carried out in the United Kingdom. The plaintiff urged the jury to regard these studies as trustworthy because they were conducted not by drug companies, as most trials are these days, but by independent researchers. Although the plaintiff lawyer did not mention it, the CATIE study cost $42 million, involved 1,493 subjects and 400 researchers from fifty-seven sites across the country and was the largest comparative-effectiveness trial in the history of the mental health field. The rationale for the study lay in the ambiguity of clinical data concerning the comparative effectiveness and side effects of four drugs (SGAs) that had been introduced in the 1990s.

Results from CATIE and CUtLASS were published in the mid-2000s, near the time when the patent for Risperdal would expire. Both trials found that Risperdal and the other SGAs were no better than the older FGAs on measures of efficacy or tolerability. Additional studies pointed out that SGAs had a number of side effects of their own, in addition to the side effects associated with the FGAs. For most, this was an unexpected finding because prior studies of SGAs, such as the ones that supported the recommendations of TMAP, had ostensibly shown the reverse. If the scientific evidence supporting claims to SGA superiority were dubious, not to say rigged, then TMAP would look even more like a scam.

Echoing the SGA manufacturers' sustained efforts to discredit CATIE, in their opening statement counsel for the defence asserted that CATIE had many scientific failings, and they concentrated on the many published studies showing the superiority of the SGAs. As part of this, the defence put a map up on the screen showing the many places in the world where studies of Risperdal had been completed, calling it 'one of the most studied drugs in history'.

While RCT evidence would form an important part of the case, it could not, by itself, be expected to prove or disprove the defence's claim for the superiority of Risperdal as an antipsychotic agent, for several reasons. First, there is a mass of evidence, and different parts of it support different conclusions. Setting aside rigged studies, which are disseminated as marketing and therefore reach a wider audience than do independent studies, even the accuracy of conscientious research can never be fully substantiated. No clinical study is perfect, and flaws can always be identified that will encourage sceptics to deem a given conclusion invalid. There exist only a few clinical researchers fully qualified to interpret the highly specialized studies associated with antipsychotics, and those people are entrenched in disagreement with each other, sometimes made rancorous by accusations of bias. Second, use of this kind of evidence is problematic in a courtroom because conclusions reached in a court case and a clinical trial rest on different standards. Courts demand absolutes (guilty or innocent) whereas medical practitioners commonly make do with probabilities, since this is the best they have. Finally, no one can expect jurors to be able to make sense of RCT results anyway, no matter how patiently they are explained. In the end, most jurors have to decide on the basis of how well they trust the experts chosen to present scientific testimony in the courtroom.

Enter Clinical Experience

The plaintiff called to the stand Dr Jim Van Norman, a psychiatrist who completed all his training and licensing in Texas and had been practising in Travis County, where the court was located, for twenty-three years. He was director of a community mental health centre, exactly the sort of clinic that treats uninsured and Medicaid patients and that had a budget of the sort allegedly targeted by J&J through the TMAP initiative.

Van Norman said that he supervised the equivalent of fifteen full-time 'prescribers' who treat about 6,500 adults and 1,100 children per year, twice what they are budgeted to do. (In good dramatic fashion, this mention of budgetary constraint foreshadowed expressions of outrage over the alleged crime of promoting a drug that cost forty-five times as much as others that work just as well.)

The state's attorney, Tommy Jacks, asked Van Norman to think back to when Risperdal was first introduced in the 1990s: 'Do you recall any of the sales messages that you heard from Janssen representatives about their drug?' He replied:

> The biggest selling point as I recall was that . . . this medication was much more effective . . . at managing the negative symptoms . . . things like not wanting to go out and get a job or just having no enjoyment in life. . . . Risperdal was represented to me as being a safer medication than the first-generation antipsychotics, that we didn't have to worry as much about the extrapyramidal motor symptoms . . . and as an added benefit, that in the long run it was less expensive to the system because these medications were so effective, they would keep people from going into the hospital.

Jacks asked Van Norman whether TMAP affected prescription practices at his centre. 'Yes', Van Norman bluntly replied. This line of questioning was important because one of the defendant's recurrent claims was that TMAP was just a guideline and in no way constrained doctors to a particular medication choice. If TMAP was not enforced in any way, then how it was put together would be irrelevant to the allegation that the defendants had overcharged Texas by $579 million.

Van Norman explained that a physician at a clinic who chose to deviate from the TMAP recommendation, for instance by not pre-scribing an SGA as an initial treatment, had to document and justify that choice. Failure to do so could lead to sanctions and financial penalties. Physicians were, moreover, required to attend training programmes and quarterly meetings, in part to assure that they understood these rules.

Jacks asked Van Norman about his current use of SGAs and FGAs. Van Norman said he did sometimes prescribe SGAs, but that he uses the FGAs more frequently. He explained that he was greatly influenced by the CATIE and CUtLASS studies, which he described as unbiased by drug company funding. Jacks asked him if he prescribes FGAs in the same manner he did in the early 1990s, before the introduction of Risperdal. This was a question calculated to bring out an important point for the plaintiff's argument – namely, the standard SGA manufacturer's argument, the one also put forward by the defendant, that FGAs cause extrapyramidal syndrome, including the dreaded tardive dyskinesia (TD), which SGAs do not. Van Norman confirmed that he did, meaning he did not believe that use of FGAs increased the risk of TD. He added that the FGAs had an additional advantage, for they do not increase the risk of diabetes in the way that SGAs do (Koller et al. 2003), and so reduce the need to pay the costs associated with monitoring patients for lipids, glucose tolerance and weight gain.

He expanded on the side effects of the SGAs in comparison with the FGAs. He and his colleagues, he said, were frequently astonished by the speed and severity of weight gain some patients experienced on SGAs, which were as much as 20–30 lbs in three months. Further, on even the smallest doses of Risperdal (1 mg), some women developed hyper-prolactinemia, causing them to lactate, a side effect that would distress someone who is not nursing.

> Jacks asked: 'And TD? Have you seen that in [patients taking] the older drugs?'
> Van Norman replied: 'Not under my care'.

It seemed to me that the cross-examining defence attorney, John McDonald, was stunned by some of Van Norman's testimony, for it was almost certainly a radical departure from the brief that J&J would have given him. Even so, McDonald stuck to his team's strategy. He tried to discredit the witness by showing that he was speaking outside his area of expertise (Van Norman is not a clinical researcher). He reiterated the claim that TMAP never dictated what a physician could or could not do ('And to be clear, Doctor, you're not suggesting to this jury that you would ever not give a patient what you thought was the appropriate medication just because you had to fill out some additional paperwork, are you?'). He got the witness to state that he currently does sometimes use Risperdal in his practice; and he attempted to discredit the CATIE and CUtLASS studies.

Janssen's Reimbursement Department Takes the Stand

When I first began visiting pharmaceutical companies, I was baffled by the size of their departments called 'Government Affairs' or something similar. I understood that regulatory matters were complex and important to those companies, but I was not clear why dealing with them would require departments that large. Eventually I realized that government affairs departments were part of and under the supervision of marketing, as indeed has come to be the case with every other function in most pharmaceutical companies, including R&D. The close links between federal and state regulatory agencies and the pharmaceutical industry illustrate the clientelist side of the system.

The first deposition played on 12 January 2012 had been recorded earlier by Ms Nancy Bursch-Smith, and it pointed to those close links. Her job was to manage the relationship between J&J and the Texas Department of Mental Health and Mental Retardation (TMHMR).

The attorney for the state quoted J&J documents that said: '[We] put Steve Shon on the map'. (Steven Shon, described above, was the director of TMHMR during the TMAP years.) Bursch-Smith responded: 'I think that there are many companies that probably were involved with Dr Shon. I wouldn't say that Janssen held that title'. Her answer indicates that Shon was probably receiving money and gaining notoriety through his relationship with a number of SGA manufacturers.

Bursch-Smith was a member of the curiously named 'reimbursement' department. Because so much of the discussion surrounded the origin and dollar amount of checks written to Steven Shon, John Rush and others on the TMAP advisory board, one could think that a reimbursement department is the place that handled the associated paperwork. However, reimbursement actually referred to Medicaid, and Bursch-Smith's job was to figure out how to divert as many Medicaid reimbursement dollars as she could to J&J. The checks written to Shon and the other TMAP advisors were money J&J were laying out in exchange for those 'deliverables' that the trial was intended to uncover.

Bursch-Smith's inability to recall just about anything was little help to her, because the lawyer for the plaintiff had emails detailing how, in exchange for its money to Shon and Rush, J&J sought 'a favorable positioning for Risperdal'. Internal emails bearing Bursch-Smith's name or authorship also showed that J&J were not the only drug company vying for Steve Shon's affections. One email that Bursch-Smith received contained the words, 'Lilly [another big drug company] is sending their corporate jet to get [Shon] . . . You didn't sell our benefits to Shon'. Cross-examination by the defence sought to affirm Bursch-Smith's claim that J&J was not 'selling' to Shon but were involved only in an 'exchange of information'. Bursch-Smith's 'redescription' (A. Applbaum 2000) of the first in terms of the second, just as many before her called advertising 'education', reflects once again the simultaneous distinction between, and blurring of, corruption and marketing clientelism. Was the witness hiding behind the overlap, redescribing corruption as normal clientelism, or could she actually not tell the difference?

> Defence Lawyer: Why don't you believe that Janssen influenced Shon's work?
> Bursch-Smith: Because they told us they'd be making their own decisions.

The next witness was Bill Struyk, J&J's Regional Director for State Affairs for seven years.

> Plaintiff Lawyer: You were on the ground floor of the reimbursement team. What was your product?
> Struyk: Risperdal was our primary focus.
> Lawyer: [Takes out a company document] Among the credits listed as your accomplishments [is]: 'Instrumental in influencing Texas mental health care funding and treatment guidelines'.

Those guidelines are the Tri-University Schizophrenia Practice Guidelines, compiled by Allen Frances, John P. Docherty and David A. Kahn, described above. An account of the inception of the Guidelines is in Sharav (2011).

Struyk preferred to use 'education' to describe the original Tri-University symposium in 1996 as well as other activities involving Steven Shon and TMAP-allied psychiatrists. The state's attorney asked Struyk if his department's activities were directed towards increasing sales of Risperdal with the aid of the guidelines. Impatient with the questioning, Struyk twice said, in a tone of jaded irony, 'If it increased sales we were not disappointed'. The cross-examination by the defence allowed Struyk to rephrase his team's purpose: 'Our group's mission was to remove hurdles . . . Our job was to educate on mental health and to make sure drugs were available to those who needed it'.

Still pursuing the subject of funding for TMAP, the plaintiff next called the former head of the Robert Wood Johnson Foundation (RWJF), Dr Stephen Schroeder. That foundation is one of the two largest health and healthcare philanthropies in the United States, and it contributed the largest single amount in financial support of the development of TMAP. Schroeder said he did not believe that TMAP was a 'marketing effort' and he was never contacted by J&J.

The state attorney's presentation of excerpts of Schroeder's deposition began with the lawyer on the tape pointing out that J&J is the single largest financial stakeholder in RWJF. Three of the Foundation's 2009 Board of Trustees members were J&J executives.

> Plaintiff Lawyer: [I understand that] TMAP was an unusual [project for RWJF].
> Schroeder: Our projects generally didn't get into clinical condition.
> Lawyer: Why'd you make an exception in this case?
> Schroeder: I just thought the upside was really – really large.
> Lawyer: Did RWJF do due diligence into the motives of the TMAP people?
> Schroeder: We didn't look into their hearts.
> Lawyer: How about whether they [were taking] money from pharma.
> Schroeder: Well, it happens all the time. That is, most academics actually take money from the pharmaceutical industry for speaking and for travel and dinners and things like that.

The final witness was Percy Coard II. Coard started working as a drug representative for J&J and Risperdal in 1998, served as district manager from 1999 to 2002 and was then promoted to the reimbursement department.

> Plaintiff Lawyer: [reading from Coard's CV] 'Seek out additional individuals and find their importance to the system . . .' Did you understand this was among the activities you were supposed to be engaging in connection with the part of your job relating – relating to your role in 'influencing others'?
> Coard: Yes, sir.

'The system' that the lawyer mentioned referred to several entities, including hospitals, the prison system and TMHMR, where Coard had contact with Steven Shon on a regular basis. Coard described Shon and Miller as key opinion leaders.

The state's lawyer reviewed a 2002 business plan at J&J. It specified a 'threat' to continued growth: Texas Medicaid, which was third in the country on Medicaid spending, was looking to implement cost containment measures. One measure identified in the document was 'prior authorization', which means that before a 'consumer' can see a specialist or receive a specific service or treatment, the request has to pass through a layer of approval involving the payer, such as an insurance company. Medicaid is public insurance. Under the heading 'TMAP Ownership!!! – (ongoing)', the business plan suggested that TMAP and strong advocacy support would lessen the threat of prior authorization.

The discussion turned to the company's effort to place Consta, J&J's long-acting injectable version of Risperdal, 'in a favourable position in TMAP'. Coard explained how helpful Steve Shon was to him in figuring out the best way to get Consta to succeed on the market:

> Dr Shon felt a key to successfully launching Consta in Texas was to focus on in-patients. He said that it is rare for stable patients to be switched from one antipsychotic to another when they enter their community mental health centre. . . . They typically stay on what they were prescribed as an in-patient. Therefore it's imperative to drive utilization in the in-patient facilities.

Conclusion

The Risperdal case was not overly complicated to try. There were many obvious infractions and J&J had little interest in allowing a media circus to continue at their expense. As it turned out, despite the conclusive evidence of fraud, J&J settled out of court for $158 million, about a quarter of the original demand. This is a small amount when compared with the profits that companies make and with the bonuses given to executives who have already moved on and who are rarely, if ever, held criminally responsible for their actions. Criminal prosecutions and suits, then, are weak tools for constraining off-label marketing.

Although the evidence was fairly clear in the case I have described, as a rule off-label promotion is difficult to prosecute and to halt. Some of the reasons for this are laid out in Figure 1.1, and they may be divided into the proximate and the overarching. Proximate causes are acts of commission or omission taken by companies and prescribing clinicians that, from a legal standpoint, end up muddying, inadvertently or purposefully, the evidence of fraud. Overarching causes are features of the political- and cultural-economic environment that either encourage or legitimate the disputed behaviours.

Taken together, these causes reflect some of the questions raised in the Introduction to this volume and elsewhere, such as the changing relationship between the economic acquiring of wealth and the social playing by the rules that concerned E.P. Thompson (1971) in his description of the English crowd, and the degree to which economic rationality should be applied to areas of life considered vital to people's survival, such as food and medicine.

System of corruption: The practice is so widespread as to be considered the norm rather than the exception.

Legal obstacles: Company strategic documents, including those pertaining to clinical trials, are considered proprietary. Revelatory evidence about the practice generally comes from whistle-blowers within the company, whose motivations are regarded as suspect by juries.

Ghostwriting: Promotions often masquerade as disinterested science, published in reputable medical journals and disseminated to doctors by pharmaceutical reps.

Key opinion leaders: Drug and device manufacturers employ tens of thousands of reputable physicians to act as surrogate marketers and promoters of off-label uses.

Blurred boundary between education and propaganda: Related to ghostwriting, but extends also to Continuing Medical Education, disease-explaining media (brochures, websites, radio shows), informational seminars led by key opinion leaders and funded by industry.

Partial truths: Many off-label uses of drugs (whether illicitly promoted or not) prove to be medically justified, and so physicians are not quick to be suspicious of or criticize off-label promotions.

Tenuous science: Off-label promotions are most common in areas of medicine where outcomes of the procedure or treatment are ambiguous, such as psychiatry (and spinal fusion surgery).

Physician over-confidence in their own judgment and obstinate in their belief that they know all about, and so are impervious to, drug company influence.

Poor adverse event reporting: Independent research into drug safety is usually too late to catch bad practices, while physicians report only 1–5 per cent of adverse events (Healy 2012b).

Political ideology: The notion that the free market is self-correcting and always right. The drug lobby in the US Congress assures a legal attitude lenient towards companies.

Figure 1.1 Reasons why off-label promotion schemes are difficult to halt

Off-label promotion is an economic activity that happens to violate federal regulations. For those within the sector, however, it is not deviant. The testimony I have described shows how pervasive and complicated it can be in the pharmaceutical industry, and likely in any industry that is so much focused on marketing. Sometimes this sort of activity is easily visible, such as in print advertisements or on product websites. It is more difficult to identify when drug representatives talk to physicians during office sales calls or over expensive dinners, or when doctors who are paid consultants of drug companies speak at conferences or in Continuing Medical Education venues. Even more difficult to discern is the effect of rigged studies published in leading journals, which are often reprinted and disseminated widely to physicians around the world.

The trial of the J&J suit that I have described illustrates the overlap of marketing clientelism and corruption, for even the most florid of J&J's actions can be located easily on the continuum of pharmaceutical marketing practices. While the actions under investigation may be legal contraventions, they are not managerial ones. On the contrary, the marketing practices conform to business and organizational norms that are embraced as sound management. This helps to account for the fact that the activities that lead to prosecution are distinguished, if at all, by degree and not kind from other practices. If for no other reason than that competitive pressures drive companies to behave in similar ways, the marketing strategies and tactics for drugs of any given class will resemble each other. So, when Vioxx was implicated in a vast scheme of marketing fraud, including off-label promotions, industry watchers knew that the other Cox-2 inhibitors (Celebrex and Bextra) were unlikely to be far behind. Similarly, when Zyprexa (Lilly's SGA) was called to account, informed observers concluded that the other manufacturers of SGAs were guilty of similar crimes, which would become visible if the opportunity arose to subpoena their marketing records.

What I have said of Medtronic, J&J and the rest buttress a point I made earlier in this chapter. That is, the neoliberal stress on the free market can lead firms to market freely. In the case of various pharmaceutical firms, this means creating a market demand when there was none, even if it involves engaging in practices that most people would think are highly questionable. In the words 'most people', however, lies another point that I have made, one that also bears on the arguments made in the Introduction to this volume, relating to the concept of deviance. That is, the sort of practices that I have described are taken for granted within the industry, a point demonstrated by some of the testimony that I have quoted in this chapter.

Deviance, then, resembles interpretation of the results of scientific studies of drugs: those who seek simple yes-or-no answers are likely to be disappointed. Vis-à-vis marketing, practices that are deviant for some may be normal for others, and those practices may be so pervasive that, without them, the operation of significant areas of life would come to a halt, at least until new practices and procedures emerge.

As discussed in the Introduction, in complex and diverse societies, it is likely that different sets of people will see different things as deviant, just as they will see different things as wrong. Reconciling these is the function of politics and government, so that the concern with economic practices of the sort that exist in the pharmaceutical industry needs to be joined with a concern with political judgement and the factors that shape it.

Kalman Applbaum teaches anthropology at the University of Wisconsin at Milwaukee. His research concerns the commercial marketing of pharmaceuticals on the one hand, and the evaluation of safety, adherence and treatment costs and outcomes on the other. He has background and specific interest in rational drug use in psychiatry. He is co-founder of Data Based Medicine (Rxisk.org), which aims to improve the quantity and quality of adverse drug events reporting, and to implement findings in healthcare.

Notes

1. A description of how Shon allegedly peddled TMAP in Pennsylvania is in Jones (2004), and Jones is the whistle-blower who originally filed the suit against J&J in 2004 (see also Waters 2005).
2. Some well-placed anthropologists also appear to have embraced it (see Healy 2012b).

References

Applbaum, Arthur Isak. 2000. *Ethics for Adversaries: The Morality of Roles in Public and Professional Life*. Princeton, NJ: Princeton University Press.

Applbaum, Kalman. 1999. 'Survival of the Biggest: Business Policy, Managerial Discourse, and Uncertainty in a Global Business Alliance', *Anthropological Quarterly* 72(4): 55–66.

———. 2006a. 'Pharmaceutical Marketing and the Invention of the Medical Consumer', *PLoS Medicine* 3(4): e189.

———. 2006b. 'Educating for Global Mental Health: American Pharmaceutical Companies and the Adoption of SSRIs in Japan', in Adriana Petryna, Arthur Kleinman and Andrew Lakoff (eds), *Pharmaceuticals and Globalization: Ethics, Markets, Practices*. Durham, NC: Duke University Press, pp. 85–110.

————. 2009a. 'Getting to Yes: Corporate Power and the Creation of a Psychopharmaceutical Blockbuster', *Culture, Medicine and Psychiatry* 33(2): 185–215.

————. 2009b. 'Is Marketing the Enemy of Pharmaceutical Innovation?', *The Hastings Center Report* 39(4): 13–17.

Eisenstadt, S.N., and Luis Roniger. 1984. *Patron, Clients and Friends: Interpersonal Relations and the Structure of Trust in Society*. Cambridge: Cambridge University Press.

Fauber, John. 2011. 'Experts Repudiate Medtronic's Research: Medical Journal Devotes Entire Issue to Exposé', *Milwaukee Journal Sentinel* (28 June). www.jsonline.com/watchdog/watchdogreports/124676453.html (accessed 22 September 2015).

FDA (Food and Drug Administration). 2012. 'Warning Letters: Medtronic, Inc. 7/17/12'. Washington, DC: U.S. Food and Drug Administration. www.fda.gov/ICECI/EnforcementActions/WarningLetters/2012/ucm314736.htm (accessed 25 May 2016).

Gellner, Ernest. 1977. 'Patrons and Clients', in E. Gellner and John Waterbury (eds), *Patrons and Clients in Mediterranean Societies*. London: Duckworth, pp. 1–6.

Halle, Dieter, and Cris Shore (eds). 2005. *Corruption: Anthropological Perspectives*. London: Pluto Press.

Healy, David. 2006. 'Manufacturing Consensus', *Culture, Medicine and Psychiatry* 30(2): 135–56.

————. 2012a. *Pharmageddon*. Berkeley: University of California Press.

————. 2012b. Review of Janis H. Jenkins (ed.), 'Pharmaceutical Self: The Global Shaping of Experience in an Age of Psychopharmacology', *Transcultural Psychiatry* 49(3–4): 638–40.

Herman, Coleman. 2014. '$80M OtisMed False Claims Settlement Nets Whistleblower Richard Adrian $7 Mill', *Whistleblower News Review* (8 December). www.whistleblowergov.org/healthcare-and-pharma.php?article=OtisMed-80M-False-Claims-Whistleblower-Settlement_15#navbar (accessed 25 May 2016).

Jones, Allen. 2004. [Untitled]. [no city]: Posted on the Internet by the Law Project for Psychiatric Rights. http://psychrights.org/Drugs/AllenJonesTMAPJanuary20.pdf (accessed 23 September 2015)

Kleinman, Arthur. 1988. *Rethinking Psychiatry: From Cultural Category to Personal Experience*. New York: The Free Press.

Koller, Elizabeth A., James T. Cross, P. Murali Doraiswamy and Bruce S. Schneider. 2003. 'Risperidone-Associated Diabetes Mellitus: A Pharmacovigilance Study', *Pharmacotherapy* 23(6): 735–44.

Lansdale, Edward P. 2006. 'Used as Directed? How Prosecutors Are Expanding the False Claims Act to Police Pharmaceutical Off-label Marketing', *New England Law Review* 41(1): 159–98.

Resnick, Daniel, and Kevin J. Bozic. 2013. 'Meta-analysis of Trials of Recombinant Human Bone Morphogenetic Protein-2: What Should

Spine Surgeons and Their Patients Do with This Information?', *Annals of Internal Medicine* 158(12): 912–13.

Scott, James C. 1972. 'Patron–Client Politics and Political Change in Southeast Asia', *The American Political Science Review* 66(1): 91–113.

Sharav, Vera Hassner. 2011. 'Confidential Expert Witness Report Documents Psychiatrists' Corrupt Practices'. New York: Alliance for Human Research Protection. www.ahrp.org/cms/content/view/822/9/ (accessed 24 September 2015).

Stempel, Jonathan. 2012. 'Medtronic to Pay $85 Million to Settle Infuse Lawsuit', *Reuters* (30 March). www.reuters.com/article/2012/03/30/us-medtronic-settlement-idUSBRE82T1A920120330#AUVZSm8s5gIK5F ZO.97 (accessed 25 May 2016).

Stroup, T. Scott, and Jeffrey A. Lieberman (eds). 2010. *Antipsychotic Trials in Schizophrenia: The CATIE Project.* Cambridge: Cambridge University Press.

Thompson, E.P. 1971. 'The Moral Economy of the English Crowd in the Eighteenth Century', *Past and Present* 50: 76–136.

Torsello, Davide. 2012. 'Clientelism and Social Trust in Comparative Perspective: Particularism versus Universalism', *International Journal of Humanities and Social Science* 2(23): 71–78.

US District Court, District of Minnesota. 2009. Consolidated Class Action Complaint. Case 0:08-cv-06324-PAM-AJB. [Minneapolis?]: United States District Court. www.blbglaw.com/cases/00119_data/Medtronic-08-6324-ConsolidatedComplaintasfiled.pdf (accessed 28 September 2015).

Wank, David. 1996. 'The Institutional Process of Market Clientelism: Guanxi and Private Business in a South China City', *The China Quarterly* 147: 820–38.

Waters, Rob. 2005. 'Medicating Amanda: When State Mental Health Officials Fall under the Influence of Big Pharma, the Burden Falls on Captive Patients. Like This 13-year-old Girl', *Mother Jones* (May–June). www.motherjones.com/politics/2005/05/medicating-amanda (accessed 23 September 2015).

2

The Measure of Sociality
Quantification, Control and Economic Deviance

Emil A. Røyrvik

Our time is characterized by a will to quantify, measure and standardize social life, and in this chapter I argue that this gives rise to socialities conducive to the proliferation of economic activities that many see as questionable. The cultural logic of that will is marked by terms such as performance, indicator, auditing, ranking, excellence, evaluation, transparency and accountability, and it shapes and is shaped by a neoliberal sociality that destroys collectives, transforms subjectivity and substantially shapes economic activities by reorienting professional and ethical judgement.

Tord Larsen argues that different social and cultural formations are distinguished by different forms of objectification, and that '[m]odes of objectification – different ways of producing thinghood and thing-like entities like categories and classes – are part of the cultural "infrastructure" of any society' (Larsen 2012: 580). The dominant forms of objectification in our time arguably are the social processes of that quantification, measurement and standardization (see, e.g., Porter 1995; Crosby 1997; Poovey 1998; Bowker and Star 1999). This is signalled by the rise of the audit society (Power 1997) and the society of standards (Brunsson and Jacobsson 2002), the culture of management and accountability (e.g. Strathern 2000), the expanding use of measurements and indicators (Merry 2011) and the near ubiquity of ranking (Espeland and Sauder 2007, 2009). As Cris Shore and Susan Wright (2015: 22) put it, '"Governing by numbers" – reducing complex processes to simple numerical indicators and rankings for purposes of management and control – has become a defining feature of our times'.

Measurement and quantification do not just represent or order entities that already exist. Rather, they help to generate them (Larsen 2012), in the way that the notion of IQ is a product of intelligence tests, or the notions of accountability and transparency are products of various quantified reporting procedures. According to Shore and Wright (2015), these processes create both new kinds of subjectivity and new forms of power and governance, themes that I will investigate in this chapter.

In the cultural formations that have emerged, most commonly referred to as neoliberalism, the market rules and defines nearly everything of worth. The financial and the moral coalesce and create new economic and ethical conceptions and practices, new regimes of control and new institutional realities and subjectivities. Inspired by market-rule and governmentality approaches to neoliberalism, where 'governing through calculation' (see, e.g., Wacquant 2012) is central to understanding government and power within and beyond the state, I use case material from Norway to investigate those institutional realities and subjectivities, and in particular the ways that they shape economic practices.

A key part of the spread of quantification is 'management by objectives', which encourages workers to achieve objectives set by managers, often cast in terms of KPIs, key performance indicators. This system is successful, in the sense that people often will change how they work in order to meet their KPI targets. However, I argue, commonly they focus solely on meeting the targets and ignore the substantive matters that the KPIs represent, and moreover do so in ways that ignore professional and ethical judgement. This occurs not only among line workers, but also among managers, who seek to achieve objectives set by managers higher up, and by boards, political departments and governments, often with serious consequences related to dubious economic behaviour. Especially among upper-level managers, the focus on measurable performance targets can lead to the idea that, as long as they meet performance targets and contract requirements, they should have 'freedom to manage', and thus 'room to manoeuvre'. That gives rise to opportunities for corruption and various forms of mismanagement (Anders 2015) and increases the cleavage between management and workers (see, e.g., Shore and Wright 2015). The result is that the spread of management by objectives and its corollaries encourages the subordination of ethical practice and judgement to financial and managerial control and concerns. One consequence is the facilitation of improper economic activity.

The first section in what follows outlines the key notions of neoliberalism and sociality. Then I consider how management by objectives and financial performance measurements have penetrated the operation of firms at all levels, encouraging various forms of economic wrongdoing and mismanagement. Next, I describe both the fallacies of mainstream neoclassical economics and its role as a main intellectual and ideological source of neoliberalism. I then present the details of performance management and measures with case examples from Norwegian work life. In the subsequent section I analyse those cases as regimes of 'neo-management' and 'post-bureaucratic' control that use the goals of profit and productivity to govern people's subjectivity, their inner lives, emotions, values and personal relations. This is followed by a critical analysis of the emerging subjective forms associated with these changes in management. I conclude the chapter by highlighting some of the paradoxes and corollaries related to the notion of neoliberal sociality.

Neoliberal Sociality

Neoliberalism has become something of a '*rascal concept* – promiscuously pervasive, yet inconsistently defined, empirically imprecise and frequently contested' (Brenner, Peck and Theodore 2010: 184), and it might be better to think of varieties of neoliberalization than of neoliberalism in general.[1] With that qualification in mind, the emergence of a global 'culture of neoliberalism' (Comaroff and Comaroff 2001) or 'neoliberal culture complex' (Hannerz 2007) since around 1980 is well documented (e.g. Harvey 2005; Crouch 2011; Streeck 2014).

Here I approach neoliberalism in terms of both market rule and governmentality. While these construe neoliberalism in somewhat different ways, they both point to the dominance of the economic and the associated denial of the social – and with that the human collectives that spring from life outside of the market (see Bourdieu 1998). As Margaret Thatcher (1987), one of the main neoliberal political advocates, famously stated, '[T]here is no such thing as society. ... There are individual men and women, and there are families'.

The idea of market rule sees neoliberalism as a programme to 'impose market imperatives not only on all territories but also on all human activities' (Wacquant 2012: 68), which states encourage through deregulation, privatization and the creation of new markets. These policies secure the free flow of capital and safeguard financial institutions, while eliminating many areas of state provision of services. The idea of governmentality is inspired by Foucault's (2010) lectures on the birth of biopolitics, and considers neoliberalism in terms of mundane techniques and technologies of governing, a 'flowing and flexible conglomeration of calculative notions, strategies and technologies aimed at fashioning populations and people' (Wacquant 2012: 69). These appear 'in a variegated landscape of institutional, economic and political forms' (Collier 2012: 191) and they mark the dominance of formal, economistic expertise over substantive expertise and, crucially, the 'attempt to govern *through the calculative choice of individuals*' (ibid.: 190). Appropriately, governmentality approaches direct our attention to things like accountability, transparency, quality control, branding (Hannerz 2007) and the other terms that, I said, reflect the cultural logic of quantification, measurement and standardization.

I take socialities to be the different qualitative forms that relationships might have (Glaeser 2006: 70), forms that are 'the formative context-constituting coexistence in human life' (Schatzki 2008). As this suggests, we can understand the processes of social life only if we understand the socialities involved, and classic approaches to the social entail distinct forms of sociality. For example, Thomas Hobbes ([1651] 1982) understood the relationships between human beings as barbaric: fundamentally competitive, even violent. The state of nature, the war of all against all, could only be left behind through relationships of submission and domination linking every citizen to the absolute sovereign, the Leviathan. For Adam Smith ([1776] 2003) also, the basic relationship between humans was competitive, driven by self-interest. For Smith, however, we leave that state behind when the division of labour increases, for then cooperation comes to overwhelm the competition. In contrast, Rousseau ([1762] 2003) held the Romantic view that people are good when in the state of nature, but are corrupted by society. This does not, as many suppose, mean that Rousseau thought that Man was inevitably corrupted by society. Rather, he held that society corrupts only when it fails, when the social contract does not operate.[2]

As a result of the interplay of these and other views during the early stages of the emergence of capitalism, the idea developed that economic interests are the guarantee of the public good (Hirschman 1977). That is because they would constrain the passions that disrupt social life: ambition, avarice, the lust for power and sexual lust. The idea that the play of interests would restrain the evils of the passions of course seems dubious in the present, an era of capitalism without democracy or with only a managed democracy, co-opted by capital and producing an 'inverted totalitarianism' (Wolin 2008). One might rather echo Rousseau and hold that the social contract has failed, and that people are corrupted.

Financial Control and Financial Fraud

In an ethnography of corporate management (Røyrvik 2011), I argued that the last thirty years or so have seen the development and use of an increasingly large and sophisticated battery of financial indicators, accounting techniques and controls, which have embedded financial concerns and control deep into organizations and the production and labour processes. These devices may have been introduced as measures that simply report economic results, but they ended up controlling and directing the goals, ambitions, values and investments of the organizations that used them. In the aluminium company Hydro,[3] the main case I described, discussions frequently dealt with different financial instruments of control, like CROGI, EBITDA and RoaCE. The head of their magnesium division once said that 'we call it "CROGI-ism", everybody is talking about it these days' (all translations from Norwegian are by the author). CROGI (Cash Return On Gross Investment), an in-house invention, was for some years the major financial reporting and control instrument.

Some of the plant managers complained that it was unfair because, no matter how much money some plants were making, their CROGI would not be satisfactory due to the way that CROGI weighted cost overruns during the investment and building phase of the plant. That weighting was based on profitability projections expressed in internal rent requirements on new plants, and those requirements were so high that some people thought that most projects would never reach the target, and thus would not be undertaken. As one project manager only half-jokingly noted: 'With the internal rent requirements these days, it is an open question whether we can do many more projects in the future'. The internal rent, in other words, became decisive in determining what the different parts of the company sought to do.

Indeed, during my years of fieldwork, Hydro shifted its focus from downstream projects and businesses (closer to the customer) to midstream and upstream ones (closer to energy sources and raw materials), even though the majority of workplaces are found downstream. This shift meant that Hydro's business increasingly had to be conducted in places where cheap energy sources are located. In practice, this meant in developing countries with energy reserves, which commonly had weaker regulations of everything from finance and tax to labour rights, and where the chance of being involved in dubious economic activities was significantly greater than it would be elsewhere. For example, in their comprehensive investigation of Hydro, a Norwegian and an American law firm concluded that the company was involved in business activities in Libya in 2000–01 that were in breach of Hydro's own code of conduct. Their report said that those activities might be seen as problematic in light of both Norwegian and American anti-corruption laws, but it drew no legal conclusion. Two high-level Hydro directors had to resign, but Norwegian authorities chose not to investigate the case (ØKOKRIM 2009).

The corporate life of Norway provides many other examples of how the extension of financial measures in the organization, combined with the idea that higher management should be free to manage, can occasion economic wrongdoing and a reorientation of goals and values. Those examples indicate that such changes in corporate orientation can challenge ethical judgement related to investment and business operations. Although revealing no direct causality, they suggest that the emergence of neoliberal financialization and certain forms of management are associated with the increased likelihood of dubious economic activity.

The Norwegian oil and gas company Statoil has been involved in several cases of alleged and proven misconduct and corruption, from controversial tar sands (oil sands) projects to the use of bribery to secure lucrative oil contracts. The most infamous involved corruption in Iran in 2002–03. Statoil was found guilty of corruption both in Norway, where it was fined Kr 20 million, and in the United States, where it was fined $21 million and had to agree that it had violated the Foreign Corrupt Practices Act, that it was responsible for bribery to obtain contracts in the Iranian South Pars gas field and that it had used improper accounting procedures to hide those bribes (Statoil 2006). Statoil is hardly the only large Norwegian company involved in controversy. The fertilizer company Yara has been charged with corruption and bribery in Libya and India (Winsnes et al. 2015). The largest Norwegian telecom operator, Telenor, is being scrutinized for possible corruption on the part of its subsidiary in Uzbekistan, Vimpelcom, which is under investigation in three countries (Laustsen 2015).

The widespread financialization of Norway, the increasing use of economic measures and the declining use of other bases of judgement, is illustrated by a controversial case involving economic wrong and municipal government. In the early 2000s eight small, relatively rural and rich municipalities capitalized about US$ 200 million of their anticipated earnings from hydropower, and invested it in complex financial products. Following the 2008 financial crisis these became worthless. They were produced by Citigroup and bought by Terra Securities, which resold them to the Norwegian municipalities. Several long legal proceedings, both in Norway and in the United States, concluded that Citigroup had explained the very risky nature of those products to Terra Securities, but that Terra had not explained the risks to the municipalities. Those municipalities sued Terra Securities, which went bankrupt, and Citigroup was held blameless in the bankruptcy proceedings. The municipalities, however, did win their case against Terra Securities' insurance company, ACE, and received about US$10 million in compensation. 'A moral victory, but a drop in the sea', said one of the mayors (Sørhelm et al. 2014). The municipalities decided not to pay back the US$200 million they had borrowed from the banks when they capitalized their expected income, and were sued for the money. The case ended in 2015 when the municipalities agreed to pay US$80 million in a final settlement (Sundberg and Fredriksen 2015).

These examples illustrate some of the ways that organizations of different sorts in Norway have become financialized. That process has a variety of aspects, but many of them reflect the growing concern with share price and shareholder value, which, according to Karen Ho (2009: 176), prepared the way for 'dismantling the corporation in the name of the shareholder', ultimately to the benefit of finance capital. The management by objectives that I have described is the main form of organizational governance associated with financialization, which also is associated with rewarding the higher echelons of management with stock options, and offering stock at a discount to those lower on the company ladder. These more or less concerted efforts are designed to support the principle of 'value-based management' and to tie management and employees to shareholders' values and goals.

These examples also illustrate the cultural logic of contemporary neoliberal economy, a logic that led eight municipalities to use their residents' future income to speculate in highly complex financial products that they hardly understood. Although those examples are diverse, the criteria of financial and performance success that they illustrate, like the instruments used to measure that success, express the cultural logic of quantification, measurement and standardization, and the neoliberal practices and ideology in which they are embedded. Although these are presented as the route to transparency and accountability, their very focus on the technology of measurement makes them easy to abuse. As Gerhard Anders documents, the fairly simple manipulation of a financial management system set up to increase transparency and accountability enabled a small group of people in Malawi's government to divert more than €25 million of government money into private pockets. The forensic audit report delivered a 'damning verdict on financial management and audit' (Anders 2015: 39).

The hegemony of mainstream neoclassical economics is particularly important for understanding this cultural logic and its neoliberal manifestations. I turn to that now.

Formative Neoclassical Fallacies

The limitations of neoclassical economics, particularly its reliance on the ideas of the rational actor and the perfect market, have received scholarly attention from several disciplines, not least anthropology (e.g. Carrier 1998; Ho 2009; Røyrvik 2011: 46–51). In the decades following the Second World War, neoclassical economics came to dominate the discipline, the most prestigious branches of which ceased to be empirical sciences of human action. Instead, much of economics came to resemble a branch of mathematics devoted to deductive modelling, a change viewed with dismay by a number of prominent economists (Røyrvik 2011: 47).

Anthropologists Carrier and Miller (1998) have described the way our lives are increasingly made to conform to the virtuality of economic thought that those mathematical models embody, and especially the growing tendency to evaluate the world in terms of economic models, rather than evaluating the models in terms of the world. As Carrier (1998: 2) put it, neoclassical economics, with its great institutional power, is engaged in 'the conscious attempt to make the real world conform to the virtual image'. Echoing this, Karen Ho (2009: 35) argues that greater virtualism and abstraction in economics is 'creating a prescriptive model for reality', and calls it a 'virtual reality' detached from social relationships. As well, aspects of the economy have increasingly been analysed using ideas like virtualism. For example, Clegg and Courpasson (2004) characterize finance capital as taking on a 'hyperreal' quality; after the 2008 financial crisis scholars began to report that finance capital was relatively autonomous from the 'real economy' (e.g. Kallis, Martinez-Alier and Norgaard 2009); the market in complex derivatives has been described as 'illusionary' and an 'economic wonderland' of 'castles built on sand' that threaten liberal democracy (Cloke 2009). Using Baudrillard's notions of hyperreality, simulation and simulacra, Røyrvik and Brodersen (2012) argue that developments in finance capital are leading to a political and cultural economy of 'real virtuality', a concept that suggests that at least the financial sector has mobilized and materialized economic relations and spaces constituted by the play of signs and models. It signifies relations based on signs subsuming their referents and on models that are confused with and that subsume what is modelled.

Yanis Varoufakis, the former Greek Minister of Finance in the Syriza government and a Marxist trained in neoclassical economics, makes similar criticism, interestingly with reference to a classical anthropological text. He contends that economists 'belong to a sinister priesthood purveying thinly disguised, heavily mathematized superstition as . . . scientific economics' (Varoufakis 2013: 1, ellipsis in original), and invokes E.E. Evans-Pritchard's (1937) work on the Azande to describe how 'economists lose not a smidgeon of their discursive power despite their pathetic incapacity to predict economic crises or, indeed, to say anything useful about really existing capitalism' (Varoufakis 2013: 2). He poses his question by drawing a parallel between those economists and the Zande priesthood.

> *How did the priests and oracles retain their hold over the tribe's imagination given that they consistently failed to predict or avert disasters?* His [i.e. Evans-Pritchard's] explanation of the Azande's unshakeable belief in their oracles goes like this: 'Azande see as well as we that the failure of their oracle to prophesy truly calls for explanation, but so entangled are they in mystical notions that they must make use of them to account for failure. The contradiction between experience and one mystical notion is explained by reference to other mystical notions'. (ibid.)

Economics is very similar, argues Varoufakis. He says that

> when economists fail to predict some pivotal economic moment, which is always, for instance the Crash of 2008, that failure is accounted for by appealing to the same mystical economic notions which failed in the first place. Occasionally new notions are created in order to account for the failure of the earlier ones. And so predictive failure leads to more, not less, social power for the economists who are entrusted by society to offer scientific explanations of their . . . failures. (ibid.: 2)

Apparently unhappy with this state of affairs, in 2011 a group of dissident economists established the World Economics Association to reform the discipline. By 2014 it had become the second largest organization of professional economists.

As I have noted already, the mystical mathematization of economics has arguably divorced the discipline from its classic task of documenting and analysing economic behaviour, and instead married it to the modelling and moulding of the economic world to fit its concocted image. In Varoufakis's words:

> Econometrics is, believe me, the art of torturing data until it fits into *any* economic model one happens to have faith in. As if that were not enough, the social phenomena under study are heavily influenced by the dominant paradigm to which dominant economic theories are major contributors. (ibid.: 2)

To a large degree, this mathematized, performative modelling is fuelled by the long-term cultural logic of quantification, measurement and standardization and the recent ascendancy of neoliberalism, each supporting the other.

Although management by objectives was popularized by Peter Drucker in 1954, it began to acquire its current ubiquitous status in Norway, as elsewhere, in the 1980s, which marks it as both a symptom and a major element of Norwegian neoliberalism.[4] Its rise was facilitated by changes in IT since the 1970s, which have allowed greater and quicker monitoring and communications, and the proliferation of new versions of management by objectives. An example of these is called BetterWorks, presented as a 'Silicon Valley-style management system called "O.K.R.", which stands for "objectives and key results"' (Dougherty and Hardy 2015). The promoters say that we will see 'more and more systems in this field of quantified work, or people science, that are going to make the most valuable resource that we have – which is our team – more effective'. The idea is that workers, doubtless with an eye on management, will 'create specific, measurable goals and track their progress in an open system that anyone in the company can see'. Co-workers can then give each other praise (in the form of standardized 'cheers') or condemnation (in the form of 'nudges'). Each worker also has a profile, a digital tree that grows with accomplishments but shrivels with poor productivity.

The passion for measurement is nothing new, as Alfred W. Crosby demonstrated in *The Measure of Reality* (1997), a title that inspired the title of this chapter. European obsession with quantification began around 1300, when the appearance of mechanical clocks and the cannon obliged people to think of time and space as divided into discrete units. At about the same time they invented Portolan marine charts, perspective painting and, not least, double-entry bookkeeping. What Crosby described is a shift to a quantitative perception, which made modern science, technology, business practice and bureaucracy possible – a shift that that we have inherited. This shift was radical:

> When in the fourteenth century the scholars of Oxford's Merton College began to think about the benefits of measuring not only size, but also qualities as slippery as motion, light, heat, and color, they forged right on, jumped the fence, and talked about quantifying certitude, virtue, and grace. Indeed, if you can manage to think of measuring heat before the invention of the thermometer, then why should you presumptively exclude certitude, virtue, and grace? (Crosby 1997: 14)

In our own times, this desire to quantify has been amplified by new electronic technologies that I have mentioned already. So, while those Oxford scholars dreamt of measuring grace, virtue and certitude, today we routinely measure everything from IQ and emotional intelligence to competence and personal experience, as well as even more intangible qualities like moral values, well-being, trust and loyalty. As I argued above, this quantification and measurement are not passive, but are generative, for they help to constitute and change the social realities they record and represent. I turn now to showing how this plays out with respect to performance measurements and their effect on professional and ethical judgement and practice.

Performance Measurement, Valuation and Ranking

Following the financial crisis, a number of financial institutions in Scandinavia, as elsewhere, were accused of misleading sales practices, as illustrated by the case of Terra Securities and those Norwegian municipalities. In reaction, many of those institutions sought to reorient their staff away from a concern with making sales and towards a concern with satisfying customers. The customer meeting – what one bank called 'the moment of truth' – became a primary focus. One aspect of this was the introduction of new measures for evaluating staff. I was involved in a series of studies of Scandinavian financial institutions that investigated these changes in sales rhetoric and practices (e.g. Forseth, Clegg and Røyrvik 2014; Forseth, Røyrvik and Clegg 2015).

Customers were asked to evaluate their advisors after meeting with them, and the evaluations were passed on to those advisors. These were treated as measures of customer satisfaction, and management used them to rate individual financial advisers. The new procedure involved additional monitoring and control in the guise of customer orientation. However, the overt focus on customer satisfaction did not actually reduce the pressure to sell financial products, because advisors continued to have their sales monitored. The result was the continuing pressure on advisors to sell, increasing managerial control, increasing self-discipline and less time to spend talking to customers.

This expansion of valuation indicators and measures, especially those related to customer satisfaction, is part of a broader trend in Norway and elsewhere. A recent comprehensive report by Lederne (Nordrik, Wessel-Aas and Knudsen 2014), the Norwegian Organisation of Managers and Executives, has the title: 'The Orwellian Work Life?' The report is the result of focus-group interviews among the organization's members and, judged by its conclusions, the question mark in the title could have been left out. The study focuses on systems of management by objectives and human-resource management, and found that members experience these as leading to more authoritarian management, more surveillance and control, greater demands for loyalty to their employers and a decreased willingness to speak frankly to their superiors (ibid.: 2).

The report states that 46 per cent of organization members and 67 per cent of the union representatives said that Norwegian working life was developing in a more authoritarian direction. This is understandable in view of the finding that management by objectives, in combination with human-resource management and the opportunities presented by new technology, enables more surveillance and control of employees. As the report states:

> While video surveillance, time clocks and physical ransacking are typical examples of outward control, we understand inward control as the social and psychological influencing of members. The latter is created through so-called 'Commitment management', implying that goals are also set for employees' satisfaction, or identification with the organization, in the form of collective indexes for their engagement, motivation and sense of duty. This is measured through satisfaction mapping and various forms of evaluations performed by different third persons. (Nordrik, Wessel-Aas and Knudsen 2014: 7)

Among the organization's members, 49 per cent were subject to systematic evaluations, and the evaluators could be customers, collaboration partners, superiors, subordinates or peers; 48 per cent found it hard to refuse such evaluations; 44 per cent perceived several problems related to evaluations by others of their work efforts; 32 per cent said that their commitment, understood as engagement and motivation, was being measured (Nordrik, Wessel-Aas and Knudsen 2014: 5). In addition to these systematic evaluations, 55 per cent of the organization's members said that they are subject to performance measurement and reporting systems, and half of those character-ized these as extensive. Moreover, 61 per cent said that management increasingly demand loyalty, and a third of those studied (and 43 per cent of union representatives) thought that their organization does not make it easy to make critical comments related to operations (ibid.: 7).

This last point indicates the extent to which companies expect their employees to be obedient and uncritical. In an interview, one of the authors of the report, Bitten Nordvik, said:

> Employers not only control what workers should do, but also how they should think and act. Everything is standardized and streamlined, often at the expense of common sense and personal initiative. It creates resigna-tion. As one union representative told me: This resignation is interpreted by management as loyalty. (Lederne 2015)

Uncritical loyalty seems to be what neoliberal management want, and not only in commercial organizations. Management by objec-tives has also been extensively implemented in state organizations, and the Norwegian Civil Service Union is highly critical of this. In a survey among their members, 43 per cent agreed or agreed strongly that 'My work results are measured in a way that makes me prioritize doing things differently than I otherwise would have'. The leader of the Union says that these measures have become so detailed that they have turned irrational, and that because of it, employees have to 'violate professional and ethical requirements' (Skjeseth 2015).

One of the companies included in that study is Statoil, mentioned above with regard to corruption and dubious operations. Statoil rou-tinely do what are called 360-degree evaluations, in which colleagues, superiors, subordinates, customers, clients, collaboration partners and others evaluate the employee. Several of the Statoil employees who were interviewed in the survey said that such evaluations often include rumours and half-truths, which are hard to rebut. Statoil also introduced a system in which employees' immediate superiors give them a score from 1 to 5, which affects employees' pay. For those whose pay is calculated individually, about thirteen thousand in all, a score of 1 means no increase. A large majority of employees surveyed said that favouritism and the desire to punish subordinates were important in producing scores. According to Statoil, this system increases productivity, but it is unlikely to stimulate critical discussion. And it is worth noting that such systems are not being introduced only in commercial enterprises. They are, for example, used in the Norwegian postal service, the largest employer in Norway, and in the Norwegian Labour and Welfare Administration (Omdal 2014).

A similar system of evaluation is used by another of the organizations surveyed, COOP, a Norwegian retail cooperative owned by more than one hundred local cooperative stores and having about 1.3 million members. COOP has introduced continuous customer evaluations, which store members see as intrusive violations of their integrity. Customers who buy more than a certain amount can receive a questionnaire about their satisfaction with the store, including questions asking them to describe the feature of the store that they most like and most dislike. The results are posted on COOP's intranet in the form of green, yellow or red 'smileys', together with customer comments. Store managers are unhappy with this. They say that they have no way to rebut criticisms that customers might make, so that the customer evaluation becomes the truth about the store and the employees. Further, they see the evaluation procedure, as well as a grading system like the one described above, as control techniques imposed by senior managers who do not trust them (Nordrik, Wessel-Aas and Knudsen 2014). COOP's Director of Communications denies this: 'This is not a control measure or a ranking system, but a tool in our ongoing development work' (Sjoberg 2014). However, the grading system, with its perceived injustices, was utilized when they fired 150 employees at the closing of an old warehouse. Then, grades ranged from 0 to 3 and those with a grade of 0 lost their jobs. The employees, however, could not see their grade or the justification for it. The Director of Communications refused to answer questions about the grading process and the criteria used to grade employees, but said that she would not call it a grading system (Svenning 2014).

Customer satisfaction surveys create the illusion that the market decides, and hence that they are objective. Thus, they rest on the implicit assumption that the market determines the worth of everything, including managers and employees, and that the market decision is the only thing worthy of attention. These measures share with other detailed employee evaluation devices the irrational trust in numbers as representing objective truth (e.g. Porter 1995); in the case of customer surveys, that is the truth of the market. These sorts of devices, then, accord with the idea that neoliberalism is associated with market rule and with calculative technologies of governmentality. Moreover, the examples show that quantification, measurement and standardization are social processes with generative powers that co-create social realities and alter professional and ethical judgement and behaviour.

Neo-management and Post-bureaucratic Control

Performance measures and devices of the sort that I have described obviously produce simplifying, decontextualized numbers that are a useful tool for management. Less obviously, it appears that some subordinates see them as empowering and self-affirming (Shore and Wright 2015). In other words, these devices appear to be producing subordinates who want them. That desire raises the question of whether those and similar devices and technologies affect people's sense of what a person ought to be and do.

In Norway there is some public concern about the emergence of a new generation called 'the curling generation' (their parents have been clearing the path in front of them) or 'generation obedient'. This is the generation born in the 1980s and 1990s, now entering university and working life. An important commentator on that generation, Gunnar C. Aakvaag, says that they are 'intellectually toothless', politically and intellectually the most obedient and featureless of the post-war generations (Aakvaag 2013). He illustrates what he means when he says that in ten years as a university lecturer he has never received intellectual critique from his students. 'If they are not happy with the lecturer, they just leave the lecture, typically in the middle of it. They have a kind of consumer attitude towards everything, and are very concerned about their rights' (Haarde 2014).

In A.O. Hirschman's (1970) terms, these students are using the tactic of exit, rather than voice. Exit is associated with the market, where buyers and sellers who are dissatisfied simply walk away. Voice, on the other hand, is part of an effort to engage with and change a state of affairs that is not satisfactory. The student behaviour that Aakvaag dislikes, then, can be seen as a sign of a growing market mentality in higher education. Other commentators include a professor of management and organization studies, who says that today's generation is more 'adaptable', and a professor of psychology who says that they are 'more dependent than any other generation before them' (Haarde 2014). These two descriptions, albeit cast in somewhat different form, appear in what managers and young employees in many Norwegian organizations say is good about the new generation. They are adaptable and flexible and work well in teams; they are aware of their relationships with others and want substantial, regular feedback on their work from superiors, peers and others (ibid.). Being measured is a form of feedback.

Such people appear to be what David Riesman (1950) described as 'other-directed'. He argued that the rise of modern organizations and their demand that people adapt to the expectations that others have of them (e.g. to be good team players) had led to the other-directed personality type becoming dominant in the United States. Such people are not guided by tradition or inner values, but instead desire to mimic the life of others – what those people do, consume, earn, own and think. Sherry Turkle (2011) sees the contemporary generation, described above, in similar terms. That generation is heavily involved in the Internet and online life, which leads to a sociality that she describes as being 'alone together'. Others see such a life as detrimental to critical thinking and to emotional and moral depth, producing what Nicholas Carr (2011) calls the 'shallow generation'.

Such labels are simplistic and can be critiqued for being over-generalizing, but the spread of neoliberal managerial and administrative practices does seem likely to lead to the formation of corresponding subjectivities and social forms. However much neoliberalism may invoke freedom in the market, it has been marked by the rise of experts (Zizek 1999), particularly experts of the economic realm, forms of governance beyond the state (Swyngedouw 2005) and various technocratic modes of control that enact an authoritarian tendency variously interpreted as multiple versions of governance, different control hybrids or devolved democracy that combines centralized autocracy with managed democracy (Courpasson 2000; Clegg and Courpasson 2004; Wolin 2008; Clegg, Harris and Höpfl 2011).

In organizations, a key task of neoliberal management is the maintenance of control and obedience through soft power, mostly in the form of loyalty. To invoke once more the idea of exit and voice, managers frequently foster and expect loyalty (to the organization, to management, to colleagues, to a brand, a vision, a culture, etc.) to hamper exit, while they simultaneously discourage people from expressing voice by seeking to change things. Boltanski and Chiapello (2007: 78–86) discuss this soft power in their analysis of the 'new spirit of capitalism', which investigates what they call 'neo-management'. That seeks to get people to control themselves by shaping their emotions, values and personal relations in terms of the productivity and profit of the firm. Thus, in important respects the new regimes of control discussed in this chapter are another stage in the history of capital seeking to control labour, and of capital's attempt to shift the appearance of control onto others, such as labour itself, the state, consultants and auditors.

Neo-management is also closely related to what several scholars of management and administration call post- or neo-bureaucratic organization (see esp. Clegg, Harris and Höpfl 2011). For example, Michael Reed (2011: 243–45) identifies five key analytical components of neo-bureaucracy, some of which are illustrated by the cases presented previously in this chapter. First, practices of demonstrated participation and a focus on team performance facilitate continuous self-surveillance. Second, various knowledge codification systems and techniques reduce social life to organization-specific issues and problems. Third, a range of peer-group regulatory mechanisms and practices, such as organizing employees in teams, ensures high worker commitment and induces people to control themselves. Fourth, bringing together disciplinary incentives and market competition facilitates the creation of divided labour markets, especially distinguishing knowledge workers and routine operatives. Finally, managed democracy is developed and maintained through delegated autonomy and collective empowerment.

The concept of 'managementality' (Sørhaug 2004) captures the tendency of neo-management to embed control in people's psyches, and this might lead to the sort of mimetic desire we find in those who are other-directed. It amounts to desiring what you think others desire, which 'makes people *want to want*' (ibid.: 104). Managementality thus combines the discipline and self-control of governmentality with the seduction of mimetic desire. As illustrated above, this form of seduction is enabled by performance measures, human resource management, ranking and individual feedback, all fitted to the extensive commodification of the self in a consumer society.

Emerging Subjectivity and Sociality

If my description of neoliberal management is correct, we can expect that new forms of subjectivity will emerge. There is a growing literature on the effects of various measures, including objectives, indicators and incentives, on different aspects of subjectivity such as morality and identity. For example, a number of studies have shown how measurement systems like objective setting and 'motivational' incentives (economic, competitive, ranking, etc.) can lead to the manipulation of behaviour and performance (e.g. Hood 2006; Pollitt 2013), and undermine not only motivation and productivity of people at work (e.g. Kohn 1993) but also social values and the moral basis for pro-social behaviour (e.g. Bowles 2016). Just as targets may crowd out intrinsic values (Moynihan 2010), so incentives may displace 'ethical and generous motives' (Bowles 2016: 6). This has implications for both subjectivity and sociality.

A fundamental discussion of the transformation of subjectivity is presented by Dany-Robert Dufour (2008), who argues that capitalism in the postmodern, neoliberal age is producing a replacement for what he sees as the older Modern subject. The Modern subject is a combination of the critical (Kantian) subject and the neurotic (Freudian) subject, and Dufour (ibid.: 3) says that it is 'dying in the West because a different form of exchange is spreading'. At the level of reflective consciousness, neoliberalism is working to do away with the Kantian critical subject; at the level of the unconscious, it is discarding the self that Freud described as the culture-creating, neurotic subject haunted by guilt.

Dufour argues that neoliberalism seeks to replace this Modern subject with a precarious and uncritical subject that increasingly finds itself in a state of 'limit-experience', where there is an internal distance between the subject and his or her own self – between the self and the self, as it were. Unlike the Modern subject, this one is not defined by its relationship to a single, important Other, classically the Leviathan or God. Rather, it is forced to struggle to define itself. It is 'the world of a subject who finds herself in the position to having to found herself' (Dufour 2008: 71). This self-made self is fashioned from commodified and fetishized things and relations, amply provided through the endless flows of the market and what I have described as the cultural logic of quantification and measurement, audit and feedback.

Such a self is based on a logical impossibility: one cannot found and be oneself by relying solely upon oneself. One has to postulate something that does not yet exist (the self) in order to enable the action by which one can produce oneself as a subject. Dufour (2008: 70) illustrates the problem with a literary quote: 'I'll light the fire while I wait for him to get the firewood'. More fitting would be: 'I'll light the fire while I wait for me to get the firewood'. In this situation, one needs to perform acts one does not believe in, which makes one a pretender in one's own (partly) unconscious eyes. This means that the mimetic self is precarious, for it can collapse through its own scrutiny. This is the limit-experience that Dufour says is at the root of the most common psychological problems of our time:

> The subject is increasingly trapped between a latent melancholy (the depression we hear so much about), the impossibility of speaking in the first person, the illusion of omnipotence, and the temptation to adopt a false self, a borrowed personality or even the multiple personalities that are made so widely available by the market. (Dufour 2008: 71)

These spring from the need to found oneself. The consequences are often expressed in the inability to act, or even to live.

Dufour, then, presents a shift from the Modern, critical and neurotic subject to a postmodern, uncritical subject with narcissistic-cynical ('narcynicism') and near-psychotic (or schizoid) tendencies. This subject can be 'plugged into anything, [it is] a floating subject who is always receptive to commodity flows and communication flows, and permanently in search of commodities to consume' (Dufour 2008: 93). The new form of exchange that neoliberalism promotes, he argues, systematically seeks to rid people of all the symbolic weight that anthropologists, from Marcel Mauss onwards, have argued guarantees exchange. Symbolic value is dismantled, and all that matters is the neutral, monetary value of commodities. A consequence is that there is

> nothing and no other consideration (ethical, traditional, transcendent or transcendental) to stand in the way of the free circulation of commodities. The outcome is the desymbolization of the world. Human beings no longer have to agree about transcendent symbolic values; they simply have to go along with the never-ending and expanded circulation of commodities. (ibid.: 5)

Dufour's concerns about the destruction of the symbolic is inspired by Jean Baudrillard's consideration (e.g. [1976] 1993) of how ideological processes are affected by the semiological reduction of the symbolic. Baudrillard argues that the symbolic (e.g. the obligation of the gift) constitutes a higher social order than the semiotic (e.g. cash flows), but shows how the latter destroys the former. Following Kant ([1785] 2002: §36), Dufour develops his argument by saying that human beings have dignity that is irreplaceable and priceless, and so are not well equipped to live in a world of expanding commodity exchange. Likewise, the neurotic subject, with its repetitions and fixations, is not well equipped to produce the 'flexibility that is needed for multiple "inputs" into the flow of commodities' (Dufour 2008: 11).

Dufour's argument can be read as an extension of Pierre Bourdieu's claim that the essence of neoliberalism is 'a programme of the methodical destruction of collectives'. This occurs because the spread of neoliberalism is associated with political measures that 'aim to call into question any and all collective structures that could serve as an obstacle to the logic of the pure market' (Bourdieu 1998). Such structures include the nation and workers' unions, associations and cooperatives; Bourdieu also includes the family, which loses part of its control over consumption through market segmentation by age groups. Such collectives are undesirable because they contradict a central element of neoliberal thought, the apotheosis of the 'lone, but free individual' (ibid.).

Again, the cases that I have presented illustrate much of what I have described in this section. Neoliberal measurement and control regimes seek to attain the goals of profit and productivity by governing through individuals' subjectivity, and in effect display totalitarian tendencies and encourage the emergence of uncritical, precarious and adaptable subjects, and the associated socialities. And they do so while promoting the myth of that lone, free individual.

Conclusion

The proliferation of individual and social measurements, indicators and rankings that I have described takes on a distinct significance when considered in light of what I have said about the difficulty of seeking to found and generate one's own self. Numbers provided by the market, or by colleagues, peers, superiors, customers or contractors, can give one direction in one's project of self-making: even if the results are negative, at least they affirm the existence of the self. This can help to explain the multiplication, spread and appeal of these measures. The efforts to capture subjects and socialites in numbers, to pin down the elusive qualities of adaptable subjects, fluid organizations and flexible capitalism, are both a symptom and a sign of the postmodern, neoliberal condition. This is because they might provide a substitute for the authoritative figures of the Modern, guilt-ridden self and help to produce new forms of subjectivity.

Management by measurement and by objectives, together with the forms of sociality and the self that are associated with them, facilitate heedless economic activity in two different ways, as considered in this chapter. One of these concerns more senior management. For them, that system imposes contracts, incentives and KPIs but, so long as these are met, it leaves managers the freedom to manage while also giving them good reason to ignore their professional and ethical judgement. From middle management down to routine workers, the system I have described gives people good reason to manipulate their behaviour and to depart from what they might see as professional and ethical practice in order to meet KPIs, and get positive feedback on surveys and audits: this in turn helps them to keep the system happy, keep their jobs and maybe even get a bonus.

At a more profound level, following Dufour's arguments, the neoliberal replacing of Modern critically driven subjects with those who are built on uncertain self-foundations and are easily seduced by the transient appears to produce a post-moral economy consti-tuted, at least to some extent, by economic wrongdoing. With the view that people are self-regarding, cooperative and autonomous individuals, neoliberalism appears to suggest that human evolution is, as Johan Galtung (2002) once put it, a progression from the nomad to the monad. An important part of the foundation of the neoliberal edifice that I have described here is quantification, measurement and standardization, deployed in ways intended to make reality fit with the abstractions and disciplinary demands of contemporary capital-ism. Although this liberalism is neo-, it is, then, another instance of our long tradition of replacing an inconvenient reality with more congenial fictions and abstractions.

Emil A. Røyrvik is Professor at the Department of Sociology and Political Science, at the Norwegian University of Science and Technology (NTNU). His focus of research is on ethnography and anthropological theory in the context of organizational work life, managerial and expert cultures, and contemporary economic and cultural financialization. Recent publications include *Trangen til å telle: objektivering, måling og standardisering som samfunnspraksis* (Scandinavian Academic Press, 2017, ed. with T. Larsen); 'Brave New World? The Global Financial Crisis' Impact on Scandinavian Banking's Sales Rhetoric and Practices' (*Scandinavian Journal of Management*, 2015, with U. Forseth and S. Clegg). His *The Allure of Capitalism: An Ethnography of Management and the Global Economy in Crisis* (Berghahn Books, 2011) won SINTEF's award for excellence in research 2011.

Notes

The research for this chapter was conducted through the research project CUFF: The Cultural Logic of Facts and Figures: Objectification, Measurement and Standardization as Social Processes, financed by the Norwegian Research Council. Managed by Tord Larsen, it investigates how objectification, standardization and measurement cohere in modern societies in a cultural logic, are constitutive of new forms of representation and morality, and give rise to new ways of constructing thinghood and personhood. See www.ntnu.edu/sosant/cuff.

A paper based on this chapter is: Emil André Røyrvik. 2017. 'Sosialitet i målstyringens tid', in Tord Larsen and E.A. Røyrvik (eds), *Trangen til å telle: Objektifisering, måling og standardisering som samfunnspraksis.* Oslo: Scandinavian Academic Press, pp. 25–54.

1. See *Social Anthropology* 20(1–3) (2012) for a stimulating debate on neoliberalism.
2. This idea has often led to attributing the idea of the noble savage to Rousseau, an expression arguably first used by John Dryden in 1672. Rousseau, however, never used the expression himself and it does not adequately render his idea of the natural goodness of humanity. Society corrupts Man only because the social contract does not succeed. Society does not corrupt the Man per se, but does so only if society fails, and one might say that society actually failed at the time, not least regarding inequality.
3. Like several other company examples I use (Telenor, Yara, Statoil), Hydro is a private corporation with the Norwegian state as a majority shareholder who acts like other professional shareholders and adheres to open principles of good corporate governance.
4. In Norway, 'management by objectives' is 'mål- og resultatstyring', literally 'objective- and result-steering'. Its name explicitly links management by objectives and results.

References

Aakvaag, Gunnar C. 2013. 'Hva skal dagens unge bruke stemmeretten til?' *Aftenposten* (1 September). www.aftenposten.no/meninger/kronikker/Hva-skal-dagens-unge-bruke-stemmeretten-til-7295510.html (accessed 10 January 2015).

Anders, Gerhard. 2015. 'The Normativity of Numbers in Practice: Technologies of Counting, Accounting and Auditing in Malawi's Civil Service Reform', *Social Anthropology* 23(1): 29–41.

Baudrillard, Jean. (1976) 1993. *Symbolic Exchange and Death*. London: Sage Publications.

Boltanski, Luc, and Eve Chiapello. 2007. *The New Spirit of Capitalism*. London: Verso.

Bourdieu, Pierre. 1998. 'The Essence of Neoliberalism', *Le Monde Diplomatique* (December). https://mondediplo.com/1998/12/08bourdieu (accessed 10 February 2016).

Bowker, Geoffrey, and Susan Leigh Star. 1999. *Sorting Things Out: Classification and its Consequences*. Cambridge, MA: MIT Press.

Bowles, Samuel. 2016. *The Moral Economy: Why Good Incentives Are No Substitute for Good Citizens*. New Haven, CT: Yale University Press.

Brenner, Neil, Jamie Peck and Nik Theodore. 2010. 'Variegated Neoliberalization: Geographies, Modalities, Pathways', *Global Networks* 10(2): 182–222.

Brunsson, Nils, and Bengt Jacobsson (eds). 2002. *A World of Standards*. Oxford: Oxford University Press.

Carr, Nicholas. 2011. *The Shallows: What the Internet Is Doing to Our Brains*. New York: W.W. Norton.

Carrier, James G. 1998. 'Abstraction in Western Economic Practice', in J.G. Carrier and Daniel Miller (eds), *Virtualism: A New Political Economy*. Oxford: Berg Publishing, pp. 25–48.

Carrier, James G., and Daniel Miller (eds). 1998. *Virtualism: A New Political Economy*. Oxford: Berg Publishing.

Clegg, Stewart, and David Courpasson. 2004. 'Political Hybrids: Tocquevillean Views on Project Organizations', *Journal of Management Studies* 41(4): 525–47.

Clegg, Stewart, Martin Harris and Harro Höpfl. 2011. *Managing Modernity: Beyond Bureaucracy?* Oxford: Oxford University Press.

Cloke, Jon. 2009. 'An Economic Wonderland: Derivative Castles Built on Sand', *Critical Perspectives on International Business* 5(1/2): 107–19.

Collier, Stephen J. 2012. 'Neoliberalism As Big Leviathan, Or . . .? A Response to Wacquant and Hilgers', *Social Anthropology* 20(2): 186–95.

Comaroff, Jean, and John L. Comaroff (eds). 2001. *Millennial Capitalism and the Culture of Neoliberalism*. Durham, NC: Duke University Press.

Courpasson, David. 2000. 'Managerial Strategies of Domination: Power in Soft Bureaucracies', *Organization Studies* 21(1): 141–61.

Crosby, Alfred. 1997. *The Measure of Reality: Quantification and Western Society, 1250–1600*. Cambridge: Cambridge University Press.

Crouch, Colin. 2011. *The Strange Non-death of Neoliberalism*. Cambridge: Polity Press.

Dougherty, Conor, and Quentin Hardy. 2015. 'Managers Turn to Computer Games, Aiming for More Efficient Employees', *The New York Times* (15 March).

Dufour, Dany-Robert. 2008. *The Art of Shrinking Heads: On the New Servitude of the Liberated in the Age of Total Capitalism*. Cambridge: Polity Press.

Espeland, Wendy Nelson, and Michael Sauder. 2007. 'Rankings and Reactivity: How Public Measures Recreate Social Worlds', *American Journal of Sociology* 113(1): 1–40.

———. 2009. 'The Discipline of Rankings: Tight Coupling and Organizational Change', *American Sociological Review* 74(1): 63–82.

Evans-Pritchard, E.E. 1937. *Witchcraft, Oracles and Magic among the Azande*. Oxford: Oxford University Press.

Forseth, Ulla, Stewart R. Clegg and Emil A. Røyrvik. 2014. '"The Moment of Truth": Valuation Devices to Promote Customer Orientation and "Right Selling" in Finance'. Presented at the Latin American and European Meeting on Organization Studies, Havana (2–5 April).

Forseth, Ulla, Emil A. Røyrvik and Stewart R. Clegg. 2015. 'Brave New World? The Global Financial Crisis' [*sic*] Impact on Scandinavian Banking's Sales Rhetoric and Practices', *Scandinavian Journal of Management* 31(4): 471–79.

Foucault, Michel. 2010. *The Birth of Biopolitics*. New York: Picador.

Galtung, Johan. 2002. Lecture at KNUS conference, Trondheim (27 September).

Glaeser, Andreas. 2006. 'An Ontology for the Ethnographic Analysis of Social Processes: Extending the Extended-Case Method', in T.M.S. Evens and Don Handelman (eds), *The Manchester School: Practice and Ethnographic Praxis in Anthropology*. Oxford: Berghahn Books, pp. 64–93.

Haarde, Margrethe Zacho. 2014. 'Curling-kongene', *Dagens Næringsliv* (29 November). www.dn.no/magasinet/2014/11/28/2140/Arbeidsliv/curlingkongene (accessed 12 February 2016).

Hannerz, Ulf. 2007. 'The Neo-liberal Culture Complex and Universities: A Case for Urgent Anthropology?', *Anthropology Today* 23(5): 1–2.

Harvey, David. 2005. *A Brief History of Neoliberalism*. Oxford: Oxford University Press.

Hirschman, Albert O. 1970. *Exit, Voice, and Loyalty: Responses to Decline in Firms, Organizations, and States*. Cambridge, MA: Harvard University Press.

———. 1977. *The Passions and the Interests: Political Arguments for Capitalism before its Triumph*. Princeton, NJ: Princeton University Press.

Ho, Karen. 2009. *Liquidated: An Ethnography of Wall Street*. Durham, NC: Duke University Press.

Hobbes, Thomas. (1651) 1982. *Leviathan*. Harmondsworth: Penguin.

Hood, Christopher. 2006. 'Gaming in Targetworld: The Targets Approach to Managing British Public Services', *Public Administration Review* 66(4): 515–21.

Kallis, Giorgos, Joan Martinez-Alier and Richard B. Norgaard. 2009. 'Paper Assets, Real Debts: An Ecological-Economic Exploration of the Global Economic Crisis'. *Critical Perspectives on International Business* 5(1/2): 14–25.

Kant, Immanuel. (1785) 2002. *Groundwork for the Metaphysics of Morals.* Translated and edited by Thomas E. Hill Jr and Arnulf Zweig. Oxford: Oxford University Press.

Kohn, Alfie. 1993. 'Why Incentive Plans Cannot Work', *Harvard Business Review* 71(5): 54–63.

Larsen, Tord. 2012. 'Introduction: Objectification, Measurement and Standardization', *Culture Unbound* 4: 579–83.

Laustsen, Eliese. 2015. 'Ny henvendelse om VimpelCom-saken', *Dagens Næringsliv* (14 February). www.dn.no/nyheter/ politikkSamfunn/2015/02/14/1344/Vimpelcom/ny-henvendelse-om-vimpelcomsaken (accessed 14 February 2016).

Lederne. 2015. 'Belønner lydighet, stilner kritiske røster', *Norsk Ledelsesbarometer* (4 January). http://lederne.no/2015/01/belonner-lydighet-stilner-kritiske-roster/ (accessed 15 January 2015).

Merry, Sally Engle. 2011. 'Measuring the World: Indicators, Human Rights, and Global Governance', *Current Anthropology* 52(3): 83–95.

Moynihan, Donald. 2010. 'A Workforce of Cynics? The Effects of Contemporary Reform on Public Service Motivation', *International Public Management Journal* 13(1): 24–34.

Nordrik, Bitten, Jon Wessel-Aas and Alf Kåre Knudsen. 2014. *Norsk Ledelsesbarometer 2014: del II – Det orwellske arbeidsliv?* Copenhagen: Lederne. http://lederne.no/wp-content/uploads/2014/12/Norsk-Ledelsesbarometer-2014-hovedrapport.pdf (accessed 15 January 2015).

ØKOKRIM. 2009. 'ØKOKRIM etterforsker ikke Libya-saken'. Oslo. www.okokrim.no/id/976BCB58EF71C750C12575B7002C5FEC (accessed 22 Apr. 2015).

Omdal, Sven Egil. 2014. 'Smilefjes på handelslaget', *Adresseavisen* (6 December): 54.

Pollitt, Christopher. 2013. 'The Logics of Performance Management', *Evaluation* 19(4): 346–63.

Poovey, Mary. 1998. *A History of the Modern Fact: Problems of Knowledge in the Sciences.* Chicago, IL: University of Chicago Press.

Porter, Theodore. 1995. *Trust in Numbers: The Pursuit of Objectivity in Science and Public Life.* Princeton, NJ: Princeton University Press.

Power, Michael. 1997. *The Audit Society: Rituals of Verification.* Oxford: Oxford University Press.

Reed, Michael. 2011. 'The Post-bureaucratic Organization and the Control Revolution', in Stewart R. Clegg, Martin Harris and Harro Höpfl (eds), *Managing Modernity: Beyond Bureaucracy?.* Oxford: Oxford University Press, pp. 230–56.

Riesman, David, with Reuel Denney and Nathan Glazer. 1950. *The Lonely Crowd: A Study of the Changing American Character.* New Haven, CT: Yale University Press.

Rousseau, Jean-Jacques. (1762) 2003. *Émile, or Treatise on Education.* Amherst, NY: Prometheus Books.

Røyrvik, Emil André. 2011. *The Allure of Capitalism: An Ethnography of Management and the Global Economy in Crisis*. Oxford: Berghahn Books.

Røyrvik, Emil André, and Marianne Blom Brodersen. 2012. 'Real Virtuality: Power and Simulation in the Age of Neoliberal Crisis', *Culture Unbound* 4: 637–59.

Schatzki, Theodore R. 2008. *Social Practices: A Wittgensteinian Approach to Human Activity and the Social*. Cambridge: Cambridge University Press.

Shore, Cris, and Susan Wright. 2015. 'Governing by Numbers: Audit Culture, Rankings and the New World Order', *Social Anthropology* 23(1): 22–28.

Sjøberg, Jeanette. 2014. 'De misliker å bli målt på jobb', *Aftenposten* (3 December). www.aftenposten.no/okonomi/De-misliker-a-bli-malt-pa-jobb-7810514.html (accessed 12 February 2016).

Skjeseth, Alf. 2015. 'Presses av målehysteri', *Klassekampen* (12 March): 8–9.

Smith, Adam. (1776) 2003. *The Wealth of Nations*. New York: Bantam.

Sørhaug, Tian. 2004. *Managementalitet og autoritetens forvandling: ledelse i en kunnskapsøkonomi*. Bergen: Fagbokforlaget.

Sørhelm, Tone Iren, Thomas Solberg, Jostein Nissen-Meyer, Anders Park Framstad and Andreas Wolden Fredriksen. 2014. '50 millioner er en dråpw i havet for Terra-kommunene', *E 24* (5 May). http://e24.no/lov-og-rett/50-millioner-er-en-draape-i-havet-for-terra-kommunene/22955016 (accessed 15 January 2015).

Statoil. 2006. 'Horton Case Settlement: Stock Market Announcement'. Stavenger: Statoil ASA. www.statoil.com/en/NewsAndMedia/News/2006/Pages/HortonCaseSettlement.aspx (accessed 10 January 2015).

Strathern, Marilyn (ed.). 2000. *Audit Cultures: Anthropological Studies in Accountability, Ethics and the Academy*. London: Routledge.

Streeck, Wolfgang. 2014. *Buying Time: The Delayed Crisis of Democratic Capitalism*. London: Verso.

Sundberg, Johann D., and Andreas Wolden Fredriksen. 2015. 'Terra-kommuner punger ut 650 millioner i forlik', *E24* (5 June). http://e24.no/lov-og-rett/dnb/terra-kommuner-punger-ut-650-millioner-i-forlik/23465008 (accessed 27 April 2017).

Svenning, Lene. 2014. 'Karakterer på jobben. Er du verdt en ener eller en femmer?' *HK-nytt* (23 April). http://hk-nytt.no/arbeidslivet/karakterer_på_jobben_256122.html (accessed 15 January 2015).

Swyngedouw, Erik. 2005. 'Governance Innovation and the Citizen: The Janus Face of Governance-beyond-the-State', *Urban Studies* 42(11): 1991–2006.

Thatcher, Margaret. 1987. Interview with Douglas Keay. *Woman's Own* (31 October). www.margaretthatcher.org/speeches/displaydocument.asp?docid=106689 (accessed 15 February 2015).

Turkle, Sherry. 2011. *Alone Together: Why We Expect More from Technology and Less from Each Other*. New York: Basic Books.

Varoufakis, Yanis. 2013. 'Being Greek and an Economist while Greece Burns: An Intimate Account'. Presented at the Modern Greek Studies Association meeting, Bloomington, Indiana (14–16 November). https://varoufakis.files.wordpress.com/2013/11/mgsa-talk-nov-2013.pdf (accessed 8 February 2016).

Wacquant, Loïc. 2012. 'Three Steps to a Historical Anthropology of Actually Existing Neoliberalism', *Social Anthropology* 20(1): 66–79.

Winsnes, Eirik, Siri Gedde-Dahl, Øystein Kløvstad Langberg and Ingvild Bruaset. 2015. 'Økokrim tiltaler fire Yara-direktører for korrupsjon', *Aftenposten* (2 January). www.aftenposten.no/okonomi/Okokrim-tiltaler-fire-Yara-direktorer-for-korrupsjon-7435558.html (accessed 15 January 2015).

Wolin, Sheldon S. 2008. *Democracy Inc.: Managed Democracy and the Specter of Inverted Totalitarianism*. Princeton, NJ: Princeton University Press.

Zizek, Slavoj. 1999. *The Ticklish Subject: The Absent Centre of Political Ontology*. London: Verso.

3

Under Pressure

Financial Supervision in the Post-2008 European Union

Daniel Seabra Lopes

This chapter is about financial supervision and reform at the level of the EU (European Union). The first thing to say is that financial supervision and reform at an international level are relatively new, reflecting the world of globalized and liberalized capital flows that we live in today. There are many labels for such a world, and 'neoliberal' is surely one of them.

Since the mid-1970s, finance has evolved in a transnational environment characterized by floating exchange rates and fiat-money regimes sustained by debt relations, while former distinctions among banking, securities and insurance are dissolving. This environment appears to be inherently unstable, as testified by a long series of crashes and bankruptcies, culminating in the 2008 global financial meltdown. Control over international finance has thus progressively become a matter of concern, though one that is mostly addressed through a variety of soft-law instruments – regulatory guidelines rather than requirements – that coexist with dissimilar national policies and what is known as regulatory arbitrage (Riles 2014). Some argue that, in such circumstances, effective financial control is impossible to achieve, the best alternative being the sort of surveillance expressed by the idea of financial supervision. Consequently, 'post-mortems of each and every financial crisis point (rightly or wrongly) at supervisory failures and the cry for changes resonates loudly' (Masciandaro and Quintyn 2013: 4).

As noted in the Introduction to this volume, one of the particularities of neoliberalism is a preoccupation with issues of right and wrong in the economy. Among other things, this means acknowledging the past failures in financial regulation and supervision that led to those crises, and seeking to perfect financial norms and regulations. In tune with this, I shall consider some organizational and regulatory implications of the 2008 financial collapse, symbolized by the bankruptcy of the investment bank Lehman Brothers. As will become clear, official reaction to the crisis amounted to creating more supervisory institutions and issuing more regulatory norms, an effort to find a technical solution to a global problem with significant socio-political dimensions. Put differently, that reaction reaffirmed the general understanding of economic wrong-doing as the violation of clear rules, an understanding that slights the socio-techno-political factors that lead economic actors to indulge in potentially wrongful practices, as well as underestimating the complexities associated with applying regulatory norms (as testified by a series of would-be prosecutions of global banks mentioned in this volume's Introduction).

By focusing on institutional and regulatory transformations since 2008, and primarily in the EU, this chapter intends to expand this analysis and consider a few additional aspects of contemporary financial governance. For instance, regulatory norms, whether clear or unclear, usually imply a scope of application, normally a national jurisdiction and a particular market segment. In other words, those norms operate in terms of boundaries, while a significant part of what passes for financial innovation sets out to explore the differences among the jurisdictions and segments that those boundaries imply or the interstices between them. Thus, financial innovation usually involves either hopping from one normative framework to another or entering a sort of regulatory no man's land. The notion of regulatory arbitrage, alluded to above, points precisely to the open and often legitimate exploration of regulatory loopholes and discrepancies for business purposes. Thus, financial actors became accustomed to using foreign offshore accounts and special-purpose vehicles to perform operations that would be highly taxed or even prohibited in their own countries, or to offering their clients products that look like savings deposits subject to retail banking regulation but that contain elements drawn from securities markets.

Much of what passes for legitimate financial innovation today, however, is likely to be labelled financial misdemeanour in the near future. This is so because of an essential characteristic of the neoliberal approach to dubious economic activity, the necessary presence of a lag between the moment when certain practices are seen as business as usual and the moment when they are condemned as wrong or criminal. If a normative framework exists, the transmutation of financial innovation into wrong-doing may involve the perception of norm violation. However, given the proclivity to regulatory arbitrage, a substantial part of financial activity remains poorly regulated or totally unregulated, as was the case of over-the-counter and derivatives markets before 2008 and of high-frequency algorithmic trading before 2014. It is no wonder, then, that regulators and others concerned with finance appear sceptical about regulatory clarity or efficacy, while at the same time continuing to make more rules. One goal of this chapter is to try to make sense of this apparent contradiction.

The chapter is based on the analysis of events related to recent organizational and regulatory steps taken by EU authorities with the aim of supervising financial activity and restricting financial wrong-doing. It is difficult to get access to financial regulators and do field work among them. Thus, I have relied on documentation available from institutional websites, occasional interviews with people and attendance at events. As well, I joined a summer course on financial regulation and supervision presented by one of my main informants in this project, a Portuguese securities regulator with extensive experience of EU forums and working groups. All this enabled me to get a clearer picture of the contemporary supervisory worldview, its intricacies and dilemmas.

The next section of this chapter considers some of the political effects of the 2008 crisis that may distinguish it from previous financial crises. The following section integrates some of the post-2008 institutional transformations into a longer chain of historical events, drawing on the concept of continuous change (Arrighi 1994). This genealogical sketch of financial supervision will be complemented by a more relational approach to be developed in the subsequent three sections. Each of these sections is devoted to a particular movement involving the combination of potentially tense elements: the cat-and-mouse game between innovation and wrong-doing, the interplay between national sovereignty and international harmonization, the predominance of technical facticity over fictionality. Taken together, these provide a socio-political framework that may help us to understand the prevalence of both dubious financial innovation and its partial remedies in contemporary neoliberal contexts; or, why regulators keep issuing more rules while being sceptical about the efficacy of those rules. The final section summarizes the main argument and the impasses presently being experienced by European financial supervisors.

The 2008 Crisis and its Effects

Following the announcement of Lehman Brothers' bankruptcy, the Wall Street crash of 15 September 2008 was presented as a critical event destined for the history books. Comparisons with the stock market crash of 1929 and the ensuing New Deal became commonplace, as were recommendations regarding changes that should be implemented in the near future. The necessity of substantial financial reform was reinforced by several bank bailouts funded with public money. And, to be fair, the efforts made to amend things have no parallel with any financial collapse since 1929.

The scope of reform is perhaps the first peculiarity of the 2008 crisis that deserves attention. Internationally, a new oversight body, the Financial Stability Board, was set up with the support of the G20, and the Basel III Accord was drafted by the Basel Committee on Banking Supervision. In the United States, the Dodd-Frank Wall Street Reform and Consumer Protection Act of 2010 created new federal supervisory organizations, tightened the leverage and capital requirements for banks, restricted the exploration of legal interstices for financial-innovation purposes and paved the way for rescuing bankrupt institutions without recourse to public money (Morris and Price 2011). Though legally limited to the country where the global financial meltdown originated, the Act soon became a mandatory reference for regulators of other countries and for international organizations.

On the other side of the Atlantic, the EU set up new mechanisms of financial stability, while directives and regulations focusing on financial markets, banks, ratings agencies and venture capital were revised (European Commission 2012). Most notable was the emergence of a new complex of supervisory authorities, the European System of Financial Supervision, intended to monitor national authorities, control systemic risks and technically assess the deliberations of the European Commission, the Council and the European Parliament. This System comprises one macro-prudential authority, the European Systemic Risk Board, and three micro-prudential authorities: the European Banking Authority, the European Securities and Markets Authority and the European Insurance and Occupational Pensions Authority.

All these efforts at financial reform testify to the impression that economic wrongdoing becomes apparent mostly in retrospect, in the light of new facts that cast doubt on practices that formerly were acceptable: what once was seen as ingenious financial innovation (e.g. piling up securitized debt) and strategic arbitrage (e.g. creating special-purpose vehicles to transfer credit risk) could later be frowned upon or even banned. Yet the 2008 stock crash was only a part, in fact a relatively benign one, of a chain of turbulent financial events with growing normative, institutional and societal impacts. Concern over investor loss due to abrupt asset devaluation was quickly superseded by the notion that both state policies and market practices were strongly conditioned by liquidity problems stemming from creditor–debtor relations (Graeber 2011; Riles 2013). The crisis, therefore, continued, with doubts regarding the effectiveness of ongoing financial reforms being openly voiced not only by specialized journalists and academics (Westbrook 2009; Nesvetailova 2010; Esposito 2011; Graeber 2011) but also by major figures of the world financial system. These included the director of the International Monetary Fund, Dominique Strauss-Kahn, who displayed his scepticism at a press conference in October 2010 (International Monetary Fund 2010).

By that time, the Euro crisis had emerged, with several highly indebted countries within the single-currency area (Greece, Ireland, Portugal, Cyprus and Spain) reluctantly accepting aid from a troika made up of the International Monetary Fund, the European Commission and the European Central Bank. As well, international money markets never recovered their old levels of activity, and they were further hampered by the Libor manipulation scandal in 2012, which strengthened the impression that little had changed in the sector since 2008 (Admati and Hellwig 2013; Lanchester 2013a, 2013b). In his last speech as Governor of the Bank of England, Mervyn King (2013: 6; see also Lanchester 2013b) assumed that both the size and the complexity of trans-sector financial conglomerates had become so serious a problem for governments and regulators that solving it would require the work of a whole generation. In other words, financial reform would become a permanent feature of a world dominated by hypertrophied banks. The absence of what Donato Masciandaro and Marc Quintyn (2013: 4) called a clear postmortem could thus be considered a second hallmark of the 2008 crisis.

Indeed, in Europe, a banking union has recently been established alongside the new European System of Financial Supervision. In order to reduce the chance of further systemic crisis, the European Central Bank has assumed direct supervisory powers over relevant banks that formerly were held by national authorities. At the same time, and following the Libor affair, new regulatory principles for index production were discussed by several authorities worldwide, while studies were conducted on the new financial frontiers represented by shadow banking and high-frequency trading, about which regulators seemed to know very little.

The long duration of the crisis, together with the fact that its consequences spread beyond the realm of banks, stock exchanges and insurance companies to affect larger sectors of the economy and society, also seems to have encouraged the emergence of new political movements that were primarily concerned with financial issues. It would thus be possible to see politicization and moralization as a third, and last, peculiarity of the 2008 crisis.

Changes and Continuities

It is still too soon to tell whether the considerable scope of reform, the permanent state of crisis and the growing politicization of finance described in the preceding section will lead to substantial change (for a sceptical view, see Roitman 2014). One thing is certain, though: much of what has been done since 2008 is in line with the way finance has been perceived and handled over the last four decades (Dymski and Kaltenbrunner 2017).

In this regard, it may be useful to recall the distinction between continuous and discontinuous change that Giovanni Arrighi (1994) used with regard to capitalist cycles of accumulation. Arrighi employs the concept of continuous change to characterize the expansionist periods of capitalist empires, when investment flows to the production of commodities along a single path of development. Discontinuous change, on the other hand, would occur when the world economy shifts to a new developmental path. According to Arrighi, such shifts are characterized by the growing importance of finance, as the productive sectors that remained aligned with the declining economic paradigm produce lower and less attractive returns. He says that this has been occurring since the 1980s, with the decline of US hegemony. Arrighi does not say much about the evolution of finance in these periods, but rather adopts a conventional Marxian stance that focuses on material production rather than what is seen as fictitious capital. I think, however, that the idea of continuous change may be useful to approach financial reforms under neoliberalism, and possibly to characterize any period of financial expansion within Arrighi's scheme as well.

To talk of continuous change in finance means to talk of evolutions and innovations within an established framework of power, without any precipitous jump into a novel situation. Such a jump is likely to occur eventually, though most probably only after all other options have been discarded. In order to illustrate this, let us take a closer look at some of the organizational reconfigurations since 2008.

As mentioned above, one of the consequences of the financial collapse was a new set of supervisory institutions at the level of the EU, the European System of Financial Supervision. I said that it has three micro-prudential organs acting in cooperation with national supervisors alongside one macro-prudential entity. This System began to function in 2011. However, due to the Eurozone sovereign debt crisis in 2012, banking union was proposed, in order to disconnect state and bank indebtedness, which were linked because bank failures were being alleviated with public debt. Accordingly, in November 2014 the European Central Bank took on the direct micro-prudential supervision of 120 banking groups. The fact that an existing institution, the European Central Bank, had to be equipped with direct supervisory powers nicely exemplifies a process of continuous change, in which innovations keep in line with previous political decisions and extant organizational frameworks. There was, in truth, no proper alternative, as the European Central Bank was the only institution that the European treaties contemplated as a possible transnational banking supervisor (for a comprehensive discussion of this process, see Fontan 2017).

A closer look at the European System of Financial Supervision shows that this institutional cluster also has clear antecedents in the supervisory committees devised by the Lamfalussy Process in 2001, which aimed to stimulate convergence among the national structures of financial regulation and supervision then existing in the EU (OJEU 2009).[1] The Lamfalussy Process reproduced a widespread supervisory model that separates banks, securities firms and insurance companies. That model developed in the nineteenth century, when the three market segments were independently regulated, offered distinct products through their own channels and were managed according to their own accounting, business and risk concepts (see Herring and Carmassi 2007). Such sectorial supervision models began to be made irrelevant by the emergence of the first trans-sector financial conglomerates in the 1960s, not to mention the market developments that followed the progressive liberalization and internationalization of finance that began in the 1970s. It is not surprising, then, that by the time of the establishment of the new European System of Financial

Supervision in 2011, a number of European countries had already replaced the sector model with different cross-sector arrangements. The group involved in the creation of the System nevertheless considered that it could be risky to implement a different model when under such pressure to react to potentially systemic events.

I shall return to the genealogy of international supervisory institutions and other financial reforms. However, first I want to provide the analytical coordinates that constitute the spine of my argument, though it is probably more useful for raising questions than it is for answering them. The co-ordinates consist of a sequence of pairs identifying previous points of negotiated compromise that may be turning into points of tension and disruption: innovation and deviance, national and international, facticity and fictionality.

Innovation and Wrongdoing: A Cat-and-Mouse Game

As already noted, the line separating financial innovation from financial wrongdoing is thin. In certain cases, crossing it involves the perception of a distance between (normative) words and (normal) practice.

Consider false reporting and data manipulation, which have been central to a number of recent financial scandals. Official rules and other regulatory documents unanimously recommend the adoption of mechanisms such as the 'four-eye principle' (the checking of automated computation processes by at least two different people or parties), 'Chinese walls' (the rigorous separation within the organization of, say, traders and accountants) and 'whistle-blowing mechanisms' (anonymous denunciation procedures). However, many supervisors acknowledge that such mechanisms are ideals that tend to be ignored whenever stronger motivations arise. Concerning Chinese walls, in 2014 a Portuguese securities-supervision officer who also coordinates a group at the new European Securities and Markets Authority told me:

> The simplest definition of the economy tells you that it is about incentives. All else is rhetoric. And incentives, for these people [in the financial sector], are about earning money. If they believe that Chinese walls are interrupting the flux conducive to profit, you may be certain that any Chinese wall will disappear immediately!

The same distance between words and practices also surfaces in the official discourse of central bankers, whose role now seems to be little more than obsessive reaffirmation of the solidity and stability of the banking sector until its fragilities can no longer be hidden, and they become evident to everyone. All this introduces a strong note of scepticism that, I think, constitutes a hallmark of post-2008 supervisory feelings deserving further elaboration (see below).

However, in many cases, financial innovation also evolves in a sort of regulatory no man's land, using new technologies and theoretical models to mix up boundaries instituted by previous regulation or simply to enter new, uncharted territories. The waning of sectorial models of supervision described in the previous section is precisely a consequence of a series of innovations and arbitrage procedures that explored regulatory vacuums and loopholes, rendering former distinctions between banking, insurance and capital markets increasingly fuzzy and even leading to disputes among supervisory authorities regarding who should supervise what. Regulators were thus forced to come up with new norms and, in countries such as the United Kingdom and the Netherlands, to reorganize the whole supervisory system around a different model.

Financial authorities usually distinguish between illegal practices involving some sort of lying (such as ignoring Chinese walls, cooking the books, etc.) and legal arbitrage practices in which the parties try to follow legislation while also taking advantage of the differences between regulatory regimes. This is a pragmatic distinction, with the decision that something is illegal being based on the interpretation of applicable law. Regulatory arbitrage, on the other hand, is more open-ended. It can be acceptable and legal, but it may lead to practices that later would be made illegal. This is not to say that all regulatory arbitrage inevitably leads to crime: financial regulators deny this as a gross over-simplification of a complex matter. However, once it is accepted as normal practice, arbitrage introduces a peculiar dynamic akin to that of a musical fugue. Under such circumstances, supervisors are condemned to follow, at a distance and with a considerable delay, the activity of financial parties while also assisting governments in the production of the legal documents that either authorize or criminalize that same activity.

In this respect, an interesting discussion emerged during a summer course, in 2014, on the regulation and supervision of financial markets that was run by a Portuguese securities regulator who also collaborated with both the European Securities and Markets Authority and the European Systemic Risk Board. This official acknowledged that financiers would always come up with something that regulators had not thought of, which meant that norms would have to be constantly revised and new regulatory layers added to the old ones. 'Codes usually tend to come after the problems have arisen', he said, adding that 'companies will find a way to circumvent – and that is why new codes and new versions of older codes are always emerging'. At this point, a young Dutch participant suggested that all this seemed like a game. The officer concurred, with a smile: 'You're right, and players are trying to play the game to their advantage'.

The metaphor of the cat-and-mouse game (Riles 2014; Thiemann and Lepoutre 2017) may, therefore, be appropriate, with regulators persistently trying to catch up with the market. Another appealing metaphor would be that of an arms race, with the regulators and supervisors striving to keep up with the conceptual and technological advances deployed by market actors. The state of high-frequency trading illustrates this idea of a game or race. In that summer school, it was presented as a recent activity which was being studied by the European Securities and Markets Authority, based on data from twelve European trading venues relative to May 2013. Although the report was about to be published (see ESMA 2014), our instructor admitted that high-frequency trading would have changed by the time it appeared, which meant that more information would need to be collected.

The nature of the cat-and-mouse game reflects two complementary aspects of neoliberal policies. The first is the deregulation that enabled the free circulation of capital and the creation of genuinely global financial markets from the 1970s onwards. The second is the fact that, although financial markets have become global, supervision and regulation remain largely confined to national borders, though some degree of harmonization has already been achieved. This leads us to the second of my three pairs of coordinates.

The National and the International: A Delicate Compromise

Globalization of finance is commonly viewed as an achievement of neoliberalism. This is true, but we need to ask what it means to say that finance has (once more) become global. The answer lies, I think, in the ability to trade in any type of financial market from virtually anywhere in the world. Suppose that Maria, with a bank account in Brazil, wants to buy a stock that is traded on the London Stock Exchange. Maria tells her bank manager, who will forward the request to, say, the bank's international department. They, in turn, will communicate, either directly or through an intermediary bank, with a British bank that has direct access to the London Stock Exchange, and that bank will lodge the buy order on the exchange. Suppose further that the order is matched with a corresponding sell order coming from Toshiro in Japan and entering the London Stock Exchange through a similar chain of banks. The result is that Maria in Brazil is indirectly connected with Toshiro in Japan. Moreover, such a connection is possible between any two people anywhere, providing that each has an account at a bank that can deal with other banks and thus, ultimately, with stock exchanges. The globalization of finance lies in the possibility of such connections virtually everywhere, mainly through the intermediation of banks.

Those connections operate at the global level, but using them depends on the national level, in this case sets of national financial regulations. Consider reporting requirements, which are crucial for carrying out financial transactions, including buying and selling stocks. In some countries, reporting forms only allow the identification, as counter-parties, of the two banks that deal directly with the stock exchange, as if Maria and Toshiro never existed. In other countries the forms require that the whole sequence of intermediaries be disclosed. Such different national regulatory specifications thus are resources that financial actors and their lawyers explore and exploit for business purposes. As a consequence, regulatory arbitrage goes international, with off-shore and other tax havens appearing as sovereign intermediate points where information can be concealed from financial supervisors and state authorities. This said, global finance could never occur on the basis of national regulatory specifications alone: some standardization is required. Moreover, and as seen in the previous section, a good part of arbitrage procedures is likely to come to be seen as financial wrongdoing, which encourages coordination among different national authorities. All this leads to what could be called a delicate compromise between national sovereignty and international harmonization, also a hallmark of finance under neoliberalism.

The establishment in 1974 of the Basel Committee on Banking Supervision, an influential forum of central bankers hosted by the Bank for International Settlements, may be seen as a step towards a transnational discussion of financial stability issues raised by the dollar and oil crises of the early 1970s. There, a new language of standards, guidelines and codes of conduct, now commonly known as 'soft law' because of its voluntary character, began to be designed with the aim of harmonizing financial operations in the new world of floating exchange rates and fiat money regimes (Borio and Toniolo 2006: 2; Cooper 2006). Central bank policies and practices became more technical and detached from political measures, while these, in turn, became more subject to the influence of specific corporate interests. Gradually, financial supervision became an autonomous area, no longer dependent on the fiscal or monetary policies of states (Masciandaro and Quintyn 2013: 3). This was associated with the creation of a growing number of international organizations. The Bank for International Settlements supported the creation of the Financial Stability Forum in 1999, a council that was composed of the finance ministers and central bank governors of the G7 countries and that preceded the aforementioned Financial Stability Board, founded in 2009. The emergence of the European System of Financial Supervision also finds its proper place within this genealogy of post-Bretton Woods deliberative processes originally hosted by an international network of colleges, summits and roundtables that became progressively surrounded by a more stable set of institutions favouring regulatory convergence.

The growing autonomy of financial supervisors does not mean, of course, that their relationship with political actors ceased. Rather, it was reconfigured along new lines, flexibly combining both the public and the private, the national and the international (see Wedel 2009). Meetings between leading bankers and leading politicians started to occur within the exclusive circles of that international institutional network, with some prominent figures assuming different roles across the deliberative complex. Such is the case with Baron Alexandre Lamfalussy, an academic, a private banker and a central banker. He served at the Bank for International Settlements between 1976 and 1993, which he left to found the European Monetary Institute (forerunner of the European Central Bank), and later was involved in the 2001 regulatory convergence process that came to bear his name. Another such figure is Jacques de Larosière, a French civil servant and administrator sometimes depicted as an *ancien régime* character. In 2009 and 2010 he coordinated a high-level group set up by the European Commission and charged with designing the new European System of Financial Supervision, which was established shortly thereafter.

Deliberation, informed discussion with a view to reaching a compromise, has been the dominant practice within this international framework of financial institutions, and a necessary complement to their proclaimed independence from national governments. However, that independence is tempered by the fact that firms and whole economic sectors have an interest in the outcome of those deliberations, an interest commonly represented by the authorities of the countries where those firms and sectors are based. Since 2008 this translated into different regulatory responses by different countries in the EU regarding issues such as short-selling, shadow banking, credit default swaps and offshore banking. It is no coincidence that the three new European micro-prudential authorities were set up in London, Paris and Frankfurt, cities that were the three most conspicuous financial rivals within the EU. Likewise, it is no coincidence that, to avoid the appearance of factionalism or favouritism, none of the new supervisory authorities was headed by an English, French or German director. This sort of political compromise has been part of the European project since its creation, but the coordination difficulties experienced by the new European supervisory authorities leave international regulators with the sense that the development of a single financial market is much slower than that of the single market for goods and services.

Facticity and Fictionality: End of Predominance

This section turns to the relationship of finance in the neoliberal era with technicality or facticity (see MacKenzie 2009). Facticity has become the common language of international finance and the basis for many of those soft-law instruments that make up what is now known as regulation and supervision, contributing to their supposed clarity and impartiality. For the same reason, it has played an important role in the globalization of finance. It is possible, then, to see the dissemination of numerical facts as just another effect of the post-Bretton Woods institutional evolutions described above. In truth, however, quantification has a genealogy longer than that of neoliberalism (see Hacking 1990; Foucault [1978] 1991; Desrosières 1993; Porter 1995; Rose 1999; Hoskin and Macve 2000; Hoskin 2004), which means that the rise of neoliberalism can be seen as a consequence of the expansion of specific management techniques throughout the nineteenth and twentieth centuries. Furthermore, facticity brings forth its own, specific tensions, such as those between experts and ordinary people, and between facts and fictions. For these reasons, it is useful to give facticity its proper place in this analysis.

First and foremost, financial facticity is a source of trust, a vital asset for banks under fiat money regimes and fractional reserve systems. The very existence of banks and supervisory authorities thus requires economic and accounting indicators that represent market conditions and that have the status of facts, of things that can safely be taken for granted and used as the basis for further activity (see MacKenzie 2009). Of course, trust in those numbers is, ultimately, a social fact that relies on things such as timely reporting, institutional reputation, articulation protocols and specific governance mechanisms. In practice, facticity is produced by the extensive circulation of Excel spreadsheets and other templates through electronic networks according to regular rhythms of reporting, contributing to the organization of work and to the performance of intra- and inter-institutional articulations and hierarchies. This kind of reporting is the bulk of the work carried out inside financial organizations, with timely provision of quantitative assessments being frequently associated with the display of signs of transparency and good governance.

When searching for the effects of the 2008 events in the domain of facticity, it is, again, easy to find continuities with the past in conceptual and methodological frames, in established information channels, even in organizational design. At the same time, it is also possible to see a growing number of obstacles along the road of financial facts. Even if one admits that maintaining the facticity of finance has always been a delicate endeavour and that the apparent objectivity of numbers quickly vanishes at the level of situated practice (see Lopes 2011, 2015), it has become even more delicate since 2008. This can be demonstrated with two examples: one is the operationalization of the notion of systemic risk through the implementation of a new instrument, the banking stress test; the other is financial benchmarks, especially credit ratings and reference rates such as Libor and Euribor.

One of the main lessons of the 2008 financial collapse is that we live in a world dominated by a handful of megabanks with the potential to cause systemic risks on a global scale. Unlike the classic run on a single bank, systemic banking crises spread, by definition, to other institutions and they may affect not only liquidity but also currency and sovereign debt. Luc Laeven and Fabian Valencia (2008: 5) situate the beginning of such crises in 1970, and identify 124 similar events between 1970 and 2007, a period that nicely matches the historical frame of the present volume. Well before 2008, then, academics and financial regulators were aware of systemic risk (see Crockett 2000; Borio 2003; Herring and Carmassi 2007), as well as the type of supervision it required, what is now known as a macro-prudential approach, a strategy originally tested by the Bank of International

Settlements in the 1980s (Maes 2009). After 2008, the idea of systemic risk was further reinforced and operationalized through the creation of supervisory bodies intended to monitor it at the national and European levels (de Larosière 2013), a process that was still underway in 2017 as setting up the institutions and procedures needed for adequate monitoring had proved to be more difficult than expected.

The key instrument that financial supervisors use to manage systemic risk turned out to be the bank stress test, designed to assess the resilience of bank balance sheets in the face of unlikely but serious adverse events, like a major economic collapse or a natural catastrophe. Adopting stress tests has led, however, to ambiguous outcomes (see Langley 2013). While the tests apparently raised confidence in banks in the United States, the first exercises conducted by the EU exacerbated the general impression of crisis and uncertainty.

One reason for this is institutional flux: the 2009 and 2010 exercises were organized by the Committee of European Banking Supervision; the 2011 exercise was conducted by its successor, the European Banking Authority; the 2014 exercise was conducted by the European Banking Authority in conjunction with the European Central Bank Single Supervisory Mechanism; and the 2016 exercise was conducted, again, only by the European Banking Authority. Furthermore, the growing sovereign debt crisis in Europe contributed to scepticism about the 2011 evaluation (de Larosière 2013), with high-ranked banks such as Dexia filing for bankruptcy shortly after publication of very good results, and two Cypriot banks being rescued by European funds within two years of getting satisfactory results (EuroFinuse 2013: 14).[2] More recently, the assumption of direct supervisory powers by the European Central Bank was resisted by influential countries, especially Germany, which led to the 2014 stress tests allegedly being designed to conceal significant problems in certain banks (for a different and more optimistic view, see Violle 2017: 433). Consequently, the institutional and methodological structures associated with systemic risk management were met with a considerable degree of scepticism in Europe, with stakeholders openly questioning and even mocking the efficacy of the stress test and its vulnerability to market interests represented by national supervisory authorities.

The case of financial benchmarks, though originating outside the supervisory realm, also merits attention, as it reinforces the impression of fragility and error in the realm of facticity. The sudden devaluation of asset-backed securities and collateralized debt obligations that had been given high ratings was at the heart of the 2008 financial meltdown and dealt a major blow to the credit ratings agencies, whose reputation had been good. In the end, regulators continued to endorse the use of ratings when assessing securities as collateral, although now people had a clearer notion of the system's fallibility. Problems with the reliability of financial benchmarks were further intensified by the Libor manipulation scandal, which erupted in 2012 after an investigation led by the UK Financial Services Authority revealed evidence of regular rigging of the rate by Libor panel banks, at least since 2005 (see Wheatley 2012), and suspicion soon extended to Euribor and other reference rates (see European Commission 2012: 2; Lopes 2017). The result was the inclusion of financial index manipulation in the revised EU Market Abuse Directive and extensive reviews of financial benchmarks carried out under the auspices of political bodies such as the European Commission and the European Parliament, and of financial bodies such as the International Organization of Securities Commissions, the European Banking Authority and the European Securities and Markets Authority.

Still, it is possible to conclude that nothing has substantially changed. Regulators remain faithful to the production of reputedly impartial technical assessments, and Libor and Euribor continue to exist, though the underlying interbank money markets remain only sporadically active and efforts to find replacements are underway. There seems to be, in truth, no immediate alternative to facticity and technical normativity, which remain deeply embedded in normal financial practice and institutional design. However, the proverbial trust in numbers appears to have decreased since 2008, with eyebrows now rising suspiciously at graphs, numbers and terminologies whose complexity and incomprehensibility were formerly accepted as signs of expert knowledge (see Tett 2009: 10, 131). Financial facticity is thus in tension with what could be called, following anthropologists of money (e.g. Guyer 2004; Maurer 2005) and some philosophers (e.g. Searle 2005), the fictional character of money and its doubles. The fictional status of money for those scholars reflects the fact that money is, ultimately, a social convention. It is this fictional element that justifies radical questions about money and finance, such as: are stress tests and financial benchmarks trustworthy because they are accurate representations of markets, or are markets the outcome of techniques of representation? Thus, while there appears to be no immediate alternative to financial facticity, people seem to stumble across more and more fictions along this road of facts.

Conclusion: Coherence Lost?

Notwithstanding its recurrent crises, finance in the neoliberal era appears to have stabilized around three related movements, each with its own points of tension. The first is the interplay of innovation and wrongdoing prompted by the practice of regulatory arbitrage, which is tolerable but has the potential to lead to the future perception of delinquencies and misdemeanours. The second movement is the development of an international framework seeking to free finance from politics and to harmonize it through soft law. This development has, however, been hindered by national governments seeking to defend the specificities of their own financial regulation and by the instrumental use of state sovereignty by influential financial conglomerates to create zones of fiscal liberalization and thus extend regulatory arbitrage across national borders. The third and last movement is the predominance of technical knowledge and numerical accuracy over social conventions, promoting an image of facticity as the concrete stuff that finance is made of.

The conjunction of these movements has been complex and has led to different sorts of economic wrongdoing, ranging from open fraud to the ingenious exploration of regulatory loopholes and to putting pressure on regulators to grant legal exemptions. Despite this complexity, the evolution of these parallel movements enabled the globalization of finance, though the consequences of the financial crisis seem to have increased the tensions within each movement and rendered their conjunction more problematic. For instance, strong state intervention after the crash introduced some novel elements within the tension between the national and international levels. One of these elements appears to be a re-politicizing of finance, with state positions no longer motivated predominantly by corporate interests in the way that they had been since the 1970s, but also motivated by the effects of the crisis on their countries. Another element, however, points in the opposite direction, to constrain the politics of finance. That is the fact that states, at least in Europe, are under greater pressure to conform to the demands of regulators at the level of the EU, most obvious after the granting of direct supervisory powers to the European Central Bank. The consequences of the crisis also increased the tension between facticity and fictionality, for it became apparent that the technical expertise and numerical indicators that had been the main glue of the global financial system under neoliberalism are no longer as clear-cut or trustworthy as they were once thought to be.

To a large extent, official reactions to these circumstances translated into more normative material, thus reaffirming the common understanding of wrongful behaviour as the violation of clear rules. However, the status of such rules appears to be changing, along with regulators' position on the subject. For instance, the flow of new standards, recommendations and guidelines coming from European institutions is impressive – what some call a 'regulatory tsunami'. Moreover, such soft-law instruments are becoming less voluntary and more mandatory: as one securities supervisor I spoke to put it, the 'comply or explain' principle must now be taken to mean 'comply or comply'. At the same time, supervisors appear more sceptical of the efficacy of these rules, testifying to a growing distance between the words of regulatory texts and normal banking practice. The most conspicuous example of this is the existence of institutions that are too big to fail and too big to prosecute, which is leaving many financial regulators with a sense of impotence.

In sum, contemporary financial supervision appears to be marked by the inevitability of errors on the part of supervisors and regulators, and of dubious innovation on the part of market actors. True, all this adds to the same sense of economic deviance and instability that has accompanied the expansion of neoliberalism, but now it is official: wrongs and errors form part of the worldview of financial supervisors and any illusion of control over financial institutions through perfected norms is gone. In this respect, the current European situation bears some similarity to the situation in Japan following the disaster at the Fukushima nuclear plant (see Riles 2013). The efficient-market hypothesis that sustained the world of financial derivatives has been discredited, giving way to a loose epistemological combination of quantitative and qualitative outputs, and that involves both expert and lay people – though only to a certain degree and only under conditions established by regulators themselves. A sign that the lines separating different financial experts from lay financial users are becoming fuzzier in Europe is that more and more technical issues have become the subject of political discussion; even the Treasury of the United Kingdom (HM Treasury 2013: 28) refers to the 'political visibility' of bank's balance sheets as one positive outcome of European stress tests.

Since 2008 some of the former coherence appears to have been lost, however there has been no major discontinuity of the sort that would, following Janet Roitman (2014), amount to crisis. Rather, the general picture now is one with more contrasting tones: crisis continues – crisis did not occur – crisis is over – crisis is yet to come.

Acknowledgements

The preparation of this article involved both empirical and theoretical research that would have not been possible without the support of two Portuguese Foundation for Science and Technology (FCT) grants with the following references: SFRH/BPD/78438/2011 and PTDC/IVC-ANT/4520/2014.

Daniel Seabra Lopes works as a researcher in the CSG-SOCIUS research centre at the School of Economics and Management, University of Lisbon. He is also Assistant Professor at the Lisbon School of Economics and Management. He does ethnographic research on retail credit, banking and financial supervision, and has published papers in *Economy and Society*, *European Societies*, *Cultural Studies*, *Social Anthropology* and the *Journal of Cultural Economy*.

Notes

1. Alongside this process of institutional harmonization, some important regulatory steps were taken, like the Markets in Financial Instruments Directive (MiFID), revised in 2014, as well as the project of a European directive regulating insurance businesses (Solvency II), which came into effect in 2016.
2. These and other drawbacks were acknowledged by participants in a 2013 EU conference and public consultation dedicated to the European System of Financial Supervision (see European Union 2013).

References

Admati, Anat, and Martin Hellwig. 2013. *The Banker's New Clothes: What's Wrong with Banking and What to Do About It*. Princeton, NJ: Princeton University Press.
Arrighi, Giovanni. 1994. *The Long Twentieth Century: Money, Power and the Origins of Our Times*. New York: Verso.
Borio, Claudio. 2003. 'Towards a Macroprudential Framework for

Financial Supervision and Regulation?' Working paper 128. Basel: Bank
for International Settlements.

Borio, Claudio, and Gianni Toniolo. 2006. 'One Hundred and Thirty Years
of Central Bank Cooperation: A BIS Perspective'. Working paper 193.
Basel: Bank for International Settlements.

Cooper, Richard N. 2006. 'Almost a Century of Central Bank
Cooperation'. Working paper 198. Basel: Bank for International
Settlements.

Crockett, Andrew. 2000. 'Marrying the Micro- and Macroprudential
Dimensions of Financial Stability'. Delivered at the Eleventh
International Conference of Banking Supervisors, Basel (20–21
September). Basel: Bank for International Settlements. https://www.bis.
org/review/rr000921b.pdf (accessed 18 February 2016).

Desrosières, Alain. 1993. *La politique des grands nombres: histoire de la
raison statistique*. Paris: La Découverte.

Dymski, Gary A., and Annina Kaltenbrunner. 2017. 'How Finance
Globalized: A Tale of Two Cities', in Ismail Ertürk and Daniela Gabor
(eds), *The Routledge Companion to Banking Regulation and Reform*.
London: Routledge, pp. 351–72.

ESMA (European Securities and Markets Authority). 2014. 'Economic
Report: High-Frequency Trading Activity in EU Equity Markets'. Paris:
European Securities and Markets Authority.

Esposito, Elena. 2011. *The Future of Futures: The Time of Money in
Financing and Society*. Cheltenham: Edward Elgar.

EuroFinuse (European Federation of Financial Services Users). 2013.
'EuroFinuse's Response to the European Commission Consultation on
the Review of the European System of Financial Supervision'. Brussels:
European Federation of Financial Services Users. http://ec.europa.eu/
internal_market/consultations/2013/esfs/docs/contributions/registered-
organisations/eurofinuse_en.pdf (accessed 18 February 2016).

European Commission. 2012. 'Restoring the Health and Stability of the EU
Financial Sector'. Brussels: European Commission.

European Union. 2013. Public Hearing on Financial Supervision / Review
of the European System of Financial Supervision. Brussels: European
Union. https://scic.ec.europa.eu/streaming/index.php?es=2&sessionno=
6f67057b6a3671fe882f6d4f27d547be (accessed 18 February 2016).

Fontan, Clément. 2017. 'The New Behemoth? The ECB and the Financial
Supervision Reforms during the Eurozone Crisis', in Ismail Ertürk and
Daniela Gabor (eds), *The Routledge Companion to Banking Regulation
and Reform*. London: Routledge, pp. 175–91.

Foucault, Michel. (1978) 1991. 'Governmentality', in Graham Burchell,
Colin Gordon and Peter Miller (eds), *The Foucault Effect: Studies
in Governmentality*. Chicago, IL: University of Chicago Press, pp.
87–104.

Graeber, David. 2011. *Debt: The First 5,000 Years*. Brooklyn: Melville
House.

Guyer, Jane. 2004. *Marginal Gains: Monetary Transactions in Atlantic Africa*. Chicago, IL: University of Chicago Press.

Hacking, Ian. 1990. *The Taming of Chance*. Cambridge: Cambridge University Press.

Herring, Richard J., and Jacopo Carmassi. 2007. 'The Structure of Cross-sector Financial Supervision', *Financial Markets, Institutions & Instruments* 17(1): 51–76

HM Treasury. 2013. 'UK Response to the Commission Services Consultation on the Review of the European System of Financial Supervision. London: HM Treasury. http://ec.europa.eu/internal_market/consultations/2013/esfs/docs/contributions/public-authorities/hm-treasury-united-kingdom_en.pdf (accessed 19 February 2016).

Hoskin, Keith. 2004. 'Spacing, Timing and the Invention of Management'. *Organization* 11(6): 743–57.

Hoskin, Keith, and Richard H. Macve. 2000. 'Knowing More as Knowing Less? Alternative Histories of Cost Management Accounting in the US and the UK', *Accounting Historians Journal* 27(1): 91–149.

International Monetary Fund. 2010. Transcript of a press conference by International Monetary Fund managing director, Dominique Strauss-Kahn. Washington, DC: International Monetary Fund. www.imf.org/external/np/tr/2010/tr100710.htm (accessed 15 January 2016).

King, Mervyn. 2013. 'A Governor Looks Back – and Forward'. Delivered at the Lord Mayor's Banquet, London (19 June). London: Bank of England. www.bankofengland.co.uk/publications/Documents/speeches/2013/speech670.pdf (accessed 19 February 2016).

Laeven, Luc, and Fabian Valencia. 2008. 'Systemic Banking Crises: A New Database'. Working paper 08/224. Washington, DC: International Montary Fund.

Lanchester, John. 2013a. 'Are We Having Fun Yet?', *London Review of Books* 35(13): 3–8.

———. 2013b. 'Let's Consider Kate', *London Review of Books* 35(14): 3–8.

Langley, Paul. 2013. 'Anticipating Uncertainty, Reviving Risk? On the Stress Testing of Finance in Crisis', *Economy and Society* 42(1): 51–73.

Larosière, Jacques de. 2013. Speech delivered at the Public Hearing on Financial Supervision in the EU, Brussels (24 May). Brussels: European Commission. http://ec.europa.eu/internal_market/conferences/2013/0524-financial-supervision/docs/speech-de-larosiere_en.pdf (accessed 18 February 2016).

Lopes, Daniel S. 2011. 'Making Oneself at Home with Numbers: Financial Reporting from an Ethnographic Perspective', *Social Anthropology* 19(4): 463–76.

———. 2015. 'Number Interception: Knowledge, Action and Culture within Financial Risk Management', *Journal of Cultural Economy* 8(2): 202–17.

———. 2017 'Libor and Euribor: From Normal Banking Practice to Manipulation to the Potential for Reform', in Ismail Ertürk and Daniela

Gabor (eds), *The Routledge Companion to Banking Regulation and Reform*. London: Routledge, pp. 225–39.

MacKenzie, Donald. 2009. *Material Markets: How Economic Agents Are Constructed*. Oxford: Oxford University Press.

Maes, Ivo. 2009. 'On the Origins of the BIS Macro-prudential Approach to Financial Stability: Alexandre Lamfalussy and Financial Fragility'. Working paper 176. Brussels: National Bank of Belgium.

Masciandaro, Donato, and Marc Quintyn. 2013. 'Financial Supervision as Economic Policy: Importance, Key Facts and Drivers'. Research paper 2013-139. Milan: Paolo Baffi Centre, Bocconi University.

Maurer, Bill. 2005. *Mutual Life, Limited: Islamic Banking, Alternative Currencies, Lateral Reason*. Princeton, NJ: Princeton University Press.

Morris, Nathan L., and Philip O. Price (eds). 2011. *The Dodd-Frank Wall Street Reform and Consumer Protection Act*. New York: Nova Science Publishers.

Nesvetailova, Anastasia. 2010. *Financial Alchemy in Crisis: The Great Liquidity Illusion*. London: Pluto Press.

OJEU (Official Journal of the European Union). 2009. 'Commission Decision of 23 January 2009 establishing the Committee of European Securities Regulators, Commission Decision of 23 January 2009 establishing the Committee of European Banking Supervisors, Commission Decision of 23 January 2009 establishing the Committee of European Insurance and occupational Pensions Supervisors', *Official Journal of the European Union* 52L(25): 18–32.

Porter, Theoder M. 1995. *Trust in Numbers: The Pursuit of Objectivity in Science and Public Life*. Princeton, NJ: Princeton University Press.

Riles, Annelise. 2013. 'Market Collaboration: Finance, Culture, and Ethnography after Neoliberalism', *American Anthropologist* 115(4): 555–69.

———. 2014. 'Managing Regulatory Arbitrage: A Conflict of Laws Approach', *Cornell International Law Journal* 47(1): 63–119.

Roitman, Janet. 2014. *Anti-crisis*. Durham, NC: Duke University Press.

Rose, Nikolas. 1999. *Power of Freedom: Reframing Political Thought*. Cambridge: Cambridge University Press.

Searle, John R. 2005. 'What Is an Institution?', *Journal of Institutional Economics* 1(1): 1–22.

Tett, Gillian. 2009. *Fool's Gold: How Unrestrained Greed Corrupted a Dream, Shattered Global Markets and Unleashed a Catastrophe*. London: Little, Brown Book Group.

Thiemann, Matthias, and Jan Lepoutre. 2017. 'Stitched on the Edge: Rule Evasion, Embedded Regulators, and the Evolution of Markets', *American Journal of Sociology* 122(6): 1775–821.

Violle, Alexandre. 2017. 'Banking Supervision and the Politics of Verification: The 2014 Stress Test in the European Banking Union', *Economy and Society* 46(3–4): 432–51.

Wedel, Janine R. 2009. *Shadow Elite: How the World's New Power Brokers Undermine Democracy, Government, and the Free Market.* New York: Basic Books.

Westbrook, David A. 2009. *Out of Crisis: Rethinking our Financial Markets.* Boulder, CO: Paradigm Publishers.

Wheatley, Martin. 2012. *The Wheatley Review of LIBOR: Final Report.* London: HM Treasury.

4

Of Taxation, Instability, Fraud and Calculation

Thomas Cantens

Did Nero really live up to his cruel reputation? In AD 58, he proposed to the Senate that indirect taxes (customs taxes and duties on imports) should be abolished, thus conferring 'a most splendid boon in the human race', according to Tacitus (1942: Book XIII, Chap. 50). Did these words originate with Tacitus himself, or was he quoting Nero, who had a penchant for flights of lyricism? Tacitus reveals only that the senators were unwilling to consent to the idea, on the grounds that it could imperil the greatness of Rome and its empire. They also argued that the tax-farming system had been established by consuls and plebeian tribunes, the implication presumably being that any moves to abolish it would eliminate a source of revenue for an elite of tax-collecting publicans towards whom the senators were, at the very least, sympathetic.

Although the senators rejected the abolition of indirect taxes, few could have objected to Nero's subsequent order that they be calculated using transparent methods and pursuant to well-publicized laws, with the amount collected never exceeding the figure for the previous year. We do not know whether this push for transparency heralded a new era in relations between tax collectors and taxpayers, since the only documented outcomes are the published laws themselves, such as the *Monumentum Ephesenum*, a copy of which was discovered in Ephesus in 1976 and which sets out the customs duties and taxes imposed in the Asian provinces.

Taxation is a *sine qua non* of contemporary societies, which have forgotten the fiscal revolts of their ancestors and are becoming evermore refined in technical, legal and bureaucratic terms. Taxation is an economic relationship commonly linked to ethical terms, such as the 'tax optimization' of multinationals, 'fraud' by taxpayers or 'corruption' in tax and customs administrations. This ethical link is all the more familiar to us because the global economic crisis has brought tax issues to the forefront of public debate. As well, of course, barely a day goes by without each of us having to pay a tax – VAT, fuel and telephone taxes, income tax, etc. These all present opportunities to avoid paying tax, and hence also raise ethical questions.

More generally, taxation evokes ethical concepts of limits and decency, either in what can be claimed from individuals or in what individuals can retain, legally or illegally, of the wealth created in the course of their interactions with the rest of society. Peter Sloterdijk (2012) notes that the rate of personal income tax, which is what can be claimed by the rest of society, has varied widely in the past century or two, from 3 per cent in the United Kingdom in 1850 to 90 per cent in the United States during the New Deal era; however, because he does not explore the way that income itself was calculated, it is difficult to compare tax rates. As to what can be retained, in some countries some practices that could strictly be considered as illegal are so widespread that they are considered acceptable, which allows tax officials few means to combat fraud to achieve the revenue targets set by the administration (e.g. Cantens 2013).

Those concepts of limits and decency arise when states take measures to counter the aggressive tax strategies of multinational companies that force territories to engage in tax competition.[1] They arise as well when Warren Buffett (2011) and Bill Gates (BBC 2012), two of the richest men in the world, living in one of the wealthiest and most liberal societies in the world, express a desire to pay more tax during periods of crisis. Their demands caused an international sensation but led to nothing in the way of concrete action. And, once more, they arose when the French government sought to raise the marginal rate of tax levied on the wealthiest people to 75 per cent, which opponents said was confiscatory. In December 2012, France's Constitutional Court rejected the draft bill, but without considering the point. Instead, it decided that the proposed tax would be iniquitous because it based tax calculations on the individual and not the fiscal household (see Conseil Constitutionnel 2012: paras 67–74). The government redrafted the bill, retaining the rate of 75 per cent on the wealthiest citizens. In 2013, the Council of State ruled that the rate was confiscatory, and should be no more than 66 per cent.[2] The result was a top rate of 50 per cent as income tax, and a further 25 per cent as social levies.

Taxation takes place not only in the law but also in the market, and this is more dramatically true now than ever. In his 1979 lectures on biopolitics, Michel Foucault argued that the era of economic liberalism that opened in the eighteenth century transformed the nature of the market. Since the sixteenth century the market had been 'a site of justice' (Foucault 2008: 31), where buyers and sellers agreed on a fair price for goods, an agreement guaranteed by the state.[3] This reflected the view that the market was risky and that buyers were to be protected. Gradually this was replaced by a different view of the market, which held that it was natural and ruled by scientific laws that those like the Physiocrats sought to discover. In this new view, the market was a 'site of truth', a 'site of veridiction' (ibid.: 32, 34), where transactions are not fair and just but only normal and true.

Foucault's argument can be extended to contemporary neoliberalism, in which the market is a source of truth, for instance by revealing the validity of a state's economic actions. So, should a state decide to apply a new taxation scheme, the market will reveal whether the scheme is valid or not through the flow of wealth and economic actors to or from the country. In this view, the problem with a fraudulent act is not that it is unjust, but that it violates the natural laws of the market or rests on misleading people about the calculations based on them.

In such a context, how do we think of taxation, fraud and misconduct? What is thinkable and acceptable, and what is not? Are there alternatives to taxes on income? Should we encourage democratic donations, as Sloterdijk suggested? Perhaps the estates of the deceased should be handed over in their entirety to the state. As was the case in Nero's time, questions about and calls for radical measures are doomed to failure; taxation seems always and forever to be a carefully weighed-up solution to the state's need for wealth.

It is the case, then, that in talk about taxation, the question of what is acceptable and what is not is not the same as the question of what is fraudulent or corrupt and what is legal. In this chapter, I approach the question of fraud and corruption indirectly, by beginning with the question of what are the acceptable and unacceptable ways of generating collective wealth – effectively state revenue. I hold taxation to be a particular form of governance that structures the ethics of relations between individuals and the community, and that this form of governance is linked to calculative thinking. I am, thus, less interested in the amount of state revenue at issue than I am in the ways that calculative thinking shapes our understanding of what is acceptable taxation and what is not.

The first section of what follows argues that the collective decision to create collective wealth has been realized in different ways, one of which, taxation, addresses an instability peculiar to the dominant contemporary model of the economy. In particular, taxation has become a restraining force, a force of inertia that counters the instability that characterizes economies based on the idea of development or progress. The second section describes an important historical change in efforts to realize collective wealth; that is, the move away from a levy on individuals themselves (e.g. a poll tax) to a levy on their material possessions or the monetary equivalent. This change facilitates the replacing of flat amounts levied on all with a calculation of how much to levy, and hence leads to the framing of acceptable taxation in calculative terms.

Taxation, however, does not take its calculation of things to the limit, since it harbours a paradox and an anomaly. The paradox is that in order to protect the right of ownership it must weaken that right. The anomaly is that the governance of things clashes with a right of ownership of things that can be transferred following the death of the owner. The limits on calculation that these two things induce is manifest in the fact that the calculations often end up being constrained by negotiation, and that this constraint is based on the individual being taxed rather than on what that person owns.

The third and fourth sections examine this negotiation and its associated constraints, and argue that the result is the drift or corruption, in the primary meaning of the term, of the system of governance. That is, while taxation is fair in the sense that everyone is equal before it, not everyone is equal in its calculation. The consequence is that, because the morality of taxation has come to be seen to rest on its calculation, the concept of dubious or wrongful economic activity needs to be extended beyond that associated with fraud or deception in taxation. It needs as well to be extended in ways that allow us to consider the practicalities of that calculation, and especially the ways that people can arrange their affairs and present themselves to tax authorities in ways intended to assure that the calculation will result in the least possible tax liability. If they are successful, what they have done is acceptable as the rules of calculation have been applied, even if what they have been applied to makes their results improper. The result of this is that we have drifted away from evaluating taxation in terms of a common agreement on what should be done in society to serve the collectivity, and instead drifted towards evaluating taxation in terms of how it is calculated.

Taxation and Instability

Taxation has not always been the sole means of filling state coffers, with practices such as euergetism (see Veyne [1976] 1990), voluntary donations and use of the public domain also laying a claim to this honour. In the *Encyclopaedia*, Jean-Jacques Rousseau (1767: Vol. 2, 37–38) wrote that the public desmene is 'the most honest and most secure of all means to provide for the State's needs'. He held that tax is a 'deplorable resource' (ibid.: Vol. 2, 45), used to serve the need for armies and fortifications, a need that arises only because the country's citizens lack patriotism and seek luxury. As Rousseau illustrates, taxation was long regarded as a solution to short-term problems, and the public desmene was thought to be the simplest way of supplying the authorities with wealth.[4]

While taxation is seen as an integral part of modern countries, in some ways we still view it as a solution to problems arising from instability. War is one of those instabilities, but so is a citizenry's rising needs and expectations. Rousseau held that a perfectly stable, static economy was best.[5] However, his liberal contemporary, David Hume, was thinking in terms of a more unstable economy, one which led to economic development, though he did not use that phrase (Brewer 1998: 79–80). Hume (1826: Vol. 3, 302) considered that 'luxury', manufactured goods that 'gratify the senses' and that people seek to own, drives economic change, which departed from Christian and republican views that luxury has a negative effect on morality and from pure liberal views that exclude morality from economic reasoning (McArthur 2014). In his *Treatise of Human Nature*, he argued that the love of acquisition is the only impulse that cannot be constrained by others or by our natural sympathies, and must be limited in some other way.

That way of limiting is private property and its peaceable transaction; in other words, the right of ownership guaranteed by the state and commercial trade (Hume 1826: Vol. 2, 253–302). This trade would lead to the growth of personal wealth, thus helping to satisfy the acquisitive desire, while the fact that what is traded is owned by individuals would help to keep the desire in check. Moreover, Hume (1826: Vol. 3, 368–73) advocated trade between countries as well as within them, for that stimulates the spirit of progress and development generally. In 'Of Commerce', he put it this way:

> And this perhaps is the chief advantage which arises from a commerce with strangers. It rouses men from their indolence; and presenting the gayer and more opulent part of the nation with objects of luxury, which they never before dreamed of, raises in them a desire of a more splendid way of life than what their ancestors enjoyed. And at the same time, the few merchants, who possess the secret of this importation and exportation, make great profits; and becoming rivals in wealth to the ancient nobility, tempt other adventurers to become their rivals in commerce. Imitation soon diffuses all those arts; while domestic manufactures emulate the foreign in their improvements, and work up every home commodity to the utmost perfection of which it is susceptible. (Hume 1826: Vol. 3, 297)

The ideas of Hume and his fellow liberals ultimately won out over Rousseau and a string of thinkers going back to Plato and others in ancient Greece. The idea of economic stability gave way to one of economic instability, cast in terms of progress, development and growth, with the market being both an instrument of that instability and a mechanism by which imbalances are corrected. From this, according to Norbert Elias (2000: 344–62), there emerged fiscal systems that are characteristically Western, in which taxes must be high enough to fund a state that both invests and regulates, and that is capable of off-setting inequalities in the distribution of wealth and providing a consistent range of public services. Together with the monopoly on violence, the monopoly of taxation was crucial for state formation.

What generally characterizes neoliberal governance, then, is that it seeks to reconcile the real condition of the economy with what is seen as the optimal condition and establish a certain relationship with time.[6] The Walras equilibrium is not the stability that was desired by the ancient Greeks;[7] instead, it is the best instability, one that will produce the greatest overall profit. In this way, economic growth and development arise from the disequilibria of individual innovations and opportunities, and the circulation that arises from that. In this situation, taxation is a form of inertia, one that rests on the assumption of a surplus, which is wealth that arises out of individual gain and profit but that is not part of the Walras equilibrium because it is achieved at the expense of society, and hence is fit for being diverted to the state treasury.[8]

While Rousseau and his predecessors may have viewed instability as a temporary condition brought about by something like war, we are now faced with continuous instability, valued as dynamism and quantified as progress and growth, with taxation being a state-generated moment of inertia that is proportional to the economic mass circulating and accelerating within the capitalist system. This proportionality points to the importance of calculation – the use of numbers to describe the world in its instability and predict its future state.[9] This, then, is no echo of Pythagorean efforts to reveal the natural perfection of numbers, in pursuit of a harmony through which society should be governed (see Wersinger 2008). Rather, this calculation is probabilistic, dealing with and being shaped by imperfections in reality, and doing so not with reference to the ideal polity, but to the ideal conditions of material livelihood. From such a foundation, corruption and fraud are not undesirable because they debase a stable present, but because they disrupt the calculation of the future. Such economic activity hinders the ability to identify and fulfil ideal conditions, and so disrupts what is to happen. This neoliberal view, then, treats what had been an ethical issue of right and wrong in terms of calculation and predictability.

Taxation and the Realm of Ownership

I have described the relationship between taxation and instability. I turn now to its relationship with wealth, which I construe broadly to mean what people possess and what can be taken from them. The form wealth takes and its social valuation allows the decency of that wealth to be negotiated. The results of this negotiation can be qualitative, in the sense that people decide that some actions are acceptable for generating wealth and some are not. As well, the results can be quantitative, in the sense that people can decide that there is a minimum level of wealth to which all are entitled and a maximum beyond which additional wealth is not justifiable. If wealth is seen in terms of objects, they can be valued in market terms, so that these limits become calculable.

It is important to remember, however, that taxation emerged as a reflection of both material and social factors. So, value could be viewed as a quality, a judgement or a moral assessment, but it must be approached as a property of objects or beings, measurable and intrinsic in exactly the same way as a physical property, in order to construct a fiscal zone where value can circulate. Foucault (1966) posited that the idea of wealth in the seventeenth and eighteenth centuries entailed the existence of an arena where ideas of price and value (and, he might have added, taxation) could expand and intermingle in order to build an economy.

Given that the idea of wealth historically has been so fluid and complex, it has taken a variety of forms and, consequently, a variety of things have been deemed capable of being taxed. We appear to own ourselves, which implies that being human is taxable. In ancient Rome, slaves who had been freed were taxed, in order to limit their access to political society (see Livy 1924: Chap. 16; Gibbon 1776: 41–42). Existence itself has been taxed, in the form of a monetary head tax collected in French colonies or in the form of a temporal head tax collected in Peru in the 1950s, which obliged people to work on major construction projects (e.g. Nugent 2013). The two could be combined, as in the Cameroons, where French colonial authorities annually varied the days of labour and the amount of money levied on each person, depending on whether the need for money or for manpower was greater (see, e.g., Ministère des affaires étrangères 1926: 8 ff.). Of course, death also has been taxed, the property of the deceased being taken by the collectivity. Particularly in colonial settings, this can be seen as the domination of the state even over death as the ultimate liberation. As Boudicca is reported to have put it: 'Not even death is free with them [the Romans]; you know how much we pay even for the dead. Among the rest of humanity death frees even those who are slaves; only among the Romans do the dead live for their profit' (Dio 1925: Vol. 8, Book LXII).

While these taxes generated revenue, they were commonly prompted by the political desire to achieve certain ends, in the way that the Roman tax on freed slaves reflected the desire to exclude them from political life. In Cameroon in 1921, the head tax was extended to include women. This was intended to discourage men from practising polygamy, which was taken to be undesirable because the polygamous had fewer children than the monogamous. In the words of the Cameroon budget, '[t]hose individuals with the most women have a proportionally tiny number of children and, without dwelling on the reasons, we can safely state that measures which restrict polygamy are wholly justified from a social and fiscal point of view' (Territoires du Cameroun 1922: 7; unless noted otherwise, all translations are by the author and Stella Hamill). It was also in the colonies, ideal venues for experiments of all kinds, that taxation brought about the introduction of money and wages, since the obligation to pay taxes in cash meant that local populations were obliged to become part of the colonial capitalist economy.

These economic considerations were themselves overshadowed by the establishment of a political order based on a shared vision of society, with the colonial authorities more interested in civilizing people than collecting money. Money was a more reliable means of purchasing goods than trading-post exchanges, and material ownership and diversity ultimately represented the apogee of civilization for the colonial powers.[10] This nascent taxation of markets in colonial empires also heralded the start of political and economic globalization in terms of both the forms of trade and its regulation.

Material objects constitute the taxable wealth of the present day in a world that has become totally commensurable through the advent of a 'trading science' (e.g. Skornicki 2006; Charles, Lefebvre and Théré 2011). Contemporary monetary taxation which is levied, for example, on a profit is in essence merely a commensurability applied to the material world, while the profit is a material possession. During the era of the slave trade, Montesquieu ([1748] 1989: 222) believed that revenue should be raised through a tax on goods rather than a head tax on slaves, arguing that '[a]n impost by head is more natural to servitude; the impost on commodities is more natural to liberty because it relates less directly to the person'. Guillaume Thomas Raynal (1773) similarly criticized the head tax as being unjust in its scope and distribution, and overly complicated to collect.[11] The two men criticized the same tax for dissimilar reasons, separated as they were by the difference between the concept of the state before and after the French Revolution, and the progression is a familiar one. The older moral and political considerations, in this case concerning servitude, gave way to economic and calculatory concerns in the sense that taxation must be just. This was justice not only in the political meaning of the word, but also the need to be simple and efficient, a justice that can be expressed pragmatically as avoiding the negative impact on distant territories of inefficient rentier taxation.

When it comes to the shift from the taxation of human beings to the taxation of what they own, it is people's material possessions that dispossess them of their fiscal nature: the more they own, the less they themselves are taxable. The last to be liberated in this way were the slaves and indigenous people who owned nothing. The right of ownership also gains significance in step with the amount of what is owned. This has little to do with the desire for riches, however, since it is initially limited to universal possession as a bedrock for production and trade, as explained above in respect of the colonies. This ownership of material objects could no longer be subject to intellectual constraints as it had been for the ancient philosophers.

The right of ownership nevertheless poses a paradox. The relationship between taxation and private property is unique in that the former protects the latter by removing part of it. Rousseau's 'Discourse on Political Economy' refers to the incongruity that exists between the idea of living together and defending private property by virtue of a social contract on the one hand, and the ethical dictate to refrain from coercion or subjugation on the other. Rousseau proposed a solution to that paradox, namely that taxation should be understood as an extension of the right to use property rather than a restriction, because it regulates and thus sanctions the transmission of property between the deceased and the living, whereas the ownership of a good should logically cease upon the death of its owner.

This positing of tax as an extension of the right of use is unsatisfactory in two respects. Firstly, it presupposes a questionable form of social stability, which Rousseau (1767: Vol. 2, 36) explicitly promoted when he wrote:

> Nothing is more fatal to morality and to the Republic than the continual shifting of rank and fortune among the citizens: such changes are both the proof and the source of a thousand disorders, and overturn and confound everything; for those who were brought up to one thing find themselves destined for another; and neither those who rise nor those who fall are able to assume the rules of conduct, or to possess themselves of the qualifications requisite for their new condition, still less to discharge the duties it entails.

Secondly, the recent work by Thomas Piketty (2013) explains why the inheritance of capital is a source of social deregulation, a problem that taxation has failed to resolve in Western societies over the past three centuries. Long-term returns on capital exceed economic growth, and so the preservation of transmitted capital escalates inequalities to a degree that many feel unacceptable because it means that labour is worth less than capital, and the entire process of education and entrepreneurship is devalued.

Yet if taxation cannot be regarded as an extension of the right of use, where does that leave the question of transmitting rights of ownership following the owner's death? The fact that there is no reasonable response to this question means that there is no escaping the fact that the legitimization of taxation in modern societies, despite its paradoxical relationship with the right of ownership, does not derive from moral or political principles. Rather, it derives from negotiated calculatory practices.

In material terms, taxing individuals in the manner of a poll tax constitutes political domination by one group over another, justified by the claimed moral or intellectual superiority of the dominant group, a claim that can be challenged. The taxation of wealth built on things is different: people assumed to be equal are differentiated according to the duty they have towards the community in accordance with a calculation alone. The values that govern that calculation may continue to be established by a social elite, but that group no longer stands out as a category that one must resemble. Rather, it is the key party in a common effort to bring about the improvement of all, which makes peaceful political subversion more complex.

This has changed the nature of wrongful economic activity and understandings of it. Famously, Foucault ([1975] 1995: 76) noted a change in the seventeenth and eighteenth centuries that resembles what happened to taxation: criminality no longer focused so much on people but on their property. This leads to a distinction between different sorts of illegality. There is a popular illegality (e.g. theft), which is severely penalized because it is an attack on private property, and a bourgeois illegality (e.g. tax evasion), which is not severely penalized because it tends to retain it. This differentiation of illegalities also entails negotiation of the respective penalty, involving an arithmetic calculation between a loss and a remedy. As Nietzsche (Neitzsche and Samuel [1887] 1918: 48) observed, the idea that a material penalty is imposed on the grounds that it would have been possible for the perpetrator not to commit an act is particular and relatively modern; the idea that such a penalty could derive from an arithmetic calculation of equivalences is even more modern. This constitutes a shift from an idea of justice in the political sense as a leading principle structuring the polity to an idea of accuracy or calculation established as a leading principle, the justice of which would merely be an effect.

Taxation as the Negotiation of Just Calculation

The distinction between popular and bourgeois illegality points to the fact that formal legality may be less important than the degree to which acts are acceptable socially. This in turn points to the fact that taxation is always a negotiation. This is the corollary of the interdependence of taxation and the circulation of wealth. The right of ownership (the *sine qua non* of the social contract) and the importance of the circulation of wealth (the *sine qua non* of capitalism) are so strong that they are not negotiable. Consequently, what we owe the collectivity in the form of tax must be negotiated, and the just calculation of tax makes it acceptable. Here I want to consider this acceptability by calculation.

What aspects of taxation can be negotiated? Tax is based on law, but the relationship of the tax system and law is unusual. Especially, tax authorities exercise coercive powers when they identify and punish violations of the law, which makes them similar to bodies such as the police. However, they are unlike police because they are also supposed to monitor the implementation of the provisions of the tax code. Unlike laws that the police enforce, customs tariffs and tax codes specify what must be, rather than what must not be, and do so precisely. They define the nature of taxes and how the tax base should be calculated, as well as providing lists of exemptions and sanctions. Also, unlike laws that the police enforce, tax and customs codes impose a positive obligation on individuals. The result often is various forms of suspicion. For instance, all a person's income is taxable unless that person can prove otherwise; and all objects presented at a border are presumed to be commodities and subject to duty unless the owner can prove otherwise.

This interplay of legislation and coercion reflects the fact that the tax system is to be applied to people who are not identical (e.g. in terms of income) and that taxes levied are just if they are based on calculations which are fair in the mathematical sense and are applied to figures (e.g. of income) which are as accurate as possible. The real collective negotiations about collective wealth revolve around these calculations.

One consequence of the importance of calculation for defining a fair or just tax system is that the practicalities of taxation are growing evermore technical in terms of both the material resources involved, especially the rise of information technologies, and the legislation applied, especially the vast array of formal rules, standards and structures. This trend is evident at the national level in the technological progress made by all countries' tax and customs authorities. It is evident at the international level in things like the G8 and G20 debates on international rules governing the exchange of tax information and the World Trade Organization's Rules on Customs Valuation.[12] Tax experts use 'professionalization' to refer to the way that taxation is becoming increasingly technical in its physical and abstract manifestations.

At the time when bookkeeping was making its first appearance in French legislation, Rousseau offered a pessimistic assessment of the capacity of technologies to assure that taxes are collected fairly, accurately and without fraud or corruption:

> Books and auditing of accounts, instead of exposing frauds, only conceal them; for prudence is never so ready to conceive new precautions as knavery is to elude them. Never mind, then, about account books and papers; place the management of finance in honest hands: that is the only way to get it faithfully conducted. (Rousseau 1767: Vol. 2, 39)

Rousseau's comment, in his 'Discourse on Political Economy', is interesting because it goes against professionalization, against basing reform on technical applications rather than ethical considerations. And as Rousseau predicted, the increasingly technical and calculative nature of taxation gives rise to novel avoidance strategies rather than doing away with the grey areas that have always existed between law and practice.

In less developed countries, corruption has been an argument used to justify taxes that are simple and easy to collect, even though the taxes might end up being unfair. Very few African countries tax real estate, for example, which would require establishing a land registry and a system of assessing the value of property. This would be expensive, and many argue that such a system would invite corruption by tax officials. However, countries quickly imposed taxes on mobile telephony, which is easy to collect because the tax is commonly levied on mobile telephone companies, which recoup it from their customers. The result is not very fair, for the tax on mobile phone use is paid by the less wealthy, who account for the majority of the population in such countries, while tax on real estate would mostly affect the better off.[13]

As with those mobile telephone companies, tax authorities' concern with ease and security of collection often leads to some people and organizations having a distinct relationship with those authorities. There is nothing new in this, for it is as old as tax farming. A common modern manifestation is the collection of sales and value-added taxes. Here, private companies collect the tax on behalf of the government and pay it to them. In such a system, tax authorities are likely to be concerned with the reliability of those intermediaries. In Cameroon, this concern has led the government to identify certain companies as 'citizens' enterprises', more reliable collectors of VAT than others (often firms linked to multinational corporations). In wealthy countries, tax authorities embrace approaches such as 'administrative audits' and 'risk management', with large enterprises (those that pay the most tax) often benefiting from special and more lenient tax regimes. For instance, an importer who has been audited repeatedly and found to be reliable may receive fewer checks by customs officials than other importers. Such a system induces compliance, but the inducement often can end up favouring the larger firms and wealthier people. This favouring appears inherent in the operation of a department of the French tax authority that has, since 2013, been 'regularizing' the situation of French taxpayers who have concealed wealth abroad and who now wish to bring it back to France. The taxes due on the wealth are not up for negotiation, but the possibility of avoiding fines can be a strong inducement to comply with the tax code.

This difference in the approach to the larger and the wealthier, as compared to ordinary individuals, is an overt part of public policies. On its website, the Australian Tax Office encourages taxpayers to obey the code, but does so in different ways (Australian Taxation Office n.d.). On the page dedicated to individuals the tone is threatening: '[W]e will continue our compliance efforts to tackle fraudulent returns, identity theft and errors, and incorrect claims for work-related expenses'. On the other hand, the section dedicated to 'public and international groups' is friendlier, describing four core values: 'Excellent working relationships: The value of conversation. Customised service for Australia's largest taxpayers: Your contribution is recognised. Transparency: You know where you stand you can also find out what attracts our attention. Tailored engagement: Your circumstances are understood'. This is not just a matter of public presentation. 'Large taxpayers units' have been established in many tax administrations since the 1990s, and the IMF usually recommends them to developing countries as a first step in the 'segmentation' of taxpayers (see Benon, Baer and Toro 2002).

This differentiation is justified in terms of calculation. It would be impossible for tax authorities to check every single tax return submitted to them or for customs authorities to check the value of everything shipped across the border. Tax and customs authorities have to make choices, but their overriding duty is to ensure that the cost of scrutiny to the authorities and to taxpayers are proportionate to the cost of fraud. This calculation is often specious, since no authority could have the data that would justify the decision to carry out a certain number of checks on certain taxpayers.

One reason for this sort of differential treatment is the common assumption that larger amounts of wealth are more difficult to manage than are smaller amounts and are less easy for the state to monitor, and that their owners should thus be eligible to negotiate with tax inspectors. Accordingly, it should come as no surprise that a study was published by the OECD on how to 'engage in dialogue' with high net worth individuals in order to promote compliance with fiscal obligations (OECD 2009: Chaps 3, 4), and that the annex to that study presents the approach of the Focus Group on High Net Worth Individuals as one that 'concentrates on cooperative compliance approaches' (ibid.: 87).

The simple fact that high net worth individuals or entities are encouraged to discharge their obligations through dialogue rather than coercion reveals weakness on the part of the state. It also implies that the wealthy are either incompetent or immoral. They may not be competent to understand and keep track of both their wealth and the relevant tax codes, and so may involuntarily fail to discharge their obligations; they may deliberately set out to exploit the complexity of the tax code or take advantage of competition between different tax regimes. The result, however, is that the richest individuals are exempted from the most stringent forms of scrutiny on the basis of mere hypotheses, even though the wealthy who hide, say, a fifth of their income will deprive the public of more tax revenue than will ordinary people who do the same thing.

The overwhelmingly technical nature of taxation, the complexity of tax collection procedures and the uneven ability of tax subjects to negotiate with political and administrative authorities have led to a ranking of taxpayers. This distinction between morals and calculation creates new forms of illegality beyond those set out by Foucault and referred to above. These illegalities are also organized, perhaps once again, according to the complexity of the calculation. The more complicated it is to calculate the wealth of individuals, the more such individuals are given the leeway to negotiate the part that will be taken from them and used for the benefit of the community. Conversely, less wealthy individuals and those who partake less of the dynamism and opportunities of liberal capitalist society are less able to negotiate, because they are caught up in structures that report their wealth automatically and quantitatively to the state.

The consequences are significant. Firstly, tax collection procedures allow for the fact that taxation is not a precise science and that, importantly, it is least precise when dealing with those who should, by rights, contribute the most. The wealthy never pay more than they wish, which reduces the scope for debate about what wrong activity could even be. Secondly, as a practical matter, taxpayers are not evaluated in terms of their honesty, but in terms of their access to *in camera* proceedings where they can influence administrative law-making and can, therefore, take advantage of the complexity of the tax system. Decisions on matters such as domestic tax and customs procedures are shaped by the fact that it is only the wealthy who can band together and influence the forms of control to which they are subject. This sort of influence is illustrated by an annual report that the World Bank publishes, *Doing Business*. It ranks countries according to their level of liberal democracy and economic openness, but these are defined by surveys carried out among local affiliates of multinational companies that are capable of comparing the administrative practices with which they are faced and judging them according to their own criteria. Those rankings encourage countries to adopt the administrative reforms, practices and legal frameworks of countries with high rankings, and so that report becomes an integral component of legal decision making (e.g. Michaels 2009).

The ease with which individuals, companies and capital can now move around, together with the associated emergence of competition among different tax jurisdictions, has given rise to new, international and even less public arenas of negotiation, access to which demands even more in the way of material resources. This access, however, ensures that those who have it are part of the small group that is most conversant with, and most influential in shaping, the conceptual language of tax systems. Moreover, because taxation is a form of calculation, it has a fluidity and abstraction that encourage international communication and conformity. New systems of sovereignty and ethics are manifesting themselves through the production and dissemination of international standards, assisted by experts who spread the good news about these technical developments to less wealthy tax authorities. This Esperanto of fiscal governance is the basis of the paradigms we see embodied in 'best practices' and normative technical standards that define the thin line between compliance and deviance.

Conclusion

Was the emperor Nero counting on his tax proposal being rejected, or was it genuine? After all, this is the same Nero who obliged senators to do battle against honest horsemen in his amphitheatres (Dio 1925: Book LXI), who expropriated the belongings of citizens 'who had celebrated triumphs' and gave them to a gladiator and a lyre player (Suetonius 1889: Chap. 30), who reviled all religious cults and is said to have urinated on the statue of the only goddess he ever worshipped (ibid.: Chap. 56). Was his call to abolish the taxes that embodied all that was wrong with the regime merely an exercise in political show-manship, or was he earnestly planning to introduce novel methods of wealth distribution? Of all the dictators of the Ancient era, Nero was the one who most skilfully parodied power by stage managing its manifestations, while still retaining a firm grip on the lethal tools of repression. Playing fast and loose with taxation, which rests on the boundary between reason and abundance, is a way of parodying political economics; proposing its abolition is the ultimate outrage, forcing those in power to contemplate its loss.

We shall never know for sure if Nero was genuine. Becoming Emperor at the age of seventeen, a political wunderkind nurtured and advised by Seneca, he managed to bring government finances back into the black during his first years in office. He is also well known for his *liberalitas* and redistributions of wealth to the people (see Kragelund 2000), sometimes exceeding the state's resources, which ultimately led the political structure to decay, the governors to revolt and Nero himself to suicide.

Nero's tax proposal is a good illustration of how taxation is both a fundamental tool of power and a symbolic and morally charged force with practical outcomes, the technical implementation of which presents a challenge to hierarchies and social relationships. But Nero tells us more than that. He ruled with a particular violence that involved abruptly, if sometimes only fleetingly, making the unthinkable thinkable, unveiling the production of ethics and decency in material life.

Can taxation be viewed as the remaining vestige of moral intelligence in liberal societies endeavouring to rise above all forms of ideology in the name of complete individual liberty? What Rousseau believed to be superfluous and what Montesquieu saw as frivolous were not determined in any economic sense, but deemed worthy of heavy taxation on the grounds of morality. The tables have turned: moral evaluations take people's self-assessments as their starting point, but economic evaluations presume that those who are evaluated lack virtue. Accurate calculation has become an invariable prerequisite for just taxation, placing economic considerations centre stage but, despite the claims of certain critics, calculation has not triumphed over politics. Fiscal calculations have always had a political footing, despite their dependence on economic principles that are increasingly posited as self-evident truths. Using economics as the sole point of reference has not only made it harder to understand the political issues at stake in tax calculations, but has also ensured that only experts are in a position to formulate criticisms. The result is a declining willingness to see that tax represents a boundary between what is just and what is unjust, and that the form of taxation is a function of local circumstances and hence only one of many different possibilities.

Sloterdijk's proposal, that states encourage public donations, may already be coming to pass. However, the gift ethos he advocates seems to be realized in an amoral form. Donors are negotiating what they will give, since recipients have established a system that deprives donors of an understanding of their act of giving other than in terms of its accordance with an accuracy of calculation. Taxpayers, including multinationals, do not hire tax specialists to consider the justice of their taxes. Rather, they hire them to consider their accuracy, reducing their contributions by lawful means. Hume (1826: Vol. 3, 387) championed indirect taxation.[14] In the light of the present situation, his position must be seen as a way of referring all people to their own calculations, and thus to a form of diffuse and moderate governance among individuals themselves and a permanent and empirical process of delineation of the acceptable and the unacceptable, ensuring an equilibrium between government and people.

One final point: what if our inability to think about taxation were a harbinger of more radical changes, such as a decrease in the overall governability of contemporary free-market societies? What if the combination of the spirit of calculation, liberty and state intervention to guarantee competitive growth were to make the task of governing societies increasingly challenging? This question is pertinent, even at a time when the spread of calculation suggests that the structures of power are, to echo Foucault, extending their reach. One reason the question is pertinent is that the promise of competitive growth looks increasingly hollow. Another reason is that the venues of decision making are becoming increasingly nebulous. Power is decreasingly incarnated in a single leader, but instead increasingly belongs to an invisible elite whose wealth is difficult to assess. The third reason is that the intellectual distance between the elite and ordinary people has narrowed. Those people have access to a language of criticism that makes them less likely to accept the authority of the elite. In terms of taxation, the increasing amount of publicly accessible data ('open data'), advocated as a form of democratic transparency, will make more and more people aware of the way in which taxes are calculated. The fourth reason is the increasing division of intellectual labour. This leads to a fragmentation of outlook and orientation, to the extent that it becomes hard to find collective representative bodies with whom the elite can negotiate. Finally, to reiterate one of the themes of this chapter, the liberal elite has adopted a calculatory approach to decision making without allowing access to the raw data and methods involved in these calculations, thus creating a cohesive elite of experts on false premises. From this perspective, states will have to be much more flexible concerning the monopoly they have on knowledge about their own functioning.

Thomas Cantens is an anthropologist who is the head of the research unit at the World Customs Organization in Brussels and associate professor at the University of Auvergne School of Economics. He began his professional career as an engineer, before joining the French Customs Administration where he occupied a number of positions. Prior to joining the WCO's Research Unit in 2010, he served as a resident advisor in the Mali and Cameroon services for six years. He is the author of numerous publications on the use of quantification in public services, and on corruption and the linkages between security, trade and taxation in fragile areas. He has a degree in engineering, a Master's in Philosophy and a PhD in Social Anthropology and Ethnology from Ecole des Hautes Etudes en Sciences Sociales (Paris).

Notes

The views expressed here are solely those of the author and do not represent the official position of the World Customs Organization or its members. The author wishes to thank the publisher's three readers for their helpful comments and Stella Hamill for her assistance with language.

1. In its 'Action Plan on Base Erosion and Profit Shifting', the OECD (2013: 8) points out 'the increasing sophistication of tax planners in identifying and exploiting the legal arbitrage opportunities and the boundaries of acceptable tax planning, thus providing MNEs with more confidence in taking aggressive tax positions. These developments have opened up opportunities for MNEs to greatly minimise their tax burden. This has led to a tense situation in which citizens have become more sensitive to tax fairness issues'. The OECD plan embeds the idea of limit, between the acceptable and the unacceptable, when it forges a category of transactions or financial structures that are 'aggressive or abusive', and calls for government actions against them (ibid.: 22).
2. The Council proposed to tax the companies that pay high salaries or extra wages. This artifice was calculatory: by taxing companies, this tax would

not be included in the marginal tax rate of individuals or households. A marginal rate of more than 66 per cent would be invalid because confiscatory; before his election, the French President, François Hollande, had promised a top marginal rate of 75 per cent; the Council's advice to tax the companies reconciled the two positions by using a calculatory artifice to make political promises comply with high-level collective norms such as those expressed in the Constitution.

3. The world is made legible through the abundance and diversity of its material productions, which can be read in the handbooks of trade written by merchants between 1650 and 1750 and that formed an *ars mercatoria*, part of the emerging culture of a petty bourgeoisie of traders (Hoock and Jeannin 1993).

4. This idea is still current, with the concept of the public desmene extended to the more contemporary concept of the public domain. For instance, Morris Silver (1983) argues, against Polanyi, that the public domain is a kind of collective taxation rather than a kind of social organization.

5. Rousseau (1767: Vol. 2, 1) starts his 'Discourse on Political Economy' with a nod to many Greek philosophers before him by distinguishing between the economy of a family and the economy of a society. He also makes, and subsequently reiterates, the point that the growth of society is an undesirable outcome, whereas the growth of the family is the opposite, for it safeguards the family's survival. It is not clear, however, how he can separate the growth of families in a society from the growth of the society as a whole.

6. That optimal condition is called the Pareto equilibrium, achieved when perfect competition leads to an equilibrium between demand and supply (including for labour) at a certain price. With this equilibrium, nobody can improve his or her situation without worsening the situation of someone else, and all economic resources are used in the most productive way.

7. Léon Walras (1874) developed a mathematical model to describe the equilibrium that markets reach when market conditions are ideal, and argued that this equilibrium is a Pareto equilibrium. His theory gave birth to the general equilibrium theory used by contemporary economists.

8. It is worth noting that the idea of surplus is exploited by Xenophon (2003), often considered as the 'first economist' (Gray 2004; Jansen 2007).

9. Note that quantification is different from the calculation that concerns me. Unlike quantification, calculation has a teleological purpose; it is related to time and uncertainty. The extension of equivalence through calculation has been dramatically extended to governance fields by international and transnational organizations such as the World Bank, the International Monetary Fund, Transparency International and the World Economic Forum.

10. Explanatory statement for the 1925 Cameroonian budget: 'Indigenous peoples are provided with food and lodging and so, having earned money by labour to pay tax, find themselves in possession of an excess of money

which is used straight away to purchase much-desired objects. These newly discovered needs will not simply disappear in future. The piece of cloth purchased this year will need to be replaced next year; an extra item will be added in response to the same impulses which prompted the original purchase; and so the trade of a country develops, at the same time as the well-being of its indigenous people gradually becomes synonymous with the meeting of needs whose number is a measure of civilisation' (Territoires du Cameroun 1925: 4).

11. After criticizing its harmful impact in economic terms, Raynal (1773: Vol. 7, Bk 13, pp. 264 ff.) draws the following technical conclusion about head tax: 'Lastly, it is a very difficult matter to levy this tax. Every proprietor must give in an annual account of the number of his slaves. To prevent false entries, they shall be verified by clerks or excisemen. Every Negro that is not entered must be forfeited which is a very absurd practice, because every labouring Negro is so much stock, and by the forfeiture of him the culture is diminished, and the very object for which the duty was laid is annihilated. Thus it happens, that in the colonies, where the success of every thing depends upon the tranquillity which is enjoyed, a destructive war is carried on between the financier and the planter. Law-suits are numerous, removals frequent, rigorous measures become necessary, and the costs are great and ruinous'.

12. In 1994, while the WTO was being set up in the wake of the GATT Uruguay Round, the members of this new international organization introduced a new system of governance to determine the value of material goods and the way in which they should be taxed at national borders. States had previously relied on their customs authorities to establish the value of the goods presented to them at border crossing points, but from 1994 these authorities were obliged to accept the figure shown on the accompanying invoice by default as the correct value, or else provide evidence to the contrary – in a reversal of the rules on the burden of proof.

13. At a seminar organized by the French Ministry of Foreign Affairs (which the author attended) in September 2006, this explanation was put forward by a French economist and expert, on the basis of his experience of implementing tax reforms in Africa.

14. Hume's main argument does not rely on justice but on the relative invisibility of this tax: people will 'confound' the tax with the 'natural price of the commodity'. The fact that Hume does not rely on justice to advocate one form of taxation or another is in accord with his not defending the existence or the necessity of any social contract and with his desire to reduce the authority of government over people (see Frecknall-Hughes 2014: 23–25). Hume's theory influenced the design of the French tax system (Orain 2010).

References

Australian Tax Office. n.d. 'Building Confidence'. Canberra: Australian Taxation Office. https://www.ato.gov.au/general/building-confidence (accessed 8 June 2015).

BBC. 2012. 'Bill Gates: I Don't Pay Enough Tax'. Interview, 25 January. London: BBC. www.bbc.com/news/world-us-canada-16714480 (accessed 16 February 2016).

Benon, Olivier, Katherine Baer and Juan Toro. 2002. 'Improving Large Taxpayers' Compliance: A Review of Country Experience.' Occasional paper 215. Washington, DC: International Monetary Fund.

Brewer, Anthony. 1998. 'Luxury and Economic Development: David Hume and Adam Smith', *Scottish Journal of Political Economy* 45(1): 78–98.

Buffett, Warren E. 2011. 'Stop Coddling the Super-Rich'. *The New York Times* (14 August).

Cantens, Thomas. 2013. 'Other People's Money and Goods: The Relationship between Customs Officers and Users in Some Countries of Sub-Saharan Francophone Africa', *Sociologus* 63(1–2): 37–58.

Charles, Loïc, Frédéric Lefebvre and Catherine Théré. 2011. *Le cercle de Vincent de Gournay: savoirs économiques et pratiques administratives en France au milieu du XVIIIe siècle*. Paris: Institut national d'études démographiques.

Conseil Constitutionnel. 2012. Décision n° 2012-662 DC du 29 décembre 2012. Paris: Conseil Constitutionnel. www.conseil-constitutionnel.fr/conseil-constitutionnel/francais/les-decisions/acces-par-date/decisions-depuis-1959/2012/2012-662-dc/decision-n-2012-662-dc-du-29-d++ecembre-2012.135500.html (accessed 5 February 2016).

Dio, Cassius. 1925. *Roman History*, edited by Earnest Cary and Herbert B. Foster. Cambridge, MA: Harvard University Press.

Elias, Norbert. 2000. *The Civilizing Process: Sociogenetic and Psychogenetic Investigations*. Second edition. Oxford: Blackwell Publishing.

Foucault, Michel. 1966. *Les mots et les choses: une archéologie des sciences humaines*. Paris: Gallimard.

———. (1975) 1995. *Discipline and Punish: The Birth of the Prison*. Second edition. New York: Vintage Books.

———. 2008. *The Birth of Biopolitics: Lectures at the College de France, 1978–1979*. New York: Palgrave Macmillan.

Frecknall-Hughes, Jane. 2014. *The Theory, Principles and Management of Taxation: An Introduction*. London: Routledge.

Gibbon, Edward. 1776. *The History of the Decline and Fall of the Roman Empire*. London: W. Strahan and T. Cadell.

Gray, Vivienne J. 2004. 'Le socrate de Xénophon et la démocratie'. *Les Études philosophiques* 69(2): 141–76.

Hoock, Jochen, and Pierre Jeannin. 1993. *Ars mercatoria: Handbücher und Traktate für den Gebrauch des Kaufmanns, 1470–1820*. Paderborn: Schöningh.

Hume, David. 1826. *The Philosophical Works of David Hume.* Edinburgh: Adam Black and William Tait.

Jansen, Joseph Nicholas. 2007. 'After Empire: Xenophon's Poroi and the Reorientation of Athens' Political Economy'. PhD thesis, Classics Department, University of Texas at Austin.

Kragelund, Patrick. 2000. 'Nero's Luxuria, in Tacitus and in the Octavia', *The Classical Quarterly* (NS) 50(2): 494–515.

Livy (Titus Livius). 1924. *The History of Rome, Book 7*, edited by Benjamin Oliver Foster. www.perseus.tufts.edu/hopper/text?doc=Perseus%3At ext%3A1999.02.0154%3Abook%3D7%3Achapter%3D1 (accessed 15 February 2016).

McArthur, Neil. 2014. 'Cosmopolitanism and Hume's General Point of View', *European Journal of Political Theory* 13(3): 321–40.

Michaels, Ralf. 2009. 'Comparative Law by Numbers? Legal Origins Thesis, Doing Business Reports, and the Silence of Traditional Comparative Law', *American Journal of Comparative Law* 57(4): 765–95.

Ministère des affaires étrangères. 1926. *Rapport annuel du gouvernement français à l'assemblée des Nations Unies sur l'administration sous mandat des territoires du Cameroun.* Geneva: Société des Nations.

Montesquieu, Charles. (1748) 1989. *Montesquieu: The Spirit of the Laws*, edited by Anne M. Cohler, Basia Carolyn Miller and Harold Samuel Stone. Cambridge: Cambridge University Press.

Nietzsche, Friedrich Wilhelm, and Horace Barnett Samuel. (1887) 1918. *The Genealogy of Morals: A Polemic.* New York: Boni and Liveright.

Nugent, David. 2013. 'Mobilizing the National Body: Taxation, Disorder and Delusion in Peruvian State Formation'. Presented at the Tax Matters workshop, Emory University, Atlanta, GA (4–6 April).

OECD (Organisation of Economic Co-operation and Development). 2009. *Engaging with High Net Worth Individuals on Tax Compliance.* Paris: OECD.

———. 2013. *Action Plan on Base Erosion and Profit Shifting.* Paris: OECD.

Orain, Arnaud. 2010. 'Progressive Indirect Taxation and Social Justice in Eighteenth-Century France: Forbonnais and Graslin's Fiscal System', *European Journal of the History of Economic Thought* 17(4): 659–85.

Piketty, Thomas. 2013. *Le capital au XXIe siècle, les livres du nouveau monde.* Paris: Éditions du Seuil.

Raynal, Guillaume Thomas. 1773. *Histoire philosophique et politique des établissements et du commerce des Européens dans les deux Indes.* Amsterdam: [no publisher listed].

Rousseau, Jean-Jacques. 1767. *The Miscellaneous Works of Mr J.J. Rousseau.* London: T. Becket and P.A. De Hondt.

Silver, Morris. 1983. 'Karl Polanyi and Markets in the Ancient Near East: The Challenge of the Evidence', *Journal of Economic History* 43(4): 795–829.

Skornicki, Arnault. 2006. 'L'État, l'expert et le négociant: le réseau de la "science du commerce" sous Louis XV', *Genèses* 65: 4–26.

Sloterdijk, Peter. 2012. *Repenser l'impôt: pour une éthique du don démocratique*. Translated by Olivier Mannoni. Paris: Libella-Maren Sell Editions.

Suetonius (Gaius Suetonius Tranquillus). 1889. 'Nero', in *The Lives of the Twelve Caesars*, edited and translated by Alexander Thomson and J. Eugene Reed. Philadelphia: Gebbie & Co. www.perseus.tufts.edu/hopper/text?doc=Perseus%3atext%3a1999.02.0132%3alife%3dnero (accessed 18 February 2016).

Tacitus, Cornelius. 1942. 'The Annals', in *Complete Works of Tacitus*, edited by Alfred John Church, William Jackson Brodribb and Sara Bryant. New York: Random House. www.perseus.tufts.edu/hopper/text?doc=Perseus%3atext%3a1999.02.0078 (accessed 18 February 2016).

Territoires du Cameroun. 1922. *Budget des recettes et des dépenses*. Yaoundé: Imprimerie du gouvernement.

———. 1925. *Budget des recettes et des dépenses*. Yaoundé: Imprimerie du gouvernement.

Veyne, Paul. (1976) 1990. *Bread and Circuses: Historical Sociology and Political Pluralism*, translated by Brian Pearce. London: Penguin.

Walras, Léon. 1874. *Eléments d'économie pure ou théorie de la richesse sociale*. Lausanne: L. Corbaz.

Wersinger, Anne Gabrièle. 2008. *La sphère et l'intervalle: le schème de l'harmonie dans la pensée des anciens Grecs d'Homère à Platon*. Grenoble: Jérôme Millon.

Xenophon. 2003. *Poroi: New Translation*, edited by Ralph Doty. Lewiston, NY: Edwin Mellen Press.

5

Marketing Marijuana
Prohibition, Medicalization and the Commodity

Michael Polson

At first glance, marijuana prohibition does not appear to fit a neoliberal mould. It is based on prohibiting and distorting markets, not on promoting them; it incites to action criminal rather than economic subjects; and it does so through expansive state policies more characteristic of Keynesian modernism. Yet, if we only understand neoliberalism in positivist terms, as a singular economic orthodoxy, we may miss its character as a class politics, which David Harvey (2006) describes as a capitalist class project to redistribute wealth upwards and, by extension, to secure the social policies that facilitate that process. This definition encourages us to understand neoclassical economics as one among many rationales that facilitate a broader neoliberal class project and invites us to consider how other rationales achieve that class project in different ways.

Accordingly, in this chapter I argue that marijuana prohibition, which began well before the neoliberal period demarcated in this collection, attained a qualitatively different character after the 1970s, a character that was increasingly framed in market terms common to the neoliberal era. In this period, marijuana prohibition led not only to marijuana commerce but also to a state apparatus to administer, tabulate and survey this market. It did this in two ways. First, it instituted this market by making it visible and measurable in reports and enforcement actions, and by crafting the market institutions of risk and price. Second, it incited the formation of market subjects, or in the terms of this collection's introduction, 'self-reliant, gain-seeking market actors'. Although this market realm had its own unique constraints, in everyday terms it was not dissimilar to those idealized in microeconomics: a market of equal buyers and sellers, operating on rationales of supply and demand, with the government positioned 'at a distance' (Rose and Miller 1992). To the degree that prohibition was an economic policy that produced and administered social life in market terms, it was consonant with the broader neoliberal class project. Also, to the degree that marijuana-related actors were market actors, they could not simply be understood as irrationally deviant. Rather, they were attached to a pervasive market logic.

Since the disruptions of the 2008 global recession the market logic of marijuana has come to the fore, as dominant policy forms such as orthodox neoliberal policies and drug prohibition are challenged. The punitive approach to ordinary crime now makes little economic sense. Bloated prisons, mandatory minimum sentences and penalization of non-violent offences, particularly those resulting from the War on Drugs, have come under scrutiny since the 2008 economic crisis in the cost–benefit tradition of US law making (MacLennan 1997). These budgetary calculations dovetailed with other developments, ranging from prisoner strikes against solitary confinement and court-ordered reductions of state prison populations to the rise of #blacklivesmatter, culminating in a surprising potential for a realignment of the US criminal justice system.

Few trends illustrate this transformation better than the case of marijuana. Since 2008, the pace of change has accelerated, with numerous reforms including decriminalization bills, the easing of marijuana research restrictions and the federal government allowing marijuana commerce on tribal lands. Between 2008 and 2016, the number of states with medical marijuana laws increased from twelve to twenty-five, and the number of states allowing recreational marijuana increased from zero to eight, accounting for over 20 per cent of the US population in 2017. From where did this sudden about-face come? Is it simply that economic rationality prevailed after seventy-five years of prohibition? If so, what relation does this new rationality have to the rationales implicit within prohibition? Are they necessarily opposed, or might they be continuous with one another?

In this chapter, I reframe marijuana legalization as a moment in a longer arc of marijuana's marketization, a process rooted in a neoliberal prohibitionism. I do this first by exploring how marijuana's status as a prohibited commodity not just criminalizes but also marketizes the plant and its social administration, leading to a unique kind of economic governance of criminalized, deviant populations. I then explore this dynamic by arguing that the escalation of the War on Drugs in the 1980s produced a field of intervention called 'the marijuana economy' and exerted a marketizing force on relations among producers. Finally, I show how medical marijuana in California, which was the first state to medicalize marijuana and thus marked an important not-for-profit exception to prohibition, interrupted marijuana's criminalized market dynamics, yet would itself be moulded into market form, culminating in the 2016 voter approval of recreational marijuana laws in California. While marijuana's legalization is a moment of discontinuity, this chapter will show that it is also *continuous* with neoliberal processes at work under the War on Drugs. Public depictions celebrating the emerging marijuana economy[1] and the 'green rush' are only the most recent efforts in a longer history of moulding marijuana to a market ideology. In the process, the potential for marijuana to be part of more radical social, economic and psychological stances is tamed.[2]

Criminal Commodities

The decision to prohibit stigmatized things and activities is not only a moral matter. It also has economic dimensions. A rendering of marijuana prohibition is incomplete without a full consideration of its qualities as a commodity.

Of course, prohibition is moral. From Lyman Beecher's denunciation of alcohol in the Second Great Awakening and H.L. Mencken's denunciation of alcohol prohibitionists as prurient Puritans to the fixation on marijuana in the US culture wars of the late twentieth century, morality has been a polarizing frame through which prohibition has been debated, and around which forces have aligned. Implicit within this moral frame are notions of individual choice. Whether one chooses to produce, transact or consume a prohibited commodity carries moral weight. But a purely moral frame can obscure the ways that marijuana prohibition is a particular kind of market intervention that produces marijuana as a commodity.

The Marihuana Tax Act became law four years after the end of Prohibition, an effort to ban alcohol in the United States that turned out to be better at producing criminals and policing apparatuses than it was at stopping drinking (Schneider 2009). Following the failure of Prohibition, there was an understanding that seeking to prohibit trade in a commodity is impossible and undesirable in a liberal market society, and hence politically fruitless (Melzer 2004). Oddly, the Marihuana Tax Act, passed in 1937, reflects this shift in thinking. While the intent was to prohibit marijuana, the legal method was taxation, which, prima facie, *permits* commerce. De facto prohibition through *de jure* taxation was first tried in a 1934 law that sought to regulate machine guns through taxation, and in 1937 was upheld by the Supreme Court in *Sonzinsky* v. *United States* (300 U.S. 506) only months before the passage of the Marihuana Tax Act.[3] The result was a new form of prohibition, one that prohibited *through* the market rather than *against* it, in ways that accorded with the market precepts of choice, individualism and consumption, rather than with the precepts of abstinence and moral composure.

Under the Act, marijuana was framed as a market commodity more intensively than it had been previously. Regulation, more aptly criminalization, construed it in terms of a series of commercial actions – cultivation, manufacture, importation, exportation, processing, distribution ('transfer'), sale and use – a construction that would underlie the 1970 Controlled Substances Act, which replaced the Marihuana Tax Act and remains the foundation of marijuana and drug laws to this day. These economic actions appeared in legal documents, enforcement apparatuses and the psyches, job classifications and risk calculations of all those concerned with marijuana. They are modalities of economization, the process through which things are identified as commodities, and interactions are identified as markets (Çalişkan and Callon 2009).

The framing of marijuana's prohibition targeted a substance and the economic actions people took regarding it. The people who took those actions were dealt with as isolated individuals whose social contexts were immaterial. The common-sense basis on which courts assessed guilt or innocence was the market choice and the utility–risk calculation of the non-social, economic individual. In other words, the rational individual of the law was indistinguishable from the rational market actor, whose individual decisions should take into account potential risks and costs (Corva 2008). This is different from alcohol Prohibition, in which the individual was a morally deficient offender who did not heed authorized definitions of substances as immoral and socially dangerous.

Cast in terms of an abstract commodity divorced from its social bearings, marijuana prohibition did not, on the face of it, target particular types of people in the way that Jim Crow laws requiring racial segregation or immigration laws like the Chinese Exclusion Act did. Rather, it targeted a commodity that circulated through diverse social spaces. Wherever marijuana travelled, criminalizing forces could follow. If these laws were enforced in one region or among one sort of people more than others, so be it.

Formally, law applies evenly and blindly across space yet, as noted in this volume's Introduction, substantively it articulates with broader dynamics of social inequalities. The ideal geography of law is contradicted by the practical geography of law enforcement, which is partial and uneven. The slippage between the ideal and practical has masked varied efforts to maintain and wield power and manage anxieties of the beneficiaries of unequal relations.[4] For instance, the overtly racist rhetoric deployed before and during Congressional hearings for the 1937 Marihuana Tax Act indexed one set of social anxieties about users and purveyors of marijuana. As a new form of racial control, marijuana prohibition came at a time when other modes of racial policing were coming into question. The Marihuana Tax Act passed in the same year that the Scottsboro Boys were mostly acquitted, providing the Communist Party USA a victory in the South, and the debate about the anti-lynching Gavagan Bill erupted in Congress, a harbinger of the mounting demands for civil rights and the ending of Jim Crow and state-permitted racial violence. Through marijuana prohibition, other anxieties over social inequality were managed, including fears over labour organization and urban residence among Mexicans in California in the early 1900s (Gieringer 2002), the moral and racial corruption of White women in the 1930s and 1940s, especially in the racially mixed environments of jazz clubs (Sloman [1979] 1998), Communist designs to destroy the American work ethic (Booth 2015), challenges to war making in the 1960s (Lee 2012), and the apparent dangers posed by urban people of colour to the moral fabric of the (White) nuclear family in the 1980s and 1990s (e.g. Bennett, Dilulio Jr and Walters 1996).[5]

With this understanding of marijuana's status as commodity and the particular form of roving, abstracting criminalization it enabled, I turn to the period of concern in this volume, beginning with the passage of the Controlled Substances Act in 1970 and its elaboration in the 1980s. This period marked a break in the history of marijuana and prohibition that was reflected in skyrocketing prison populations (King and Mauer 2006; Alexander 2012), unprecedented consolidation of federal enforcement powers (Mauer 2006) and the militarization of police (Kraska and Kappeler 1997; Andreas and Price 2001). The 1980s marked another important shift. Previously, illegal plant-based drugs had been seen as dangerous foreign imports. Marijuana fitted this model as most of it flowed into the United States from Mexico, the Andes, the Caribbean and South East Asia, and domestically produced marijuana was marginal to the overall market. For reasons I explain below, the 1980s saw the growth of substantial domestic marijuana production.

As Adam Smith argued long ago, countries that consume what they themselves produce are better off economically than those that rely on international trade. As well, he said that such domestic trade encourages the spread of liberal values and moralities of the market to the country's citizenry. Marijuana prohibition and the domestic marijuana market it fostered in the 1980s illustrate how marijuana became an important, new and unorthodox market morality for an anti-drug society and illegal producers themselves. This market morality was suited to a post-Keynesian, neoliberal age.

Prohibition Markets

Numerous factors encouraged the formation of the domestic marijuana economy in the 1980s. Most immediately, it was stimulated by increased international activity by the Drug Enforcement Administration (DEA), particularly the spraying of paraquat over Mexican crops. This undoubtedly destroyed plants but, more importantly, it led US consumers to fear tainted marijuana, thus generating market demand for domestic product. While marijuana production in the United States was small at that time, there were dedicated farmers among the countercultural back-to-the-land movement in regions far from the reach of law enforcement, like rural Oregon and California, eastern Tennessee and parts of Hawaii, Maine and West Virginia. During the 1970s, these farmers developed new horticultural practices and acquired marijuana strains more suited to northerly latitudes. These developments dovetailed with other shifts in the rural United States in the early 1980s. Natural resource extraction industries and agriculture went into crisis (for workers and farmers, anyhow) amidst major shifts in global market dynamics and the growing power of finance capital. In response to this and the growing momentum of environmentalism, pressure built towards significant deregulation of rural lands (Cawley 1993). Rural America was primed for the emergence of a new economic resource, one it found in the unexpected guise of marijuana.

Were it not for prohibition, this economy would never have grown so rapidly. The federal government, often in coordination with local and state jurisdictions, focused on supply, based on the assumption that targeting drug producers and traders would cause the price of the drug to rise, which in turn would reduce demand. In other words, the explicit aim of federal policy was to *increase* the price of drugs. While this may make them more expensive for consumers, it also made them more lucrative for producers and other commercial actors. With the drug war's escalation, the wholesale price of a pound of premium imported Colombian Red marijuana rose from $800 in the late 1970s to $4,000–$6,000 in the mid-1980s. Domestically produced *sinsemilla* (seedless) marijuana, once nearly worthless because its appearance put off consumers accustomed to the imported bricks of marijuana from Central and South America, similarly spiked in price. Although estimates are unreliable, the government's National Narcotics Intelligence Consumers Committee estimated that domestic production had doubled between 1986 and 1989, some of the most intensive years of drug-war activity, and that by 2002 it had risen to nearly five times 1986 levels (Gettman 2007). Despite the growth of production and producers, prices stayed stable and high, even as indoor production techniques spread to suburban and urban areas. In this way, the marijuana economy became a core American industry in a time characterized by farm crisis, deindustrialization and the ecologically devastating financialization of natural resources.

Yet, with marijuana eradication having only minimal impact on the total crop, supply-side interdiction did not raise prices by restricting supply but by increasing the perception of risk (Polson 2013). In 1984, federal legislation authorized an increase in marijuana-related penalties, allowed the seizure and forfeiture of related property and implemented mandatory minimum sentences, which were increased in 1986. While possession of marijuana could lead to a prison term of between fifteen days and three years, cultivation and sales could send a person to jail for life, thus heightening the risks and rewards for upstream economic actors. Spectacular raids, from the Lower East Side of New York City to the mountains of Hawaii, held prohibition up for all to see and increased the perception of risk.

As Christina Johns (1992) suggested, the War on Drugs required a new actuarial practice, as estimates of the marijuana economy relied upon contradictory claims that the war was both succeeding and failing. Seizure estimates had to be high enough to prove the efficacy of prohibition but low enough to justify further funding. The numbers resulting from this delicate actuarial logic became a kind of market index. This sort of discursive–actuarial production of the marijuana economy was just as important to market dynamics as were risk-induced price effects, arrests and laws.

This transformation in calculative techniques and approach is evident in the 1982 Domestic Marihuana Eradication/Suppression Program (DMESP) report. The report was part of an effort by the Reagan administration to standardize data collection and assessment, and to establish an intelligence database on domestic marijuana. As a knowledge-producing apparatus, replete with acronyms and statistical figures, it revealed the contours of a previously unassessed entity: the domestic marijuana economy. Specifically, the report marvelled at the fact that the amount of domestically produced marijuana that the DMESP had physically eradicated, which was a mere fraction of the gross product, was 38 per cent more 'than was previously *believed to exist*' (DEA 1982: iii). The DMESP, in other words, discovered and quantified the marijuana economy in a way that radically transformed previous understandings and approaches. To the government, marijuana was suddenly abundant and in need of immediate rectification. Although the formulas used to calculate gross product would shift over time, 1982 marked the year when the federal government became not only the arbiter of knowledge about the marijuana economy, particularly through the press release and press conference, but also the producer of the data that underlay that knowledge. As the producer, tabulator and arbiter of that knowledge, the federal government gave birth to the marijuana economy as a discursive field into which interventions needed to be made successfully, but not too successfully.

The governmental administration of the marijuana economy required a massive institutionalization of prohibition. In anti-crime and anti-drug laws in 1984, 1986, 1988 and 1989, the Reagan and Bush administrations consolidated a drug-war apparatus that would reach from the White House down to local law enforcement. This was achieved in part by breaching jurisdictional and institutional boundaries, such as: facilitating cooperation between the Coast Guard and the Navy around drug interdiction, and between military intelligence and state and local law enforcement; forming task forces spanning local, state and federal agencies, such as the High Intensity Drug Trafficking Area committees organized under the Office of National Drug Control Policy; and allowing direct military involvement in domestic anti-drug operations (see Stelzer 1996; Campbell 2009). The anti-drug enforcement apparatus was facilitated by restricting judicial discretion in sentencing, such as in setting mandatory minimum sentences in drug cases, and in measures like California's Proposition 190 that established citizen review of judges and stronger methods to discipline judges. The institutionalization of prohibition extended down to the level of workplaces and social service agencies (Garriott 2011) and, by extension, employees and clients. Federally coordinated prohibition consistently produced risk across the United States, and with it a consistently growing marijuana economy.

The foregoing argument contrasts with the popular 'balloon effect' theory, which argues that drug markets are produced through the unintended consequences of enforcement activities – push down on one area and another pops up (Seccombe 1995). The prohibition apparatus is not simply repressive; rather, it is *productive* of the marijuana market discursively, institutionally and economically. This surprising, perhaps ironic, outcome alters two common conceptions of neoliberalism and the War on Drugs.

First, market prohibition may contradict orthodox neoliberal economics but it aligns with neoliberalism's substantive marketization of society. No longer performing its Keynesian role as regulator and macroeconomic coordinator, neoliberal government was retooled to 'promot[e] the prosperity of the commonwealth', as Adam Smith ([1759] 2002: 95) enjoined. This accords with recent scholarship arguing that the neoliberal state, rather than disappearing or being reduced to a minimum, actually increases its capacity to establish and facilitate markets and incite market behaviours through governance at a distance (Ferguson 2010; Peck 2010; Gane 2012). Prohibition appears to contradict this capacity. It is an illiberal, anti-market policy that violates the sovereignty of the consumer, seller and buyer. This contradiction only holds, however, if we assume that prohibition actually prohibits, instead of produces, markets. Rather, as I suggested, the post-1980 escalation of marijuana prohibition let loose the invisible hand of the market. Prices rose, a domestic-producer economy boomed and countless individuals sought their fortune. Though delimited by governmental enforcement actions, as are formal markets, the marijuana market mirrored free-market principles. It was unregulated, operated through a logic of supply, demand and market exchange, and was, in neoliberal fashion, governed at a distance through prohibition's formation of risk and reward, disincentive and incentive, rule and exception. This prohibition, then, worked *through* the market, not against it, and in doing so it fostered market growth.

Second, while the War on Drugs can have a moralistic, neoconservative face, it is not inconsistent with the less apparent moral precepts of neoliberalism. Commonly regarded as the outcome of a neoconservative culture war and its moral crusade to save the (White) nuclear family, especially its children – as represented in Nancy Reagan's Just

Say No campaign and periodic drug-related moral panics – the War on Drugs is in fact a 50-year policy regime with both neoconservative and neoliberal expressions. Important differences exist between neoconservatism and neoliberalism, yet these differences are two expressions of a capitalist class project, namely to redistribute wealth upwards (Harvey 2006) and establish a marketized society (Brown 2006). As Don Robotham (2009: 228) argues, although neoconservatism abhors 'the libertarianism and moral relativism that the market inescapably brings', it nonetheless shares with neoliberalism a common aim of ensuring capital-friendly free markets. Further, both neoliberalism and neoconservatism are underpinned by the same presumptions about the individual. Whether a criminal or a consumer, the individual is understood to be rational, choice-making, responsible and utility-maximizing (Corva 2008: 180), albeit with different orientations towards collective morality. Thus, even in repressive neoconservative regimes, subjectivity is formulated through market logics. Finally, Dominic Corva suggests that these two '-isms' are interdependent. Neoliberal economic reforms leave behind populations that must be governed 'in other ways', namely illiberally (ibid.: 177; see Beckett and Western 2001). Thus, neoliberalism and neoconservatism share class aims, epistemological assumptions and projects of governance. In these ways, we can reframe illiberal, neoconservative strategies of governance, such as the War on Drugs, not as an exception to neoliberal market fundamentalism but as tightly linked, if not mutually constitutive (see Peck 2003).

By blurring the binary between neoconservative moralism and neoliberal rationality, we can better see the moralities implicit within neoliberalism. For his part, Adam Smith did not simply argue for a free market. He argued that the government should also establish 'good discipline . . . by discouraging every sort of vice and impropriety' (Smith [1759] 2002: 95). Smith's government was one of moral enforcement and the encouragement of proper market comportment, which has been noted as one of the founding conditions of liberal economic orders (e.g. MacPherson 1962; Gidwani 2008; Losurdo 2011). Despite Smith's reinterpretation as a free-market fundamentalist, liberalism has always been moralistic and has not hesitated to use the law to enforce this morality (Thompson 1975; Linebaugh 1992; Hill 1996). This morality is occluded, however, when neoconservatism is assigned the status of 'moral' and neoliberalism is regarded as simply (and deceptively) a reflection of economic laws and universal market rationalities and behaviours.[6] The segregating of neoconservative moralities from neoliberal rationality in the case of the War on Drugs illuminates the moralizing authoritarian statecraft of neoconservative drug warriors, even as it obscures the important ways that actually existing neoliberalism supports and functions through prohibition.

In this section, I have described a domestic marijuana economy that was stimulated and facilitated by the supply-side tactics of prohibition, its risk–price effects, new calculative logics and representations, and institutionalization. I argued that marijuana prohibition produced the domestic marijuana economy, that it did not contradict the terms of neoliberal governance but were consonant with it, and that its neoconservative expression articulated with neoliberal understandings and practices. If we only focus on the articulated intentions of prohibition, we would miss its substantive achievement of neoliberal effects – not the least of which was the distant governance of the insecurity spawned in the demise of the Keynesian state.

Marketized Redistribution and the Political Economy of Producers

Having established that marijuana prohibition was productive of the domestic marijuana economy, what did this mean for those in that economy? First, it became a safety net in a period of post-Keynesian government retrenchment. Second, relations revolving around marijuana were increasingly organized in terms of market relations, causing them to be disembedded and, depending upon one's vantage point, re-embedded. Third, this marketization of relations produced forms of political action that centred on opposing government and freeing markets, thus dovetailing with the broader neoliberal drive towards government retrenchment. I approach these points by turning directly to those at the centre of the price–risk nexus, namely producers in Northern California, one of the oldest and most established marijuana regions of the United States.

The Emerald Triangle, so named for its reputation in marijuana production, is made up of parts of Humboldt, Trinity and Mendocino counties in the North Coast region of Northern California. It was one of the first marijuana-producing regions targeted by federal forces in the early 1980s. As suggested above, the federal government effectively merged law enforcement jurisdictions, which in California appeared in the form of the Campaign Against Marijuana Planting (CAMP). CAMP was based in California's Department of Justice, so that it was, technically, a state programme. However, it received 75 per cent of its funding from the federal government, which meant that it was likely to reflect federal prohibition priorities and involvement. California had been receiving federal grants since the late 1970s for fixed-wing aircraft to spot marijuana, among other things. CAMP, however, introduced helicopters, which could not only spot marijuana but, by hovering above gardens, could facilitate instantaneous eradication in otherwise inaccessible areas. Counties were enticed to participate in these efforts not only because of the overtime pay they provided to employees and the common local disdain for counter-cultural growers, but also because it added to county coffers in the period following the passage of California Proposition 13 in 1979, which restricted property taxation and hence county revenue. After federal forfeiture laws came into effect in 1984, county law-enforcement bodies also benefited from the assets seized from drug producers. Indeed, forfeiture laws enabled the transfer of seized property among federal, state and local forces, thus becoming another way that federal drug-war priorities were propagated locally.

CAMP initially focused on the Emerald Triangle, from where over 75 per cent of CAMP-eradicated marijuana came (Leeper 1990). One effect of that was the doubling of marijuana prices between 1980 and 1985, after which it stabilized at roughly $4,000–$5,000 per pound for the next two decades (Corva 2014). As Corva argues, that doubling eventually resulted in more widespread production throughout California (ibid.: 2121).

CAMP radically rearranged local marijuana production. Gerri, a woman who moved to the Emerald Triangle in 1968, recalls that marijuana had been less an economic object than a symbol of cultural resistance to conventional society. She was part of the 'back to the land' (BTTL) movement, which emerged after 1968 as a splinter of the anti-war counter-culture movement (Turner 2008). It was a Romantic movement seeking to reduce people's alienation from their labour and land by creating utopian rural communities (Anders 1990; see also Danbom 1991; Olwig 2005). To Gerri, marijuana was a 'side project' and a 'medicine' originally intended for personal consumption, self-sufficiency and communal bonding. During the 1970s, growers in the Emerald Triangle began to use seeds imported from Afghanistan, which were better suited to the region. Also, people began to grow *sinsemilla* marijuana, which was superior to the imported 'stem and seed' bricks of brown marijuana that were dominant at the time. Because the new variety was so different from what people were used to, there was no market for it. Gerri described what producers did:

We drove it by the pounds to the city and the cops didn't even know what it was. We had to introduce it to people to stop buying Mexican [product]. We actually had to go to San Francisco and show people good herb, and create the need for it. I remember going to a bar and hustling little buds to people, slowly, getting numbers. [I had to] introduce it like Campbell's soup.

By the mid-1970s, marijuana became a cash crop, which enabled BTTL communities throughout the Emerald Triangle to flourish at a time when many BTTL communities elsewhere were collapsing. It was, as one retired grower remembered, a kind of 'golden era of marijuana' when prices for the superior seedless product were rising but had not yet spiked under CAMP. Community members built schools, established community centres and numerous volunteer fire departments, began improving roads, became important in US solar-panel distribution and started model reclamation and conservation projects for the area's forests and watersheds, which had been degraded by a century of logging.

One marijuana broker and trafficker named Jim remembered that, for much of this period, the Emerald Triangle was a net importer of marijuana, with product from Thailand, Colombia, Afghanistan, Hawaii and Mexico. Jim remembers 1979 as the year when the Emerald Triangle became a net exporter, displacing Marin County as the locus of marijuana sales. Marin had been popular not only because of its proximity to urban consumers of the San Francisco Bay area but because the area's ports and boat traffic allowed the smuggling of marijuana from abroad. The geographical shift to the Emerald Triangle signalled the rise of marijuana's domestic production sector. Many growers, brokers and transporters I spoke with waxed nostalgic about this era as having been rooted in trust-based market relations, relative safety and a common system of ethical market conduct.

By 1980, marijuana eradication efforts were mounting, culminating in the launch of CAMP in 1983, driven partly by the nationally publicized murders of Kathy Davis, a social worker, and Clark Stephens, a marijuana farm worker, in 1982. The resulting political furore was stoked by California's Democratic Attorney General John Van de Kamp and Republican Governor George Deukmejian, both of whom presented themselves as tough on crime (Corva 2014). This bipartisan anti-crime politics supported and propagated the self-perpetuating drug-war loop between law enforcement and producers, whereby police attempted to eradicate marijuana and thus increased its price, stimulated more production and made more eradication possible.

The cycle of policing and economy building was critical for the Emerald Triangle in the wake of the decline of timber, which had been its core industry. Although it had been in decline through the 1960s and 1970s, between 1979 and 1982 the price of timber plummeted by 48 per cent (Wells 2014). The industry underwent a major reorganization, as timber companies became just one of many holdings of financial investment groups. Waves of lay-offs struck the North Coast and whole forests were clear-cut, 'liquidated', as timber conglomerates sought to increase investor returns (Harris 1997; Widick 2009). Workers in the timber and ancillary industries who were laid off found that marijuana was one of the few alternative industries in the region, and it soon displaced timber as the source of jobs after secondary school.

This new socio-economic order filled in the economic gaps left behind by timber and the declining welfare state. Hannah, a migrant from Southern California in the early 1980s, retreated to the Emerald Triangle after the anti-nuclear organization in which she was involved fell into disarray after being infiltrated by federal agents (Gelbspan 1991). As a single woman living at the political and geographical edge of the nation, the proceeds of marijuana became a lifeline for her. She never made it big ($36,000 was her best year), but it helped her to 'keep off welfare'.

Whether for the disaffected or deindustrialized, the marijuana economy became a safety net and employment generator. In other words, the War on Drugs served as a post-Keynesian answer to the shortcomings of neoliberal economic policy and the welfare state's decline. While neoliberal governments facilitate and even produce markets, they disavow a role in redistributive policies that correct the failings of those markets. Yet it was the supply-side strategy of the War on Drugs that led to the high prices that became the core of a market-based but government-instituted system of redistribution that functioned to manage the human consequences of deindustrialization and the withdrawal of the welfare state. That system of redistribution, however, was not based on the idea of entitlements, rights and social benefits. Rather, it was based on notions of risk, reward, criminality and the ever-present possibility of arrest, incarceration and the loss of entitlements and rights. In the Emerald Triangle, this new system enabled the pre-emptive criminalization of restive unemployed White workers and disaffected back-to-the-landers who were increasingly battling the destruction of the region's forests by a timber industry now guided by the financial logic of investor return.

More importantly, though less obviously, the marijuana economy became a place where alliances were formed between the outcasts of timber's reorganization and environmental activists. Karyl, who had been born and raised in the Emerald Triangle, remembers that it was in the economic reorganization of the early 1980s that 'locals' and 'hippies', as they often called each other, began to bridge the cultural divides that had kept them apart. Indeed, the children of back-to-the-land and local parents came together in the area's schools as they traded marijuana cultivation skills. For her part, Karyl, the daughter of Republican ranchers, married the pot-growing son of former activists in Students for a Democratic Society, symbolizing this cultural intermixing.

The potential for overt alliance came to a head in 1990 when Judi Bari, an environmentalist who advocated unity with unemployed and employed timber workers in the area, announced plans for a 'Redwood Summer' modelled on the 'Freedom Summer' of the Civil Rights movement. The Redwood Summer, and Bari's unifying vision, hobbled along after Bari was seriously injured by a mysterious, and uninvestigated, car bomb before the campaign began (Bari 1994; Harris 1997). In the same way that the contemporaneous spotted owl controversy pitted environmentalists against loggers, the foiling of Bari's vision of worker-environmentalist unity forestalled the nascent rural radicalism present in the marijuana economy from rising to the level of organized resistance to the region's still-dominant timber interests. Indeed, in the Redwood Summer the Emerald Triangle became the staging ground for the most aggressive marijuana eradication effort to date, Operation Green Sweep, which united local and state law enforcement with the US Army's 7th Infantry Division.

As a market-based policy, marijuana prohibition exerted a marketizing influence upon social relations in the Emerald Triangle. One second-generation grower, a son of back-to-the-land migrants, noted his friends' desire to 'build themselves big' with 'exorbitant castles and cars and everything [that] goes along with the lifestyle – the American dream, the consumerist mentality'. He thought that people now craved 'suburban amenities' – a big change in a region where water heaters were rare, many people used kerosene lanterns and cars were perpetually breaking down. Another environmentalist regretted the disappearance of open social relations:

Maybe only one person had a chainsaw and it would be loaned around. Two [people] would have a working vehicle and they would drive us around. It was far more convenient. First, then, people got a little bit of money and bought a chainsaw. This began the process of closing themselves off. It really wasn't obvious. It was very gradual.

For some, this marked a decline. One retired grower and schoolteacher explained: 'At parties, the only thing people [were] talking about [was] pot'. Another grower said that the atmosphere became more ominous, if not violent: gates appeared where none had existed, bullets ricocheted from semi-automatic guns, Rottweilers patrolled properties, roving hikers found themselves confronted by gun-toting marijuana grower patrols. For one marijuana broker, the rising price had two effects: it attracted more high-stakes entrepreneurs and it elevated the price to well beyond what he believed the product was worth. He retired as a broker soon after the price spiked because it violated his ethical commitments as a seller: 'I knew the value of the experience people were getting from it, and it [wasn't] worth it'.

Equally, though, others thought the change had beneficial aspects. Cole, an international trafficker, regretfully remembered his many friends who found themselves in jail or fleeing the country at the time, but he became enraptured by the thrill of outsmarting customs inspectors and evading law enforcement. He believed that the heightened risk deepened, rather than degraded, the value of trust and reputation. Another person, who grew up around organized crime on the East Coast, echoed Cole's idea: the drug war imposed a higher standard of market ethics as well as an intensification of social bonds between people, because they had more to lose. For Karyl, the locally born grower, the booming marijuana market instigated a decades-long discussion with her partner over how to instil the values of thrift, confidentiality and prudence in her children. For Gerri, the back-to-the-lander, the drug war was an opportunity to teach her children, and the community's children, about imperialism, racism and capitalism, a kind of anti-capitalist (illegal) market ethics. So, while some saw the decline of community values and social relations, others saw a time of new ethics and intensified social relations. This was apparent in the ongoing internalization of state-like infrastructural projects by marijuana-producing communities that I mentioned above: road maintenance, fire departments, community schools, health care and community centres. Amidst the rise of a marketized social life, those I have just described remind us that Polanyi's (1944) disembedding commonly involves re-embedding (Carrier 1997; Granovetter 1985).

The marketization of social life produced two noteworthy new political forms, hemp activism and civil-liberties activism. Jack Herer's *The Emperor Wears No Clothes* (1985) helped to galvanize

activists around full legalization. On the North Coast, people organized an annual Hemp Fest and a Hemp Awareness Group, and provided community support for a hemp store in Garberville, in southern
Humboldt County. Concurrently, the local chapter of the American
Civil Liberties Union formed the Civil Liberties Monitoring Group,
which was joined by the Citizens Observation Group and the local
radio station in organizing resistance to law-enforcement operations
in the area through the 1980s and 1990s. Property rights were central
to this activism and served as a defence against the predations of law
enforcement, which had to justify its invasion of privacy. Marijuana
prohibition, then, inspired an anti-state, libertarian activism that
advocated the free market and private property as the salvation and
security of those in the marijuana economy.

In sum, the marijuana economy managed the human and potential
political consequences of the decline of the welfare state and domestic productive industries, broke down and rebuilt social relations in
new marketized terms and fostered a pro-market, anti-state politics.
While these dynamics continued well into the twenty-first century,
during the 1990s another political force arose in another corner of
California, reframing marijuana not as a market commodity but as a
medicine.

Breaking the War System and Making the New Normal

After a decade of spectacular warfare throughout pot-growing regions
in the United States, culminating in joint military–police campaigns
like the Emerald Triangle's 1990 Operation Green Sweep, the drug
war became more routinized and more pervasive. Under President
Clinton, the focus turned from major raids to low-level policing
(King and Mauer 2006). The 1994 Violent Crime Control and Law
Enforcement Act institutionalized the drug war throughout the
federal government, with elements like the denial of education loans
and welfare services to (drug) felons, increased funding for police
and drug-focused 'broken-windows policing'[7] and mandatory drug
testing for those under supervised release from jail. In California,
prison construction continued to boom as White, rural, conservative
reaction mounted following the 1992 Los Angeles riots, resulting in a
3-strikes law,[8] the creation of a sexual-offender database and greater
limitations on judicial discretion. Much of this seems to have focused
on possession of marijuana, which accounted for 8 per cent of drug
arrests in 1990 but 30 per cent two decades later (Macallair and Males

2009). As for those in the marijuana economy, the dynamics of prohibition, price and production continued to generate a steady stream
of marijuana in California and throughout the country (California
was estimated to be the largest exporter of marijuana to other states;
Gettman 2006).

The relationship between prohibition and the marijuana economy
was a variant on what Nazih Richani (2002) calls a 'war system'. Like
Gramsci's (1971) 'war of position', a war system has a kind of equilibrium between opposing sides, where small manoeuvres are made but
both sides recognize the impossibility of winning decisively. Warring
conditions become a new kind of normal through which governance
and social life take shape.

For instance, the employment of marijuana-spotting helicopters
in eradication efforts led marijuana growers to move production
indoors, which produced more potent marijuana and thus created
new market demand. In turn, the development of new marijuana
detection technologies like heat-seeking radar led some growers to
build bunkers in hillsides or to grow marijuana on public land where
plants could rarely be traced to individuals. Producers might be
arrested but, lacking employment options and denied state benefits
under anti-drug legislation, they often turned back to marijuana production. As for law enforcement, officials readily admitted that they
detected only a small amount of the total marijuana being grown
and went after only a fraction of that amount. In the fiscal-actuarial
logic of drug-war funding, what was critical was not the elimination
of marijuana production, but rather the production of numbers of
arrests, plants eradicated and the value of seized property that would
justify further funding.

Richani argues that when war systems reach an equilibrium they
become especially susceptible to outside forces. This came in the
1990s, in the struggle to frame marijuana as a medical substance
instead of a commodity. There was a long history to this framing.
During the 1937 Congressional hearings preceding the Tax Act, the
American Medical Association unsuccessfully attempted to get a
medical exemption for marijuana. In the 1950s a move to medicalize, treat and provide social support for those who used marijuana
and other illegal drugs gained ground among researchers and practitioners (Edman 2009). This culminated in a stand-off between the
Commissioner of the Federal Bureau of Narcotics, Harry Anslinger,
and Dr Alfred Lindesmith, a leading medicalization proponent and
critic of Anslinger, which ended when President Kennedy pushed
Anslinger to resign (Galliher, Keys and Elsner 1998; Sloman [1979]

1998). President Johnson's Advisory Commission on Narcotic and Drug Use issued a report in 1963 (Advisory Commission 1963) that urged a shift towards rehabilitation of drug users, which led to the Drug Abuse Control Amendment of 1965 and the Narcotic Addict Rehabilitation Act of 1966, both of which built upon the 1963 Community Mental Health Centers Act (Anderson, Swan and Lane 2010). Anslinger outmanoeuvred these medicalizing moves by encouraging Congressional approval of the international Single Convention on Narcotic Drugs, which obliged signatory governments to criminalize the marijuana economy and restrict scientific research into and medical use of marijuana (Sloman [1979] 1998: 226–27). This criminal frame was institutionalized in the 1970 Controlled Substances Act and came to maturity under President Reagan in the 1980s.

Yet, the drive towards medicalization of marijuana treatment and research into the medical benefits of marijuana was not totally sidelined. In 1972, the Nixon-appointed Shaffer Commission recommended decriminalization and treatment for marijuana users (National Commission on Marihuana and Drug Abuse 1972) and in 1978 the courts mandated the establishment of a federal marijuana programme for patients claiming 'medical necessity' (Lee 2012). Medical exception was written into the Single Convention yet had not been activated prior to that point, except to authorize research into the medical effects of marijuana use at the new National Institute on Drug Abuse. To the chagrin of many anti-marijuana advocates, Institute researchers produced surprisingly positive results, lending credence to marijuana's medical value (see Munson et al. 1975; Sallan, Zinberg and Frei III 1975; Rubin and Comitas 1976; Carter 1980; Dreher 1984).

The AIDS epidemic heightened the stakes surrounding medical marijuana. Reagan's weak public health response to the epidemic led many patients to seek treatment in illegal and informal ways. San Francisco, a city with a high density of gay men, was drastically affected. When AZT, the first approved treatment for HIV/AIDS, proved to be arguably worse than the illness, it became an open secret that marijuana could help to manage the drug's side effects and, at the end of life, substitute for mind-fogging painkillers. With ready supplies of marijuana in San Francisco, Dennis Peron opened the San Francisco Buyers' Cooperative in 1991, which helped to acquire and distribute marijuana to people living with HIV/AIDS (Lee 2012). At the same time, ACT-UP, a national AIDS activism network, and marijuana and gay-rights activists began to organize around a medical necessity argument, encouraging those with HIV/AIDS around the country to flood the federal government with applications to join the federal marijuana programme that had been established under court mandate in 1978, mentioned above (ibid.).

Despite the numerous findings by the federal government of marijuana's medical efficacy in the 1970s, the National Institutes of Health had been developing a synthetic alternative to marijuana, which it would later sell to Unimed Pharmaceuticals. Synthetic THC could defuse the medical necessity argument by providing an alternative to marijuana (Werner 2001). In 1991, the medical applications of synthetic THC were expanded to cover ailments affecting those with HIV/AIDS. The result was that the federal marijuana programme was closed to new admissions. Not to be outmanoeuvred, activists campaigned for, and won, a ballot for medical marijuana in San Francisco in 1991 and then Proposition 215 on the California state ballot in 1996 to create a medical exception to marijuana prohibition (see Bock 2000; Geluardi 2010).

This authorization of medical marijuana in California was a crucial moment in turning marijuana from a market commodity into a medical substance. While the criminal-economic frame cast marijuana in terms of the economic choice of individuals, the medical frame cast it in terms of medical necessity and value. Marijuana had been a matter of cultivation, distribution, possession and (mis)use, but now was being constituted by a different array of actions and discourses, such as caregiving, medical recommendation, provisioning, titration and medication. This construction of marijuana as a medical substance provided an exception to the war system of prohibition and markets.

Since medical marijuana had an economic dimension, it is worth exploring briefly how this medical-economic system differed from illegal market dynamics, the subject positions it enabled and the political forms it inspired. First, 'Prop 215', as the medical marijuana proposition is commonly called, and its clarification in Senate Bill 420 (SB420) in 2004, stipulated that marijuana could not be exchanged for profit. It did, however, allow reasonable compensation of caregivers and others involved in marijuana provision for the costs they incurred in their activities. Second, the potential consumer or patient base of this medical exception was very large. Prop 215 allowed doctors to recommend marijuana for a series of illnesses and for 'any other illness for which marijuana provides relief', wording intended to anticipate future research that might show that marijuana could treat illnesses not listed in Prop 215. Third, SB420 required

that each county establish a medical marijuana identification programme, which obliged localities to recognize the right of patients
to medical marijuana uniformly across the state, thus suggesting a
reasonable expectation of marijuana provisioning and acquisition. It
also required law enforcement officials to recognize a doctor's recommendation as legal grounds for having marijuana, thus freeing the
growing number of people producing and consuming medical marijuana from legal jeopardy. Finally, SB420 determined that patients
and caregivers, as well as 'collectives' and 'cooperatives', would be
allowed to produce and distribute marijuana.

Cooperatives had a legal definition, but collectives did not. To
some advocates, they were simply informal associations of people
who agreed to provide marijuana among themselves, and the law's
invocation of collectives inspired a wave of associations for self- and
collective-provisioning. This entailed the organizing of labour, time
and product in a non-market form. What I have said of the terms
under which marijuana was authorized, protected, produced, distributed and consumed shows how they diverged from the more
conventional terms of the market in general, and the particular terms
of prohibition markets. Marijuana was re-signified: not a commodity with (criminalized) market attributes, but a non-profit medical
substance outside traditional market forms.

The legal authorization of medical marijuana and the growing
number of provisioning collectives put pressure on producers to
medicalize, much as they had been marketized in an earlier time.
They did so chiefly by acquiring medical marijuana recommendations from patients corresponding to the plants they grew. Whether
the marijuana was destined for patients or the underground market,
producers utilized medical recommendations to forestall, if not foil,
law enforcement. This had a profound impact on the risk profile
of marijuana growing, which, in turn, placed a downward pressure
on the prices producers could ask. For producers who wanted to
maintain their income, this meant trying to sell to those who would
distribute outside of California, where prices remained high. Inside
the state, however, these developments facilitated the transfer of
market power, particularly power over prices, from producers to
distributors. I turn to that now.

Collective non-market provisioning opened a route back to
more conventional market dynamics through the boom in medical
marijuana 'dispensaries' following SB420. Dispensaries usually
defined themselves as collectives but operated more in the manner
of a retail outlet. While the collectives comprised medical producers

and patients, dispensaries required what small businesses routinely need – like lawyers, accountants, security staff, managers and electricians. Like a non-profit business, all cash earned from marijuana sales had to be reinvested, meaning that shareholders and investors were disallowed from this emerging division of labour. So, where the proceeds of marijuana sales used to go primarily to producers and brokers, now they were distributed to an array of economic actors clustered around distribution. This was intensified by the fact that many dispensaries grew marijuana on site, thus cutting pure producers out of the market altogether. The result was that even though the price of medical marijuana to the consumer remained approximately the same as it had been under prohibition, the earnings of producers fell precipitously, from a high of $4,000–$6,000 a pound to as little as $800 a pound (which dropped even more following commercial legalization). The difference went to those involved in distribution. This had important consequences for those who had been in the marijuana economy and those who now sought to make their fortunes in the emerging legal form of the industry.

Although the storefront dispensary model was not authorized in SB420 or Prop 215, three developments pushed medical marijuana towards this commercial model. First, the Board of Equalization issued guidelines in 2007 stating that all marijuana sellers must obtain a Seller's Permit from the state to transact marijuana and collect sales tax. Second, the Attorney General issued guidelines for dispensaries and informal collectives, advising that they obtain business licences from local governments, maintain membership records and verify members' identities, track the sources and movements of their marijuana and provide security. These two decisions pushed collectives towards a business form recognizable by the government (recognition was what many operators desired) and away from informal medical collective organization. While profit was still not allowed, medical marijuana began to look more like a formal market. The third development pushing towards a commercial model was the shoring up of a retail consumer politics and identity. Throughout the 2000s, the dispensary model was increasingly adopted and advocated by groups arguing for consumer rights, such as Americans for Safe Access, which were demanding that these retail institutions be protected from regulators and law enforcement alike. Many California consumers found it easy to obtain medical recommendations and safer to purchase marijuana in dispensaries rather than on the street, thus giving dispensaries a growing consumer base from which to make claims on local governments. Although dispensaries were insecure because they were easy targets for federal raids and local persecution, they became an important arbiter of the interests of medical marijuana more broadly. Medicalization, then, was the outside force that breached the war system that existed under prohibition, yet this new system was soon drawn back into normalizing market forms, ultimately culminating in the voters' approval of recreational marijuana in 2016.

For a decade, the medical model developed as an alternative, non-market way of dealing with marijuana. Yet, the media, legislators nationwide and even advocates themselves bemoaned California's medical system as a 'mess' and a 'failure', terms that arose frequently during fieldwork. There were certainly ambiguities around medical marijuana, but the biggest issue was that collective- and self-provisioning operated in non-market terms, and so were illegible in a society that recognized the market and the business form as the primary vehicle of economic activity. It should be no surprise that by the late 2000s, marijuana was pushed towards this legible market form in order to clean up the supposed mess that medical marijuana represented. As I will explore in my conclusion, by 2010 a fully legal marijuana market was presumed to be the inevitable outcome of these developments. Although this presumption was dashed by a federal offensive against medical marijuana in California beginning in 2011, the market continued to emerge nationally, leading to the full legalization of recreational marijuana in eight states by 2016. This emerging market was accompanied by new market practices, discourses and relations, the sum of which was a new economic normality that followed the passage of marijuana from illegal to legal. Along with it came new forms of economic deviance.

Conclusion: A New Economic Deviance

In 2010, a pivotal report on the marijuana economy was released. Unlike the government reports that had been used to justify spending more on the War on Drugs, this report was issued by See Change Strategy LLC, a different kind of market intelligence group. While the DEA and other enforcement agencies measured property seized, people arrested and plants eradicated, See Change Strategy (2010) measured investments returned and augmented. It and the federal government shared a logic of escalation and market emergence (see Heyman 1999) that called for intervention – one in the form of interdiction, the other in the form of investment. The medical marijuana industry, See Change Strategy said, could reach $8.9 billion by 2016, attesting to the accuracy of the DEA's claim, some thirty years earlier, that the United States 'is becoming a major source for' marijuana (DEA 1982: 6). I highlight these similarities to suggest that even though legalization marks a significant shift in marijuana, there are continuities between the marketized relations established under the War on Drugs and what is seen by many as the inevitable formal marketization of legal marijuana.

Since the See Change Strategy report and the marijuana investor and business conference of 2011 where I became aware of it, marijuana has been through a tumultuous period. The federal government intensified its interventions during this period even as it began to liberalize its approach to marijuana. State and local governments followed this chaotic approach, unevenly deciding to move with marijuana or move against it, depending on local dynamics. Although several states (including California) have now fully legalized marijuana, at a national level it remains illegal. In such a situation, it is more correct to say that marijuana has been decriminalized for medical and commercial use rather than actually legalized. Yet, as a social process by which an object gains a particular legal meaning (Comaroff and Comaroff 2006), legalization, like marketization, has been happening for some time.

In the uneven and capricious application of regulation and prohibition, this gradual legalization is changing the nature of the marijuana market. Labourers can be unionized, economic development and tourism campaigns can be launched, a wide cast of professional services can cater to firms, professional associations can hold meetings to strengthen each emerging sector of the broader industry and even capital can accumulate with relative freedom as marijuana businesses are quietly finding ways of accessing federally insured banks despite marijuana's federally illegal status. As marijuana's market valences develop, the plant's other meanings – a sign of the counterculture, a symbol of resistance, an untaxed and home-grown medicine, an informal means of community development – diminish. Economic relations that are professional, respectable and reputable are valued, not those that exist in informal or illegal economies. Market and government discourses increasingly value economic actors who are compliant, environmentally sustainable and properly zoned over those who are labelled as irresponsible, polluting and disruptive. Market practices such as accounting, organic certification and quality-assurance testing are preferred to those that cannot be quantified, made transparent, certified or approved.

Those who violate the terms of this formalizing economy are cast as deficient and untrustworthy, even criminal. As time passes, the distinctions between good and bad market actors, discourses and practices become firmer. This new moral order is increasingly viewed as the inevitable outcome of economic rationality, while prohibition is portrayed (albeit only by some) as an irrational policy. The argument I have made, however, suggests that we interrogate, rather than simply presume, what is rational. As the Introduction to this collection suggests, expectations surrounding such things as rational behaviour, roles and policy are themselves situated and dependent.

All the while, the prohibitionist federal government lets marijuana evolve, deciding, apparently arbitrarily and often dramatically, when to intervene and when to leave things alone. That which has been criminally excluded is brought into the civic fold through a federally directed and locally enacted process of allowance: this person is proper, not that person; this way is approved, not that way; this set of rules applies, not that set. A feature of the neoliberal decentralization of policy making is that the federal government has the option of picking and choosing, targeting and allowing, such that some policy directions are enabled and others disabled. By not assuming any new national marijuana policy, this decriminalization allows the federal government in particular to appear as if it is tolerating, allowing and even enabling new freedom and liberty when, substantively, it is shifting policy elaboration onto subsidiary governments and placing individuals in jeopardy. This is the way in which the United States retreats slowly out of a failed prohibition, establishes a new normalized market and marks the new economic deviant.

The decline of the federal War on Drugs is a political activity that may differ from state to state and from county to county, according to which prosecutors or police officers one encounters and what jurisdictional powers they have, and what colour of skin or appearance one might have. The cost of these vagaries ultimately falls on individuals in the marijuana economy. Through this process, the federal government deflects charges that the War on Drugs was a mistaken policy that cost countless lives and livelihoods and years of human freedom, a policy that elsewhere might incite calls for a truth and reconciliation process or reparations. Instead, incrementally and in a monitored manner, decriminalization allows for the self-organization of marijuana's economic and social structure into the economic morality of liberalism and its categories of respectable and unrespectable, compliant and non-compliant, permitted and forbidden. Instead of reparations or reconciliation, many simply desire a piece of the pie and the ability to make a living. At some point, presumably, the federal government will intervene, standardize and regulate that which has already been moulded into economic form.

The result is that new forms of economic deviance are being formulated as marijuana passes from criminal to civil governance. The new normal, it seems, is not the drug-free nuclear family but, rather, the independent consumer. The criminalized commodity and the system of governance it enabled now melts into the general commodity culture of consumerism, with its market and government surveillance. Yet, as consumers exercise their choice and individualism, it is incumbent on us not only to ask how control and dominance are structured anew, but also what new social worlds and new kinds of transformational deviance might yet be born?

Michael Polson is a Ciriacy-Wantrup Postdoctoral Fellow in Natural Resource Economics and Political Economy at the University of California, Berkeley. His research, based on nineteen months of field work on Northern California's marijuana economy, addresses issues of governance, il/legality, property relations, medicalization and formalization. He has published on the political-economic dynamics of marijuana as it relates to real estate, land use regulations and economic development and is currently working on two other pieces on environmentalism and the transformation of Right-wing drug war politics in the rural United States. He also is working on a book manuscript for the University of Minnesota Press exploring the uneven formalization of the illegalized marijuana production sector and its ramifications for Northern California's political economy and US modes of governance.

Notes

1. 'Emerging' is commonly used to describe the legal marijuana market, yet I use it provisionally. As I make clear in this chapter, the market is not emerging, it is transforming. Talk of emergence ignores marijuana's prior social-economic existence.
2. This chapter is the result of nineteen months of fieldwork among marijuana producers, government officials and advocates in northern

California, and it draws upon broader histories, policies and events to illustrate the relation of the situation in California with the United States more broadly.

3. Over the three decades that the Marihuana Tax Act operated, it became apparent that taxation was in fact a backdoor method of making marijuana illegal, particularly given the harsh penalties contained in the 1951 Boggs Act and the 1956 Narcotic Control Drug Act. In 1969 the US Supreme Court ruled that this was the case in *Leary v. United States* (395 U.S. 6), and the Act was repealed as a violation of the constitutional protection against self-incrimination.

4. The most recent evidence of this emerged from President Nixon's domestic policy chief John Ehrlichman, who stated: 'We knew we couldn't make it illegal to be either against the war or black, but by getting the public to associate the hippies with marijuana and blacks with heroin. And then criminalizing both heavily, we could disrupt those communities. We could arrest their leaders, raid their homes, break up their meetings, and vilify them night after night on the evening news' (Baum 2016).

5. Such fears have practical consequences. An ACLU report shows that despite having equal rates of use, African Americans were four times more like than Whites to be arrested for marijuana (ACLU 2013: 4).

6. Although Margaret Thatcher and Ronald Reagan are often lumped together as purveyors of neoliberalism, there are important differences between the libertarian neoliberalism of Thatcher and the neoconservative neoliberalism of Reagan. While Thatcher's philosophy is encapsulated in her statement that 'economics are the method but the object is to change the soul' (quoted in Harvey 2006: 17), Reagan's philosophy might be summarized in reverse: 'the soul is the method but the object is to change the economy'.

7. Policing that focuses on low-level infractions, like broken windows, to promote lawfulness and expectations of active police presence. In many places, marijuana was a target of such policing.

8. Laws that require extended prison sentences for three-time offenders. California was one of the first states to pass such a law.

References

ACLU (American Civil Liberties Union). 2013. *The War on Marijuana in Black and White*. New York: ACLU.

Advisory Commission (The President's Advisory Commission on Narcotic and Drug Abuse). 1963. *Final Report*. Washington, DC: United States Government Printing Office.

Alexander, Michelle. 2012. *The New Jim Crow: Mass Incarceration in the Age of Colorblindness*. New York: New Press.

Anders, Jentri. 1990. *Beyond Counterculture: The Community of Mateel.* Pullman: Washington State University Press.

Anderson, Tammy, Holly Swan and David C. Lane. 2010. 'Institutional Fads and the Medicalization of Drug Addiction', *Sociology Compass* 4(7): 476–94.

Andreas, Peter, and Richard Price. 2001. 'From War Fighting to Crime Fighting: Transforming the American National Security State', *International Studies Review* 3(3): 31–52.

Bari, Judi. 1994. *Timber Wars*. Monroe, ME: Common Courage Press.

Baum, Dan. 2016. 'Legalize It All: How to Win the War on Drugs', *Harper's Magazine* (April). http://harpers.org/archive/2016/04/legalize-it-all (accessed 19 June 2016).

Beckett, Katharine, and Bruce Western. 2001. 'Governing Social Marginality: Welfare, Incarceration, and the Transformation of State Policy', *Punishment & Society* 3(1): 43–59.

Bennett, William J., John J. Dilulio Jr and John P. Walters. 1996. *Body Count: Moral Poverty . . . and How to Win America's War against Crime and Drugs*. New York: Simon & Schuster.

Bock, Alan W. 2000. *Waiting to Inhale: The Politics of Medical Marijuana*. Santa Ana, CA: Seven Locks Press.

Booth, Martin. 2015. *Cannabis: A History*. New York: St. Martin's Press.

Brown, Wendy. 2006. 'American Nightmare: Neoliberalism, Neoconservatism, and De-democratization', *Political Theory* 34(6): 690–714.

Çalışkan, Koray, and Michel Callon. 2009. 'Economization, Part 1: Shifting Attention from the Economy towards Processes of Economization', *Economy and Society* 38(3): 369–98.

Campbell, Howard. 2009. *Drug War Zone: Frontline Dispatches from the Streets of El Paso and Juárez*. Austin: University of Texas Press.

Carrier, James G. (ed.). 1997. *Meanings of the Market: The Free Market in Western Culture*. Oxford: Berg Publishing.

Carter, William E. (ed.). 1980. *Cannabis in Costa Rica: A Study of Chronic Marihuana Use*. Philadelphia: Institute for the Study of Human Issues.

Cawley, R. McGreggor. 1993. *Federal Land, Western Anger: The Sagebrush Rebellion and Environmental Politics*. Lawrence: University of Kansas Press.

Comaroff, Jean, and John Comaroff (eds). 2006. *Law and Disorder in the Postcolony*. Chicago, IL: University of Chicago Press.

Corva, Dominic. 2008. 'Neoliberal Globalization and the War on Drugs: Transnationalizing Illiberal Governance in the Americas', *Political Geography* 27(2): 176–93.

———. 2014. 'Requiem for a CAMP: The Life and Death of a Domestic US Drug War Institution', *International Journal of Drug Policy* 25(1): 71–80.

Danbom, David B. 1991. 'Romantic Agrarianism in Twentieth-Century America', *Agricultural History* 65(4): 1–12.

DEA (Drug Enforcement Administration). 1982. *Domestic Marihuana Eradication/Suppression Program*. Washington, DC: United States Department of Justice.

Dreher, Melanie. 1984. 'Marijuana Use among Women: An Anthropological View', *Advances in Alcohol and Substance Abuse* 3(3): 51–64.

Edman, Johan. 2009. 'What's in a Name? Alcohol and Drug Treatment and the Politics of Confusion', *Nordic Studies on Alcohol and Drugs* 26(4): 339–53.

Ferguson, James. 2010. 'The Uses of Neoliberalism', *Antipode* 41(s1): 166–84.

Galliher, John F., David P. Keys and Michael Elsner. 1998. 'Lindesmith v. Anslinger: An Early Government Victory in the War on Drugs', *Journal of Criminal Law and Criminology* 88(2): 661–82.

Gane, Nicholas. 2012. 'The Governmentalities of Neoliberalism: Panopticism, Post-panopticism and Beyond', *The Sociological Review* 60(4): 611–34.

Garriott, William. 2011. *Policing Methamphetamine: Narcopolitics in Rural America*. New York: NYU Press.

Gelbspan, Ross. 1991. *Break-ins, Death Threats, and the FBI: The Covert War against the Central America Movement*. New York: South End Press.

Geluardi, John. 2010. *Cannabiz: The Explosive Rise of the Medical Marijuana Industry*. Sausalito, CA: PoliPoint Press.

Gettman, Jon. 2006. 'Marijuana Production in the United States', *The Bulletin of Cannabis Reform* 4. [n.c.]: DrugScience.org.

——. 2007. 'Lost Taxes and Other Costs of Marijuana Laws', *Bulletin of Cannabis Reform* 4. [n.c.]: DrugScience.org.

Gidwani, Vinay. 2008. *Capital, Interrupted: Agrarian Development and the Politics of Work in India*. Minneapolis: University of Minnesota Press.

Gieringer, Dale. 2002. 'Medical Use of Cannabis: Experience in California', in Franjo Grotenhermen and Ethan Russo (eds), *Cannabis and Cannabinoids: Pharmacology, Toxicology and Therapeutic Potential*. New York: Hawthorn Integrative Healing Press, pp. 143–51.

Gramsci, Antonio. 1971. *Selections from the Prison Notebooks of Antonio Gramsci*, edited and translated by Quintin Hoare and Geoffrey Nowell Smith. New York: International Publishers.

Granovetter, Mark. 1985. 'Economic Action and Social Structure: The Problem of Embeddedness', *American Journal of Sociology* 91(3): 481–510.

Harris, David. 1997. *The Last Stand: The War between Wall Street and Main Street over California's Ancient Redwoods*. New York: Times Books.

Harvey, David. 2006. *Spaces of Global Capitalism: Towards a Theory of Uneven Geographical Development*. New York: Verso.

Herer, Jack. 1985. *The Emperor Wears No Clothes*. Van Nuys, CA: Ah Ha Publishing.

Heyman, Josiah. 1999. 'State Escalation of Force: A Vietnam/U.S.–Mexico Border Analogy', in J. Heyman (ed.), *States and Illegal Practices*. Oxford: Berg Publishing, pp. 285–314.

Hill, Christopher. 1996. *Liberty against the Law: Some Seventeenth-Century Controversies*. New York: Viking.

Johns, Christina Jacqueline. 1992. *Power, Ideology, and the War on Drugs: Nothing Succeeds Like Failure*. New York: Praeger.

King, Ryan S., and Marc Mauer. 2006. 'The War on Marijuana: The Transformation of the War on Drugs in the 1990s', *Harm Reduction Journal* 3(6): 1–17.

Kraska, Peter B., and Victor E. Kappeler. 1997. 'Militarizing American Police: The Rise and Normalization of Paramilitary Units', *Social Problems* 44(1): 1–18.

Lee, Martin A. 2012. *Smoke Signals: A Social History of Marijuana*. New York: Scribner.

Leeper, Joseph. 1990. 'Humboldt County: Its Role in the Emerald Triangle', *California Geographical Society* 30(6): 93–108.

Linebaugh, Peter. 1992. *The London Hanged: Crime and Civil Society in the Eighteenth Century*. New York: Cambridge University Press.

Losurdo, Domenico. 2011. *Liberalism: A Counter-history*. New York: Verso.

Macallair, Daniel, and Mike Males. 2009. 'Marijuana Arrests and California's Drug War: A Report to the California Legislature'. San Fransciso: Center on Juvenile and Criminal Justice.

MacLennan, Carol. 1997. 'Democracy under the Influence: Cost–Benefit Analysis in the United States', in James G. Carrier (ed.), *Meanings of the Market: The Free Market in Western Culture*. Oxford: Berg Publishing, pp. 195–224.

MacPherson, C.B. 1962. *The Political Theory of Possessive Individualism*. Oxford: Clarendon Press.

Mauer, Marc. 2006. *Race to Incarcerate*. New York: The New Press.

Melzer, Marc Aaron. 2004. 'A Vintage Conflict Uncorked: The 21st Amendment, the Commerce Clause, and the Fully-ripened Fight over Interstate Wine and Liquor Sales', *Journal of Constitutional Law* 7(1): 279–309.

Munson, A.E., L.S. Harris, M.A. Friedman, W.L. Dewey and R.A. Carchman. 1975. 'Antineoplastic Activity of Cannabinoids', *Journal of the National Cancer Institute* 55(3): 597–602.

National Commission on Marihuana and Drug Abuse. 1972. *Marihuana: A Signal of Misunderstanding*. Washington, DC: United States Government Printing Office.

Olwig, Kenneth. 2005. 'Representation and Alienation in the Political Landscape', *Cultural Geographies* 12(1): 19–40.

Peck, Jamie. 2003. 'Geography and Public Policy: Mapping the Penal State', *Progress in Human Geography* 23(2): 222–32.

———. 2010. *Constructions of Neoliberal Reason*. Oxford: Oxford University Press.

Polanyi, Karl. 1944. *The Great Transformation: The Political and Economic Origins of Our Time*. Boston, MA: Beacon Press.

Polson, Michael. 2013. 'Land and Law in Marijuana Country: Clean Capital, Dirty Money and the Drug War's *Rentier* Nexus', *Political and Legal Anthropology Review* 36(2): 215–30.

Richani, Nazih. 2002. *Systems of Violence: The Political Economy of War and Peace in Colombia*. Albany: State University of New York Press.

Robotham, Don. 2009. 'Liberal Social Democracy, Neoliberalism, and Neoconservatism: Some Genealogies', in Jeff Maskovsky and Ida Susser (eds), *Rethinking America: The Imperial Homeland in the 21st Century*. Boulder, CO: Paradigm Publishers, pp. 213–35.

Rose, Nicholas, and Peter Miller. 1992. 'Political Power beyond the State: Problematics of Government', *British Journal of Sociology* 43(2): 173–205.

Rubin, Vera, and Lambros Comitas. 1976. *Ganja in Jamaica: The Effects of Marijuana Use*. Garden City, NY: Anchor.

Sallan, Stephen E., Norman E. Zinberg and Emil Frei III. 1975. 'Antiemetic Effect of Delta-9 Tetrahydrocannbinol in Patients Receiving Cancer Chemotherapy', *New England Journal of Medicine* 293(16): 795–97.

Schneider, Jane. 2009. 'Abstinence and Power: The Place of Prohibition in American History', in George Baca, Aisha Khan and Stephan Palmié (eds), *Empirical Futures: Anthropologists and Historians Engage the Work of Sidney W. Mintz*. Chapel Hill: University of North Carolina Press, pp. 112–44.

Seccombe, Ralph. 1995. 'Squeezing the Balloon: International Drugs Policy', *Drug and Alcohol Review* 14(3): 311–16.

See Change Strategy LLC. 2010. 'The State of the Medical Marijuana Markets 2011'. [n.c.]. https://c480341.ssl.cf2.rackcdn.com/SeeChange_MedMarijuanaMkts%202011_ES%2032311.pdf (accessed 22 June 2016).

Sloman, Larry. (1979) 1998. *Reefer Madness: The History of Marijuana in America*. Indianapolis, IN: Bobbs-Merrill.

Smith, Adam. (1759) 2002. *The Theory of Moral Sentiments*. Cambridge: Cambridge University Press.

Stelzer, Edward E. 1996. 'Military Support to Domestic Law Enforcement Agencies: A Policy with Unintended Consequences'. Carlisle, PA: U.S. Army War College.

Thompson, E.P. 1975. *Whigs and Hunters: The Origin of the Black Act*. New York: Pantheon.

Turner, Fred. 2008. *From Counterculture to Cyberculture: Stewart Brand, the Whole Earth Network, and the Rise of Digital Utopianism*. Chicago, IL: University of Chicago Press.

Wells, Gail. 2014. 'Restructuring the Timber Economy'. Portland: Oregon History Project, Oregon Historical Society. www.oregonhistoryproject.org/narratives/the-oregon-coastforists-and-green-verdent-launs/the-oregon-coast-in-modern-times/restructuring-the-timber-economy/#.V26ZozUpnzt (accessed 25 June 2016).

Werner, Clinton A. 2001. 'Medical Marijuana and the AIDS Crisis', *Journal of Cannabis Therapeutics* 1(3–4): 17–33.

Widick, Richard. 2009. *Trouble in the Forest: California's Redwood Timber Wars*. Minneapolis: University of Minnesota Press.

6

Neoliberal Citizenship and the Politics of Corruption

Redefining Informal Exchange in Romanian Healthcare

Sabina Stan

In contemporary neoliberal perspectives, corruption is essentially framed in terms of the opposition between the state, political elites and public employees on the one hand, and civil society, the market and consumer-citizens on the other. Public services are by default constructed as breeding grounds for corruption, while honest (middle-class) citizens are seen as opposing corruption by demanding the rule of law, private property and market behaviour (Stan 2012). In this view, anti-corruption campaigns are the crusade of civil society against parasitic, non-market clientelistic relations (Sampson 2005). The solution to corruption is, therefore, to redraw the boundary between state and market, and public and private sectors, by extending the first and reducing the second.

This view acknowledges that corruption is a battleground of social struggles. Anthropological studies of corruption have, however, proposed that the manner in which this happens may in reality be more complicated than that. The most notable such studies have come from a renewed interest in political anthropology among those studying post-socialist and post-colonial societies, and calling for an anthropology of the state (Verdery 1996; Gupta 2012). Akhil Gupta in particular argues that the degree to which discourses of corruption and accountability become politically significant depends not only on pressures from global organizations such as the World Bank or Transparency International, but also on the degree to which groups affected by corruption organize themselves at national, regional and local levels. For example, in the case of the 'routinized practices of retail corruption' in India, Gupta (2012: 99, 100) finds that urban, middle-class political activism at a national level and agrarian mobilization at a regional level were important for making anti-corruption and clean government an important political issue. Most interestingly, Gupta also finds that these groups demanded an end to corruption in the name of the inclusive citizenship put forward by India's populist democracy. In this case, therefore, struggles around corruption were not so much about retrenching the realm of the state as about extending it, most notably by extending access to the public goods and services distributed by the state (i.e. citizenship). In a similar vein, we could read Schneider and Schneider's (2005) analysis of mafia practices in Italy as illustrating another possible use of corruption in struggles around citizenship. In this case, ruling elites encouraged corruption in order to maintain their dominance, most notably by stifling labour protest intended to bring about a more inclusive definition of citizenship. In contrast to neoliberal views on corruption, these studies show that corruption and demands to end it may be pursued by a variety of actors using a variety of means.

The link between struggles around corruption and citizenship is important. Indeed, it draws our attention to the state as being not only and automatically a breeding ground for corruption (as in neoliberal perspectives) but also an arena of social struggle over the distribution of common goods (Bourdieu, Waquant and Farage 1994), which constitute both the substance of citizenship and the object of corrupt practices. Struggles around corruption, including around identifying its nature, location and culprits, may thus take several possible forms, which need to be studied empirically rather than assumed.

This chapter uses informal exchanges (or 'petty corruption') in the Romanian healthcare sector to investigate the links between corruption and neoliberal citizenship regimes, and to illustrate its contested character in post-socialist contexts. Given its role in the social reproduction of capitalist societies (Navarro 1976), and given that access to it has traditionally been seen as an important citizenship entitlement in Europe, healthcare offers a useful vantage point for grasping struggles over citizenship in the region.

In recent decades, reforms across Europe have aimed to commodify healthcare, and so challenge entitlement to healthcare services and reconfigure citizenship. I want to situate informal exchanges in Romanian healthcare in the larger context of that rise of neoliberal citizenship and healthcare reform, which has been attended by increasingly unequal access to services, by worsening employment conditions in the sector and by protest against those reforms among the public and those in the sector.

I treat neoliberalism as a set of policies that seek to encourage the development of the 'free market' by reducing state involvement in various parts of the economy and the society. In public services such as healthcare, these policies include measures such as cuts in public spending, the introduction of new public management and the privatization of service delivery, management and funding. By using the term 'neoliberal' I do not assume that all policies come as a coherent package to be adopted in one go. Rather, I contend that, while they have often been adopted and implemented in a patchy and uneven manner, these policies have also contributed in various ways to extending the realm of the market in health services. Finally, this chapter does not argue that informal exchanges are a novelty generated by neoliberal policies. Rather, it contends that their form and the way various actors in society engage with these exchanges are embedded in the larger policy frame of particular historical periods. A period dominated by neoliberal policies is one of them, and the chapter seeks to unearth what is specific about informal exchanges and corruption at this time.

In order to do this, I adopt a historical perspective that links citizenship configurations to the changing nature of informal exchanges since the fall of the Communist regime at the end of the 1980s. The chapter starts by describing the configuration of citizenship and informal relations during the socialist period and then looks at the dismantling of the socialist worker-citizenship and at the new role played by informal exchanges during the 1990s. It then links the rise of neoliberal citizenship during the economic boom (2000–08) with the increasingly divergent nature of informal exchanges, attending particularly to how they help to reproduce or, alternatively, temper inequalities of access to services. The chapter then turns to the austerity period that followed the boom, and shows that the consolidation of neoliberal citizenship and the accelerated privatizing of healthcare have led to informal exchanges taking forms that are intimately imbricated with the public–private mixes to which these reforms have given rise. It also shows that the intensification of union and popular protest against these reforms has triggered increased government attempts to identify informal exchanges as corruption, and to use them to justify further privatization of healthcare.

Worker-Citizenship, the Economy of Favours and Informal Exchanges during Socialism

During the socialist period, the regime's worker-citizenship was built around access to and security of employment, and also included free and universal access to healthcare and education, as well as access to a variety of subsidized services such as rented accommodation and holidays in socialist resorts (Kideckel 2001). However, Romania's focus on developing heavy industry and the resultant low levels of healthcare expenditure led to access to healthcare being informed by various inequalities, such as that between urban and rural areas and between workers in different sectors of the economy.

Informal exchanges between patients and healthcare personnel played an important role in moderating these inequalities. Together with informal exchanges in other areas, these were part of the larger socialist 'economy of favours' (Ledeneva 2014). Based on networks of personal relations and exchanges of favours among family, friends, neighbours and work colleagues, the economy of favours helped to compensate for the occasional bottlenecks in the distribution of goods in the socialist economy (Sampson 1983, 1986). Moreover, because favours involved the creative use of whatever resources and services various employees controlled in their workplaces, the economy of favours also had a relatively equalizing effect on access to goods and services, thereby 'reducing the privilege gap between insiders and outsiders of the centralised distribution system' (Ledeneva 2014: 16).

Although it involved the appropriation of public goods, the socialist economy of favours differs in important ways from forms of corruption in capitalist societies. This is because 'the nature of formal constraints' (Ledeneva 2014: 17) framing the socialist and capitalist societies are different. In socialist societies 'the lack of private property or clear divisions between the public and the private' provided citizens with 'a degree of entitlement to whatever the economy of favours had to offer' (ibid.). Accordingly, during socialism many citizens construed favours as the 'selfless redistribution of public funds for a moral cause' (i.e. as access to goods and services to which one was already entitled), thus distancing many ordinary exchanges of favours in which they were involved from self-serving corrupt practices (ibid.).

Moreover, during socialism, wrongdoing was not understood in the same way as capitalist corruption, with reference to the expected behaviour of a particular sector of the society (i.e. public servants misusing public resources for private gain). In addition, it was understood with reference to the expected entitlements of worker-citizens (i.e. their misuse of collective resources for personal gain beyond what they were normally entitled to through their employment). This meant that, given that all socialist enterprises were part of the collective good, the potential realm of economic wrongdoing was extended beyond public servants to include all employees.

The Communist regime came, therefore, to be caught between, on the one hand, its embedding of socialist worker-citizenship in entitlement to a package of goods and services and, on the other, its inability to ensure that everyone had access to this package. As a result, recourse to informal exchanges 'was prosecuted by authorities in only selective campaigns' (Ledeneva 2014: 16). Interestingly, a 1978 report found that most cases prosecuted through the law on illicit gains concerned ordinary workers, with cadres constituting only 1.3 per cent of total cases (*Evenimentul zilei* 2008). The regime, therefore, not only allowed the economy of favours to compensate for the deficiencies in resource allocation, but also used the potential threat of prosecution as a means to discipline various sections of its population – most notably the potentially contentious working class, and not so much the cadres.

Doctors were well placed to attract a relatively large share of resources exchanged informally, as they could dispense services vital to all citizens. Some doctors, especially those involved in what was seen as more critical hospital care, were much better placed than ordinary workers to informally appropriate goods that they could later give to others as favours or sell on the black market. Especially in urban areas, some doctors managed to live in large villas and have a prestigiously higher standard of living than ordinary workers, despite their salaries not being markedly higher than those of the workers.

Thus, during socialism the medical profession faced a continuous underfunding of healthcare services and the accompanying low levels of wages in the sector, but their participation in the economy of favours gave at least some of them access to a wider range of goods as well as money. In these cases, doctors were able to enrich themselves beyond their wages. This differed from what the economy of favours could provide for ordinary workers, thus opening doctors to accusations of bribe taking and illicit gain. Because of the risk of such accusations and the threat of legal sanctions, doctors protested against depressed employment and working conditions mostly at an individual level, either by being slack at work or by emigrating rather than by engaging in collective action.

Citizenship and Informal Relations during
Post-socialism (1990–2000)

After the fall of the Communist regime in 1989, Romania had a centre-left government led by what is known nowadays as the Social Democratic Party (Partidul Social Democrat, PSD), and it adopted a gradualist approach to the transition to a market economy. This was combined with neo-corporatist industrial relations and a weak state, which could neither resist labour's demands nor manage to build an institutional configuration favourable to labour (Bohle and Greskovits 2012). The abrupt dismantling of the planned economy and the partial liberalization of prices at the beginning of the decade prompted massive lay-offs and a sharp fall in real wages. This was only partially compensated by the redistribution of cooperative lands, the return of former workers to the countryside and the reinvigoration of subsistence agriculture (Stan and Erne 2014).

During the first half of the 1990s, job insecurity and job losses thus led to a practical dismantling of worker-citizenship. Facing massive social upheaval, post-socialist governments chose, nevertheless, not to challenge access to healthcare but instead maintained its role in post-socialist citizenship. The organization of healthcare thus underwent few significant changes during this period. However, decreasing levels of expenditure and wages in the sector led to new forms of action on the part of healthcare workers. Both doctors and nurses joined free trade unions, although their political leanings and forms of protest differed. Federaţia Sanitas, the nurses' union, entered into alliances with the ruling Social Democrats, while the Romanian Federative Chamber of Doctors Union (Camera Federativă a Sindicatelor Medicilor din România, CFSMR) sided with right-wing opposition parties.

With the reinstatement of private property and the dismantling of state and cooperative property, the realm of wrongdoing came to be redefined in ways that resemble the definition of corruption in capitalist societies, as a matter regarding the public sector rather than the mass of employees. At the same time, decreasing expenditure and wage levels adversely affected the quality of public healthcare, and informal exchanges were important for securing good care. It is in this context that we have to understand CFSMR's claim to have obtained, by the mid-1990s, the exemption of doctors from accusations of *luare de mită* (bribe taking) (CFSMR 2011). Indeed, even though most doctors continued to be public employees in the 1990s, a legislative document deemed doctors to be not public servants but liberal professionals (PR 1995). However, the status of doctors employed in public healthcare units remained ambiguous. Not only were various legislative documents subject to different interpretations by different judges, the label 'liberal professional' hardly fitted the fact that so many doctors were public service employees. The fact that doctors were not charged with *luare de mită* in the 1990s is probably due more to the government's willingness to turn a blind eye to informal exchanges in the healthcare sector than it is to the relabelling of doctors working in public healthcare units as liberal professionals.

During this same period, the growing availability of consumer goods led to an increasing use of money in informal exchanges, along with the continued use of goods and services. Poorer patients and doctors at the bottom of the medical hierarchy lacked the money that would buy the post-socialist consumerist abundance; therefore, patients often offered goods as *şpaga* (informal prestations of considerable value, whether as money or as luxury goods; Stan 2007); for instance, imported coffee or whiskey, but also things like eggs or cheese produced by subsistence farmers. Better-off patients and doctors at the top of the medical hierarchy increasingly came to exchange money, even if consumer goods complemented it in the form of gifts of gratitude. Thus, the *atenţii* (attentions) that those patients gave to doctors were more and more talked about as *şpaga*.

After the victory of the right-wing coalition Romanian Democratic Convention (Convenţia Democrată Română, CDR) in the election at the end of 1996, Romania accelerated the privatization of state companies and the liberalization of the economy. This led to a new round of inflation, rising unemployment and falling wages, as well as increased labour protest. By the end of the 1990s, worker-citizenship was in tatters, with real wage levels only 60 per cent of what they had been in 1989 and job security surviving only in the public services (Stan and Erne 2016). To replace that citizenship, the CDR government proposed a post-socialist citizenship predicated on fostering entrepreneurial skills in the capitalist market, which was expanding because of privatization.

This post-socialist entrepreneurial citizenship rested on the retrenchment of public services and the questioning of universal entitlement to them. Thus, the 1997 law on social health insurance (PR 1997) changed the funding of Romanian public healthcare services from the state budget to a National Health Fund (NHF), which collected contributions from both employers and employees.

Entitlement to public healthcare services came, then, to be based on employment, which in turn depended on an increasingly compressed labour market. The 1997 law also turned patients into consumers, as it gave those seeking healthcare the freedom to choose among doctors and healthcare units, and it introduced contractual relationships between the NHF (as purchaser) and healthcare providers.

Because it was adopted in a period of social upheaval, the 1997 law was not as thoroughgoing as it might have been. In particular, it included among those deemed to be insured, and thus eligible for healthcare covered by the NHF, some who were not, in fact, contributing employees. These included those up to twenty-six years of age if not in employment, the spouses, parents and grandparents of contributing insured persons and members of families receiving social benefits (PR 1997). Nevertheless, some people had no access to insured services and had to pay for healthcare themselves.[1] These included, for example, the long-term unemployed who had ceased to receive unemployment benefits, those living in areas lacking providers of primary healthcare services, those working in the informal economy and those engaged in subsistence agriculture (Bara, van den Heuvel and Maarse 2002: 21).[2]

Informal Exchanges and Citizenship during the Economic Boom (2000–08)

After its victory in the 2000 elections, the PSD government committed itself more firmly to the process of European accession and managed to turn Romania away from the 1990s development model that combined crumbling socialist industries and subsistence agriculture. In its place, it opted to consolidate the turn to peripheral neoliberal development (Bohle and Greskovits 2012) began by CDR. That involved encouraging foreign firms to set up businesses that employed low-skilled, low-paid workers, reducing the welfare state still further and facilitating the construction of housing, paid for with household debt (Stan and Erne 2014). This was coupled with the maintenance of the neo-corporatist industrial relations of the 1990s, which insured steady but modest wage increases during the boom years of 2000–08.

The result was a turn from internal urban–rural migration to temporary out-migration, mainly to other European countries (Sandu 2005). That migration became an important exit strategy for Romania's disenfranchised working class, as well as an important source of funds for Romania's new development model. Remittances also fed into the public services informal exchanges, as they meant that households with migrant members were likely to have the resources needed to engage in *șpaga* and so gain access to better education and healthcare services.

The consolidation of the neoliberal turn in Romania's development model also led to healthcare being, at last, gradually but steadily transformed along the same lines. At the beginning of the 2000s, doctors practising in primary and secondary care ceased to be public employees and instead became free professionals, and more and more of them set up their own private, entrepreneurial practices. By 2007, 45 per cent of general-practice and family-medicine surgeries, and 92 per cent of polyclinics, were private (INS 2013: 258). Overall, by 2008 19 per cent of all healthcare employees were in the private sector (my calculations based on INS 2016). In contrast to the situation in primary and secondary care, even at the end of 2000s most doctors in tertiary healthcare were employed in public hospitals.

The 2004 elections brought to power a right-wing coalition government and a right-wing president, Traian Băsescu. This inaugurated the 'Băsescu era' of 2004–14 (Poenaru and Rogozan 2014), which saw the extension of neoliberal reform. In their first year in power, the new government adopted a personal and corporate flat tax set at 16 per cent, which benefited business and the new 'comprador bourgeoisie' (Sampson 2002) that became politically powerful. This tax reform was also a blow to public services and to the marginalized classes dependent on the social wage provided by these services, for underfunding now became structural.

The new government radically changed both the healthcare sector and people's access to it. Concerning the sector, the 2006 law on healthcare reform (PR 2006) said that private healthcare providers could contract services with the NHF, which pitted state service units against private ones (MS 2013). Another 2006 law allowed public healthcare units to 'externalize medical and non-medical services' (MS 2006; all translations from the Romanian are by the author), so that hospitals and other units could contract them out. Concerning access, the government further reduced citizens' entitlement to public services and social benefits, now increasingly vilified as Communist-era dependency on the state (Goina 2012). Thus, the 2006 law that allowed private providers to contract with the NHF stipulated that those insured with the NHF should have access to a defined 'basic package of services', while non-insured citizens should have access to only a 'minimal package of services': emergency services and treatment for contagious diseases (PR 2006). As well, it reduced the number of categories of people considered to be insured but exempt from paying into the Fund.

These changes meant that 'the right to healthcare services provided by state healthcare units' contained in Romania's constitution (CR 2003: Art. 47) referred to a shrinking pool of public healthcare services (Vladescu and Astarastoae 2012). Also, they led to the uneven distribution of healthcare services across the country. In contrast to large cities, many deindustrialized small towns and rural areas became healthcare deserts. Together with the decline of public transport, the shortage of medical personnel meant the greater isolation of an increasingly ageing population.[3] A 2007 study of healthcare in the relatively rich north-west development region found that 16 per cent of the active population were not covered by national health insurance and almost 4 per cent were not registered with a GP (Rat 2008: 20). By contrast, the rising comprador bourgeoisie, fuelled by Romania's new development model, increasingly resorted to a strategy of 'lift-off' (Sampson 2002) from public services into private healthcare, either in Romania or abroad.

The increasingly unequal access to healthcare was compounded by the differences in people's ability to make informal payments to get better care (Stan 2012). The same 2007 study found that 46 per cent of respondents who had been hospitalized or had had a close family member hospitalized during the previous twelve months had offered money to doctors or nurses in order to receive better care (Rat 2008: 23–24). However, recourse to informal payments differed by class: 59 per cent of respondents in the richest quintile said that they had made such payments, but only 37 per cent of those in the poorest quintile had done so (ibid.: 24). Poorer patients still engaged in informal exchanges, but complemented their limited cash with goods that they had produced themselves or had obtained through other informal exchanges. As well, they tried to invoke notions of social justice by insisting that the value of informal prestations should be a function of a patient's capacity to give, and that doctors should expect little or nothing from those who were less well off (Stan 2007).

Austerity, Healthcare Reforms and Informal Exchanges

After the onset of the financial crisis and a year after being returned to power in 2008, the government signed agreements with the EU and the IMF, which led to drastic austerity reforms. More specifically, in

2010 the government cut wages in the public sector by 25 per cent and restricted the filling of positions that became vacant. The neo-corporatist social partnership model was thrown out with the adoption of a new Labour Code, which considerably restricted collective bargaining rights and trade union membership (Trif 2013).

These developments resulted in a deterioration of wage levels and working conditions in the healthcare sector, despite considerable labour militancy on the part of healthcare unions, particularly Sanitas and its umbrella confederation Fratia (Stan and Erne 2016). The government took the opportunity of austerity to try to increase state withdrawal from, and privatization of, healthcare. They proposed to get private insurers to manage the NHF, as outlined in the 2011 law on healthcare reform, to close local hospitals, to introduce co-payment for admission to public hospitals, to use private beds in public hospitals as a means of supplementing doctors' income, to turn public hospitals into associations and foundations, to realize the ambulatory turn in financing healthcare services (described below) and to introduce financial discipline in public hospitals. Following union and popular protest, the Ministry of Health temporarily abandoned or diluted these proposed reforms. Most notably, popular street protests in January 2012, in reaction to the 2011 law, led to the law's suspension, as well as to two government reshuffles and, at the end of 2012, the election of a PSD government. In 2013 a series of protests conducted by a coalition of trade unions and professional organizations led to a new collective agreement in the healthcare sector, an increase in wages for resident doctors and the opening of new positions, as well as the temporary dropping of the idea of turning public hospitals into associations and foundations (Stan 2015).

In spite of the protests, the privatization of the Romanian healthcare sector continued, and the austerity period saw a surge in the number of private hospitals. By 2012, 23 per cent of the 473 hospitals in the country were private (INS 2013), and the proportion of those in the sector working in private units rose accordingly. The result of the austerity reforms was that the previous combination of low wages, secure employment and tolerated informal exchanges in the sector was replaced by sharply lower wage levels and increasingly flexible employment in both public and private healthcare. As we will see later, this was to be complemented by increasing government intolerance of informal exchanges in the healthcare sector.

By the beginning of the 2010s, as subsistence agriculture started to lose its importance as a buffer against unemployment, out-migration became one of the acknowledged components of the entrepreneurial citizenship offered by the regime, with Băsescu publicly thanking migrants for not being a burden on Romania's unemployment fund (*Daily Mail* 2012). This citizenship was also increasingly divisive, as marginalized classes were vilified as scroungers living off the public resources produced through the efforts of honest entrepreneurs, and as ungratefully voting for the PSD candidate in the 2014 presidential elections (Poenaru 2014). This was manifest in healthcare, as more and more in the public arena advocated abolishing the remaining categories of people who were treated as insured, even though they were exempt from paying contributions (Vladescu and Astarastoae 2012). If they were to be treated as insured, they should pay.

Moreover, during the 2010s the spread of private clinics and hospitals introduced additional inequalities of access to healthcare. Better-off patients could use the private sector, as they would be able to afford the co-payments needed to supplement the costs covered by the NHF (MS 2013). However, in 2013 the Ministry of Health estimated that only 20 per cent of the population could afford the necessary co-payments (ibid.), which is not surprising in view of the fact that, at the beginning of 2010s, 42 per cent of the population was at risk of poverty and social exclusion (MS 2014).

Finally, inequalities also rose in accessing public healthcare. These inequalities were fuelled by the rising importance of money in *şpaga* that now took an additionally nasty turn. Indeed, the deterioration in wage levels in public hospitals led to a rise in predatory informal exchanges whereby some healthcare personnel, most notably doctors (Stan 2012), engaged in what in local parlance is called 'the conditioning of the medical act' on receiving sums of money, which for poorer patients were often prohibitive.

Informal Exchanges and the Fuzzy Border between Private and Public Healthcare

It is in this context that *şpaga* entered as a powerful signifier in debates around healthcare reforms. Thus, the two authors of the 2011 healthcare reform law (Vladescu and Astarastoae 2012) said that the introduction of regulated competition among private insurers was a means to eradicate *şpaga* in public hospitals. Those authors and, subsequently, the Ministry of Health (MS 2013), made the same case for the ambulatory turn mentioned above; that referred to shifting many of those with chronic conditions from hospitals to outpatient care, and because outpatient services were primarily private, it would effectively privatize a substantial amount of healthcare. In addition, the authors of the 2011 law argued that eliminating *şpaga* would eliminate inequalities of access to healthcare services (Vladescu and Astarastoae 2012), thus blaming those inequalities on *şpaga*, rather than on the neoliberal healthcare reforms and the depletion of public health services.

The existence of *şpaga* in the healthcare services in the 2010s does not indicate that greater privatization would eradicate informal exchanges. Especially in rural areas and small towns, *şpaga* persisted in both primary and secondary healthcare, in both the public and the private sector, that catered to the poorer population of these areas. Indeed, being usually small entrepreneurial practices, private practices in these areas rarely had patients who could afford out-of-pocket costs for treatment, and instead contracted a lot of services with the NHF. As well, doctors would refer patients who needed specialist consultations and treatments to services that also were contracted out with the Fund. The overall effect was that *şpaga* served to ensure not only better care, but also that patients' consultations would be reimbursed through the NHF rather than leaving them out-of-pocket.

The other area where we find *şpaga* is public hospitals. Following measures allowing them to charge patients for services not found in the basic NHF package, public hospitals also came to resemble small-scale entrepreneurial practices in their combination of services covered by the NHF (and thus, in principle, free at the point of delivery for insured patients) and those covered by out-of-pocket payments. Here we find the same functions of *şpaga*: to ensure better care, to have medical consultations reimbursed by the NHF rather than being paid out-of-pocket, and to have doctors refer patients to other specialist services that are also contracted out with the Fund.

An additional manipulation of the fuzzy border between private and public care is found in situations where doctors working both in public hospitals and private clinics shuffled patients between the two in a bid to increase their income on the back of public funding. Thus, these doctors could refer patients they first see in their private practice to the public hospital, thereby transferring some of the costs related to treatment to the public system (where they could also pocket *şpaga* for their interventions). In the other direction, the same doctors could refer their patients from the public hospital to their private practice, where they could sometimes cover part of the costs through the NHF and also charge patients co-payments (MS 2013).

The only area where *şpaga* is not known to be widespread, despite occasional claims to the contrary, is in the big private medical centres and hospitals – what I call corporate healthcare. In these, corporate control seeks to make sure that resources flow into the company's pockets, not those of the staff, and *şpaga* is effectively forbidden, even in cases where patients are willing to give it. However, some of the doctors working in private corporate care also work in public hospitals and, as I described, could engage in shuffling patients between the two systems and, in the process, draw on *şpaga*.

Thus, the forms taken nowadays by *şpaga* are closely related to the manner in which the Romanian healthcare system has been reshaped over the past few decades, most notably in terms of the specific mixes of public and private provision and funding seen above. This means that, while already present during socialist times, current *şpaga* practices could only very partially be considered as a 'legacy of socialism'. Instead they should be seen as also including important elements of 'innovation' triggered by the neoliberal transformation of the Romanian healthcare sector.

Protest and the Criminalization of Informal Exchange in Austerity Times

There is more to *şpaga* than simply a question of how its forms reflect neoliberal healthcare reforms. Indeed, the ways in which *şpaga* has been used in media debates and some state actors' interventions in the healthcare sector speak to us also of struggles around healthcare reforms and of *şpaga*'s role in attempts to contain union and popular protest.

A case in point concerns what has been seen by many union leaders as the political use of corruption accusations in order to discipline the labour movement and its leaders. In 2010, new laws on corruption and the integrity of those engaged in 'public functions and dignities' identified union leaders among those so engaged. One year later, the National Agency for Integrity (Agenţia Naţională de Integritate, ANI) undertook to verify the wealth of fifteen union leaders (Adevarul 2011). Union leaders saw this as a government attack on the labour movement, meant to discredit the union leaders who were active in the 2010 street protests organized by Romania's main union confederations. A trade union leader described the ANI's action against union leaders as 'a follow-up of last year's protests. All [union leaders] on the list have been very active in trade union actions' (ibid.).

Also in 2011, the National Anti-corruption Directorate (Direcția Națională Anticorupție, DNA) staged a *flagrant* (sting operation) that caught Marius Petcu, the leader of both the Sanitas union federation and the Fratia union confederation, taking bribes from a private businessman for the building of a new training centre for Sanitas (ARC 2011). Petcu was arrested for corruption, convicted and sentenced to seven years in prison. Petcu's daughter, as well as other insiders and sympathizers of Sanitas, claim that his prosecution was politically motivated, as his arrest took place 'only eight days after the demonstration where Marius Petcu announced a general strike in the healthcare sector' (Petcu 2013).

Austerity also saw the intensified use of claims that healthcare employees, and especially doctors working in public hospitals, were profiting from untaxed informal payments to counter the assertion that wages in the sector were too low (Stoica 2012). Many doctors saw these claims as a media campaign against the medical profession. As one commentator put it, 'in the case of doctors, demonizing them has become a national sport' (Ene Dogioiu 2013a). For another commentator, 'the medical profession is widely seen as corrupt', and 'the venal doctor . . . has become a fixture of sting operations by tabloid papers and the TV news' (Stancu 2014). The Romanian media has become concentrated in the hands of a few powerful people with close links to the country's main political parties, and many doctors saw the media corruption stories as a sign of the links between media owners and a government seeking to discredit doctors' claims for better wages and working conditions.

This view was not entirely unwarranted. Since 2009, several stings in which doctors working in public hospitals were caught receiving and even asking for *șpaga* have been conducted by the DNA and have appeared prominently in newspapers and on television. More importantly, the DNA's efforts to include doctors working in public hospitals in its anti-corruption campaign ultimately led the agency to request a clarification of their legal status. At the end of 2014, the High Court of Appeal and Justice responded by stating that doctors working in public hospitals are civil servants and are thus forbidden to accept 'supplementary payments and donations' from patients (*Hotnews* 2015). For the first time, therefore, doctors working in public hospitals were clearly identified as being subject to laws against *luare de mită*.

In parallel with the DNA's efforts, right-wing commentators in the media blamed the ills of the healthcare sector on those in it, rather than on government policies toward it. One of the most vocal,

President Băsescu, said that the problems arise not only because of informal payments, but also because of mafia-like structures connected to various political interests – by which he apparently meant those opposed to his government and its austerity policies. In a speech in August 2010, Băsescu said that he knew of doctors who were 35 or 40 years old who were leaving the country, not because they cannot succeed on a material level, but 'because of stifling structures that do not permit new doctors to progress in their career' (Agerpress 2010). Other right-wing commentators echoed this, saying that doctors were leaving the country 'because here their chances of professional development are blocked by the clans that took control over most of the hospitals' (Ene Dogioiu 2013a). That same commentator referred to 'those who for the last twenty-three years [i.e. since 1989] have kept the Romanian healthcare system on the breakdown line, have humiliated doctors, humiliated patients, and drained the healthcare money into private pockets, transforming the system into a feud of all sorts of mafias' (Ene Dogioiu 2013c). A former president of the NHF, and member of Băsescu's party, declared at the end of 2013 that 'the interests in the healthcare system and in education are enormous because they produce enormous benefits for "health barons" [*baronetul sănătăţii*]. For this reason it is difficult to change anything' (quoted in Ene Dogioiu 2013b).

These allegations of significant corruption resonate with the populist discourse of President Băsescu, who presented himself as a modern crusader against corruption and the 'wretched system' (*sistemul ticăloşit*), and who, like the national hero Vlad the Impaler, impales corrupt politicians (Leca 2012). More interestingly, Băsescu claimed that the 2012 protests against the 2011 law were the work of 'the mafia system [*sistemul mafiot*] in healthcare' (Fierbinteanu 2014). In his view, then, opposition to the further privatization of the sector sprang from the desire to continue to receive gifts and bribes. Following this logic, Băsescu later on implicitly acknowledged his government's attempts to make *şpaga* illegal, and presented them as a legitimate response to protesters' refusal to acquiesce to the reform law of 2011: 'I have a lot of respect for doctors, but I assure them that if they had not rejected so vehemently the healthcare law proposed in January 2012, they would have earned as much as they earn now in the context where they have the risk of prosecution' (ibid.).

It is not clear if the protests of January 2012 against the 2011 law had the potential to sustain an alternative view of the problems that Romania's healthcare system confronts. Doctors were not prominent in the protests, which were dominated by the remnants of the old socialist classes (workers, intellectuals and pensioners) and the newly disenfranchised middle classes of post-socialist neoliberal times (Stoica 2012). The demands of these two groups reflected their different positions in Romanian society as well as their different views of citizenship. Many of the middle-class protesters were among the better-off patients who had already lifted off from public health services and would have agreed on the president's view that the latter's problems lay in the informal exchanges between doctors and patients. While agreeing on that point with the president, the middle classes, represented by various NGOs, were moved to protest mainly because of what they saw as the undemocratic behaviour of Romanian politicians (Gotiu 2012). They wanted Băsescu and his PDL government to step down, and many condemned the political class as a whole. Protesters from the old socialist classes wanted this and more. Many of them were among the poorer category of patients who understood informal exchanges not so much as the justification for the privatization of an inherently corrupt public healthcare sector, but as a means to fairer access to services. For them, the problem of the Romanian healthcare sector lay in the retrenchment of state involvement in the sector, as they held that the previous twenty years had seen the abusive and illegitimate appropriation of state assets by the new ruling elite who were plundering the country. Thus they also demanded job creation and decent wages, the end of healthcare privatization, increased funds for education and healthcare, and the return of the control of the country to its ordinary citizens.

The alliance of these two segments of the country was too fragile to survive. In autumn 2013 there were two important protests in Bucharest that met neither physically nor symbolically: against the Rosia Montana gold mining and the Pungeşti Chevron fracking projects, and against employment and working conditions in the healthcare sector. Between them, they managed to reduce the anticipated degradation of the environment and of employment and working conditions in healthcare, but they produced no united front that could significantly alter the direction of reforms in these two areas.

Conclusion

This chapter has described the evolving links among citizenship, government policies and the configuration of informal exchanges in the Romanian healthcare sector. That description shows that post-socialist informal exchanges in healthcare are not so much a legacy of socialism (see also Zerilli 2013) or an invariant and intrinsic characteristic of the state and its public services as a function of the evolving reconfigurations of citizenship and the struggles that social actors wage around it. Indeed, these reconfigurations were driven in part by the desire to commodify healthcare work and to privatize access to healthcare services, and they have been resisted by sections of the public and those in the sector. That resistance reflected ideas about what citizenship and work in the sector should entail, and also ideas about whether or not informal exchange should be a criminal offence. Echoing points made in this volume's Introduction, what I have described for Romania shows that the nature of, and reaction to, informal exchange in the healthcare sector reflect both economic and political forces at work in the country.

Informal exchange in Romania's public service resembles what is described in Eastern Europe (Stepurko et al. 2015) and even Southern Europe (Mossialos, Allin and Davaki 2005). One might, then, be tempted to treat what I have described as characteristic of areas that are peripheral to global capitalism. However, the link between that informal exchange and the mixture of private and public realms that is a recurring feature of neoliberal reforms suggests that the periphery of global capitalism that is pertinent is not the geographical one of regions like Eastern and Southern Europe. Rather, it may be the political-economic one of the border between the public and the private – a border that neoliberal reform has made evermore fuzzy, even in the heartland of global capitalism.

Sabina Stan is a Lecturer in Sociology and Anthropology at Dublin City University. Her research has dealt with the post-socialist transformation of Romanian agriculture, and more recently with healthcare reform and informal payments in the Romanian healthcare system, transnational healthcare practices in Europe, the rising European healthcare system and collective action in response to healthcare privatization and mobility in Europe. She has published with CNRS Editions (Paris) and Routledge, as well as in journals such as *Labor History*, *Social Science and Medicine* and *Journal of the Royal Anthropological Institute*.

Acknowledgements

This work was supported in part by the European Research Council grant 'Labour Politics and the EU's New Economic Governance Regime (European Unions)', grant agreement ERC 725240.

Notes

1. In 2004, 34 per cent of Romania's total healthcare expenditure was from private sources (Vladescu, Scintee and Olsavszky 2008: 45), which at that time was mainly patients making out-of-pocket payments.
2. The 1997 law allowed self-employed persons and farmers to avail themselves of the national health insurance, given that they pay their contribution. However, because of their very low income levels, few of them did so. At the end of the 1990s, subsistence agriculture rose to around 40 per cent of total employment (Stan and Erne 2014: 29).
3. In 2012, access to NHF services covered 94 per cent of the population in urban areas but only 75 per cent in rural areas (MS 2014).

References

Adevarul. 2011. 'Averile a 15 lideri sindicali sunt verificate de ANI', *Adevarul* (16 February). http://adevarul.ro/news/eveniment/averile-15-lideri-sindicali-verificate-ani-bogdan-hossu-ordin-primit-sus-1_50acee6e7c42d5a6638c0f07/index.html (accessed 22 June 2015).

Agerpress. 2010. 'Presedintele Colegiului Medicilor, mahnit de declaratiile lui Traian Basescu', *Ziare.com* (5 August). www.ziare.com/social/spital/presedintele-colegiul-medicilor-mahnit-de-declaratiile-lui-traian-basescu-1033658 (accessed 22 June 2015).

ARC (Alianta pentru o Romanie Curata). 2011. 'Marius Petcu, fost lider CNSRL Fratia, condamnat la sapte ani inchisoare pentru coruptie', *Romaniacurata.ro* (8 December). www.romaniacurata.ro/marius-petcu-fost-lider-al-cnslr-fratia-condamnat-la-sapte-ani-inchisoare-pentru-coruptie/ (accessed 30 March 2016).

Bara, Ana Claudia, Wim van den Heuvel and Johannes Maarse. 2002. 'Reforms of the Health Care System in Romania', *Croatian Medical Journal* 43(4): 446–52.

Bohle, Dorote, and Bela Greskovits. 2012. *Capitalist Diversity on Europe's Periphery*. Ithaca, NY: Cornell University Press.

Bourdieu, Pierre, Loïc Waquant and Samar Farage. 1994. 'Rethinking the State: Genesis and Structure of the Bureaucratic Field', *Sociological Theory* 12(1): 1–18.

CFSMR (Camera Federativa a Sindicatelor Medicilor din Romania). 2011. *Organizare interna*. Bucharest: CFSMR. www.cfsmr.ro/subpagina/organizare-interna (accessed 22 June 2015).

CR (Constitutia Romaniei). 2003. *Constitutia Romaniei*. https://www.ccr.ro/constitutia-romaniei-2003 (accessed 22 June 2015).

Daily Mail. 2012. 'Romanian President Praises Countrymen for Doing British Jobs in Attack on "Lazy Westerners"', *Mail Online* (6 August). www.dailymail.co.uk/news/article-1300807 (accessed 22 February 2016).

Ene Dogioiu, Ioana. 2013a. 'Cea mai justificata greva din lume', *Ziare.com* (24 June). www.ziare.com/social/spital/cea-mai-justificata-greva-din-lume-1242666 (accessed 22 June 2015).

———. 2013b. 'Dezvaluiri grave in sanatate: De ce mor pacientii? De ce tac medicii?', *Ziare.com* (4 December). http://www.ziare.com/social/spital/dezvaluiri-grave-din-sanatate-de-ce-mor-pacientii-de-ce-tac-medicii-cat-si-cine-fura-interviu-1271086 (accessed 22 June 2015).

———. 2013c. 'Medicina pentru export', *Ziare.com* (27 July). www.ziare.com/stiri/spitale/medicina-pentru-export-1248291 (accessed 22 June 2015).

Evenimentul zilei. 2008. 'Controlul averilor, un veac de esecuri' *Evenimentul zilei* (7 August). www.evz.ro/controlul-averilor-un-veac-de-esecuri-815433.html (accessed 22 June 2015).

Fierbinteanu, Cristian. 2014. 'Băsescu: sistemul mafiot din sănătate a stimulat bine Piaţa Universităţii împotriva Legii Sănătăţii', *Mediafax* (27 April). www.mediafax.ro/politic/basescu-sistemul-mafiot-din-sanatate-a-stimulat-bine-piata-universitatii-impotriva-legii-sanatatii-12534702 (accessed 30 March 2016).

Goina, Calin. 2012. '"Cine nu sare, nu vrea schimbare!" O analiza a miscarilor de protest din ianuarie-ferbruarie 2012 din Cluj', in Catalin Augustin Stoica and Vintila Mihailescu (eds), *Iarna vrajbei noastre: Protestele din Romania, ianuarie-februarie 2012*. Bucharest: Paideia, pp. 198–231.

Gotiu, Mihai. 2012. '"PDL şi USL, aceeaşi mizerie!" Ce vor protestatarii: Lista de la Cluj', *Voxpublica* (16 January). http://voxpublica.realitatea.net/politica-societate/psd-si-usl-aceeasi-mizerie-ce-vor-protestatarii-lista-de-la-cluj-72824.html/attachment/proteste-cluj (accessed 22 June 2015).

Gupta, Akhil. 2012. *Red Tape: Bureaucracy, Structural Violence and Poverty in India*. Durham, NC: Duke University Press.

Hotnews. 2015. 'Medicii nu pot primi primi plati suplimentare sau donatii de la pacienti – decizie Inalta Curte'. *Hotnews* (7 August).

www.hotnews.ro/stiri-esential-20343594-medicii-nu-pot-primi-
primi-plati-suplimentare-sau-donatii-pacienti-decizie-inalta-curte.htm
(accessed 19 January 2016).

INS (Institutul National de Statistica). 2013. *Anuarul statistic 2013*.
Bucharest: INS.

———. 2016. FOM103C – Civil Economically Active Population by
Activities of National Economy at Level of CANE Rev.1 Section and
Ownership Type. Tempo Online. Bucharest: INS. http://statistici.insse.
ro/shop/index.jsp?page=tempo3&lang=en&ind=FOM103C (accessed 30
March 2016).

Kideckel, David. 2001. 'The Unmaking of an East-Central European
Working Class: Knowledge and Subalternity in Post-socialist/Neo-
capitalist Societies', in Chris Hann (ed.), *Postsocialism: Ideals, Ideologies
and Practices in Eurasia*. London: Routledge, pp. 114–32.

Leca, Iulian. 2012. 'Traian Basescu si sistemul ticalosit', *Ziare.com* (22
October). www.ziare.com/basescu/presedinte/traian-basescu-si-
sistemul-ticalosit-1197106 (accessed 22 June 2015).

Ledeneva, Alena. 2014. 'Economies of Favors or Corrupt Societies?', *Baltic
Worlds* 1: 13–21.

Mossialos, Elias, Sara Allin and Konstantina Davaki. 2005. 'Analysing the
Greek Health System: A Tale of Fragmentation and Inertia', *Health
Economics* 14(S1): S151–68.

MS (Ministerul Sanatatii). 2006. *Ordin Nr 886/2006*. Bucharest: Ministerul
Sanatatii. http://lege5.ro/Gratuit/geydcnbrgm/ordinul-nr-886-2006-
privind-externalizarea-serviciilor-medicale-si-nemedicale-din-unitatile-
sanitare (accessed 22 June 2015).

———. 2013. 'Comunicat de Presa: Finantarea din Fondul Unic de Asigurari
Sociale de Sanatate a furnizorilor de servicii medicale din sistemul privat'
(16 January). Bucharest: Ministerul Sanatatii. http://www.ms.ro/index.
php?pag=62&id=12329&pg=1 (accessed 22 June 2015).

———. 2014. *Strategia nationala de sanatate 2014–2020*. Bucharest:
Ministerul Sanatatii.

Navarro, Vincente. 1976. *Medicine under Capitalism*. New York: Prodist.

Petcu, Ana-Maria. 2013. 'Dreptate pentru tatal meu', *Mariuspetcu.blogspot*
(19 May). http://mariuspetcu.blogspot.no/2013/05/dreptate-pentru-
tatal-meu-oamenii-sunt.html (accessed 22 June 2015).

Poenaru, Florin. 2014. 'Câteva observaţii după alegeri', *CriticAtac* (17
November). www.criticatac.ro/26782/cateva-observaii-dup-alegeri/
(accessed 6 March 2016).

Poenaru, Florin, and Costi Rogozan (eds). 2014. *Epoca Traian Băsescu:
România în 2004–2014*. Cluj: Editura Tact.

PR (Parlamentul Romaniei). 1995. 'Legea 74/1995 privind exercitarea
profesiunii de medic, înfiinţarea, organizarea şi funcţionarea
Colegiului Medicilor din România', *Monitorul Oficial* 149 (14 July).
Bucharest: Monitorul Oficial RA. http://lege5.ro/Gratuit (accessed 22
June 2015).

——. 1997. 'Legea nr.145 din 24 iulie 1997, Legea asigurărilor sociale de sănătate', *Monitorul Oficial* 178 (31 July). Bucharest: Monitorul Oficial RA. www.cdep.ro/pls/legis/legis_pck.htp_act_text?idt=2557 (accessed 22 June 2015).

——. 2006. 'Legea nr. 95 / 2006 privind reforma in domeniul sanatatii', *Monitorul Oficial* 372 (28 April). Bucharest: Monitorul Oficial RA. www.cdep.ro/pls/legis/legis_pck.htp_act_text?idt=72105 (accessed 22 June 2015).

Rat, Cristina. 2008. 'Unequal Security within Public Health Care Systems: A Case Study of the North-West Development Region of Romania'. Presented at the annual conference of The Human Development and Capability Association, New Delhi (10–13 September). http://socialzoom.com/echiserv/eng/C%20Rat%202008%20HDCA.pdf (accessed 22 June 2015).

Sampson, Steven. 1983. 'Bureaucracy and Corruption as Anthropological Problems: A Case Study from Romania', *Folk* 25: 63–96.

——. 1986. 'The Informal Sector in Eastern Europe', *Telos* 66: 44–66.

——. 2002. 'Beyond Transition: Rethinking Elite Configurations in the Balkans', in Chris Hann (ed.), *Postsocialism: Ideals, Ideologies and Practices in Eurasia*. London: Routledge, pp. 297–316.

——. 2005. 'Integrity Warriors: Global Morality and the Anti-corruption Movement in the Balkans', in Dieter Haller and Cris Shore (eds), *Corruption: Anthropological Perspectives*. London: Pluto Press, pp. 103–30.

Sandu, Dumitru. 2005. 'Dynamics of Romanian Emigration after 1989: From a Macro- to a Micro-level Approach', *International Journal of Sociology* 35(3): 36–56.

Schneider, Jane, and Peter Schneider. 2005. 'The Sack of Two Cities: Organized Crime and Political Corruption in Youngstown and Palermo', in Dieter Haller and Cris Shore (eds), *Corruption: Anthropological Perspectives*. London: Pluto Press, pp. 29–46.

Stan, Sabina. 2007. 'Transparency: Seeing, Counting and Experiencing the System', *Anthropologica* 49(2): 257–73.

——. 2012. 'Neither Commodities Nor Gifts: Post-socialist Informal Exchanges in the Romanian Healthcare System', *Journal of the Royal Anthropological Institute* 18(1): 65–82.

——. 2015. 'Transnational Healthcare Practices of Romanian Migrants in Ireland: Inequalities of Access and the Privatisation of Healthcare Services in Europe', *Social Science and Medicine* 124(C): 346–55.

Stan, Sabina, and Roland Erne. 2014. 'Explaining Romanian Labor Migration: From Development Gaps to Development Trajectories', *Labor History* 55(1): 21–46.

——. 2016. 'Is Migration from Central and Eastern Europe an Opportunity for Trade Unions to Demand Higher Wages? Evidence from the Romanian Health Sector', *European Journal of Industrial Relations* 22(2): 167–83.

Stancu, Elena. 2014. 'Mass Exodus: Why Corruption in Romania's Healthcare System Is Forcing its Doctors to Work Abroad', *The Independent* (2 January). www.independent.co.uk/news/world/europe/mass-exodus-why-corruption-in-romanias-healthcare-system-is-forcing-its-doctors-to-work-abroad-9035108.html (accessed 22 June 2015).

Stepurko, Tetiana, Milena Pavlova, Irena Gryga, Liubove Murauskiene and Wim Groot. 2015. 'Informal Payments for Health Care Services: The Case of Lithuania, Poland and Ukraine', *Journal of Eurasian Studies* 6(1): 46–58.

Stoica, Catalin A. 2012. 'Fetele multiple ale nemultumirii populare: o schita sociologica a protestelor in Piata Universitatii din ianuarie 2012', in Catalin Augustin Stoica and Vintila Mihailescu (eds), *Iarna vrajbei noastre: protestele din Romania, ianuarie–februarie 2012*. Bucharest: Paideia, pp. 19–79.

Trif, Aurota. 2013. 'Romania: Collective Bargaining Institutions under Attack', *Transfer: European Review of Labour and Research* 19(2): 227–37.

Verdery, Katherine. 1996. *What was Socialism and What Comes Next?* Princeton, NJ: Princeton University Press.

Vladescu, Cristian, and Vasile Astarastoae. 2012. 'Policy and Politics of the Romanian Health Care Reform', *Romanian Journal of Bioethics* 10(1): 89–99.

Vladescu, Cristian, Gabriela Scintee and Victor Olsavszky. 2008. 'Romania: Health Systems Review', *Health Systems in Transition* 10(3): 1–172.

Zerilli, Filippo. 2013. 'Corruption and Anti-corruption Local Discourses and International Practices in Post-socialist Romania', *Human Affairs* 23(2): 212–29.

7

Neoliberalism, Violent Crime and the Moral Economy of Migrants

Kathy Powell

Over the last few decades in Mexico and Central America, neoliberal policies have driven integration into the global economy, so that the region has experienced the sorts of changes in economic thought and political economy that, as James Carrier describes in the Introduction to this volume, are generally associated with the neoliberal era. In terms of economic policy, this has involved abandoning Keynesian protectionism and nationalist development in favour of a focus on non-traditional agricultural exports, agro-industries, assembly-plant industrialization and tourism, much of which is controlled by transnational capital, and has involved the feminization of the work-force and, in many areas, the displacement of poor, small farmers (Robinson 2008).

With respect to political economy, there have been significant changes in state functions, as public expenditure on social protections has shrunk while an emergent transnational capitalist class has gained increasing influence over political elites and government policy (Robinson 2008: 178–79). As Alejandro Portes and Kelly Hoffman (2003) argue, the rise of neoliberalism throughout Latin America has brought marked changes in class structures. The paring down of state employment and distributive functions, and the privatization of state-run enterprises, has produced a steep rise in poverty, inequality and underemployment. Workers' responses to this have led to an increase in micro-entrepreneurialism, unprotected employment in the expanding informal sector, a surge in migration and, for a minority, crime, all of which reflect increasing inequality (see also Centeno and Portes 2006; Moodie 2010). As Portes and Hoffman point out, there is

> an obvious affinity between the character and spirit of neoliberal policies and the decision by at least some of the downtrodden to take matters into their own hands. . . . The new ideology preaches individual initiative and self-reliance in a context of generalized poverty and increasing inequality . . . [so] it is not surprising that a minority of the poor have concluded that the only means of survival consists of appropriating resources through illegal means. (Portes and Hoffman 2003: 69)

Moreover, over the past ten to fifteen years in particular, criminal activity has developed radically. The strengthening, diversification and transnational reach of criminal organizations operating in Mexico and Central America has secured their dominance over the region's illegal economy, and represents a challenge to states (Arias and Goldstein 2010; Gledhill 2015). The violence associated with organized crime especially affects poor communities, and has further contributed to migration, while migrants travelling north through Mexico offer organized crime more opportunities for exploitation.

Neoliberal government across Mexico and Central America has thus normalized scarce, insecure work and poverty wages, producing populations that are surplus and disposable, and contributing to a crisis of public insecurity rooted in organized criminal economies, militarized policing responses and state corruption that is widespread and intense. In consequence, poor and precarious workers struggle to secure their social reproduction in environments that are as materially uncertain and impoverished as they are physically unsafe. In areas where criminal economies and organized gangs are concentrated, crime and homicide rates are extremely high, workers and small-business owners are vulnerable to violence and extortion, and youth are likely to be recruited, or coerced, into gangs. As Josiah Heyman's chapter in this volume points out, these processes build on more than a century of capitalist displacement of rural populations in Mexico and, more recently, Central America.

It is understandable, then, that one effect of governments' neoliberal policies has been a significant rise in undocumented migration north from the Northern Triangle countries of Guatemala, El Salvador and Honduras. At the same time, as I have said, that journey has become especially hazardous as gangs expand their activities to exploit the vulnerability that illegal migration involves. This means that migrants seeking to reposition themselves within the broader regional economy as undocumented workers in the United States are exposed to violent practices by both state actors and organized crime, a context that they must both navigate and make intelligible. At the same time, the US policy of deterrence, border militarization and deportation has made migrants' chances of success in crossing the border significantly lower, locking many into cyclical journeys through Mexico where they are repeatedly exposed to predatory crime and violence. It has also reincited anti-immigrant discourse that compulsively emphasizes migrants' illegality, constructing them as criminal interlopers, and that ignores the circumstances that prompt them to migrate in the first place – circumstances in which the United States is strongly implicated.

While poverty, precarious livelihoods, authoritarian forms of policing and organized crime all have a long history in the region, the spread of neoliberalism has facilitated their development. This raises questions about the moral implications of market economy and its consequences, as the excluded seek the 'adaptive self-reliance' that neoliberal thought champions, but they are obliged to do so in ways that are illegal and violent (Gledhill 2015: 23). While neoliberal logic valorizes the rationality of capital accumulation and sets aside moral considerations with the assertion that '"free" markets produce efficient and socially beneficial results', the experience of migrants confirms that this assertion is 'entirely theoretical' (Robinson 2008: 20). In contrast, migrants rationalize their journeys and aspirations by elaborating a moral economy founded on family and community relations, and on the inherent value of their own capacity for productive labour. Yet they confront a complex set of processes that make these aspirations intensely problematic. Moreover, while those processes introduce grey areas into the relationships that are fundamental to that moral economy, particularly those of family, and lead to practices that are at times difficult to reconcile with the principles that migrants claim, they nonetheless derogate the normative ideas of the common migrant moral economy, reinforce the marginalization of migrants and multiply the dangers they face.

Neoliberalism and Moral Wrongs: Contexts of Exit

The adverse effects of neoliberal policies on poor populations in Latin America have been extensively documented, as have the many ways in which neoliberal policies have been contested. Commonly those who object to neoliberalism condemn its moral abdication as it exploits and discards the already disadvantaged, and call for a moral economy (Nash 2005) that relates economy and society in a way that allows social justice and dignity for working people – the decent type of work in secure and dignified conditions to which migrants aspire. However, the concept of moral economy is anathema to neoliberal theory. Hayek, after all, believed the idea of social justice to be a 'dangerous mirage' (Lukes 1997: 65). Moreover, the prospects of establishing such a world have receded with the spread of neoliberalism in Latin America.

In Guatemala and El Salvador, neoliberal programmes were built into peace accords after brutal civil wars. Elsewhere in the region they emerged when governments repressed the political left and other expressions of popular grievance during the Cold War: Mexico's dirty war; Honduras's transition from military rule to formal democracy while hosting the military base from which the United States conducted its counter-insurgency efforts in El Salvador and Nicaragua (Martin 2007; Robinson 2008; Moodie 2010; Reichman 2011). As Patricia Martin argues, explanations for the neoliberal turn in Latin America have tended to focus on narrowly economic causes, such as the supposed failure of import-substitution policies and debt crises. This ignores how Cold War geopolitics laid the political foundations for the emergence of neoliberalism in the region by repressing opposition movements. 'In the wake of authoritarian violence and the concomitant deinstitutionalization of the left, neoliberalism rapidly became the idiom – the practices and ideas – that wove together a new set of economic, political and cultural relationships throughout Latin America' (Martin 2007: 55) – relationships that were ultimately institutionalized in the North American Free Trade Agreement and subsequently the Dominican Republic–Central America Free Trade Agreement.

In Mexico and Central America, authoritarian violence continues to protect these sets of relationships, with considerable US support (Lievesley 2011). The provision of US military training, equipment, intelligence and policy support for Mexico and Central America through the Mérida Initiative and the Central American Regional Security Initiative has been as much about protecting neoliberal economic interests from popular dissent and activism as it has been about confronting the security threats presented by drug traffickers and terrorists (ibid.; Main 2014). The suppression of social-distributive demands that characterized the Cold War continues under neoliberalism, which sits well with political rationalities based on the defence of oligarchic privilege. Indeed, Cold War spectres continue to haunt Honduras, where the coup against President Zelaya in 2009 was led by elites alarmed by his relations with Venezuelan socialism and outraged by his support for peasant land claims and for raising the minimum wage. The coup restored the political dominance of economic elites, protected by increased police and military repression of those who protested against the coup, the abuse of political rights and corruption (Perry 2012; Main 2014; Salomón 2014).

The hostility of neoliberal governments to social and political demands, and their indifference to the material security of poorer people, is evident in the imposition of economic projects that favour elite domestic and transnational capital at the expense of working people. These include assembly-plant industrialization, tourism projects that have forced indigenous and Afro-indigenous communities out of prime areas (Garcia Soto 2014), large-scale agribusiness projects that displace peasant farmers and criminalize peasant leaders and journalists who defend them, some of whom have been assassinated (Davis 2014; Beachy 2015; McCain 2015), and the spread of special economic development zones, autonomous areas governed by corporations able to institute their own laws, taxation systems and security forces (Perry 2012; Mackey 2014; Peralta 2014). Such use of private and state force to displace populations and suppress dissent demonstrates once again that market fundamentalism need not free economic actors of state intervention, but instead can entail state repression of those made vulnerable by its imperatives – a point that Karl Polanyi made long ago (Block 2001: xxvii).

Recall that Polanyi ([1944] 2001: 136) argued that there is a double movement, as the spread of market fundamentalism has been met by countermovements demanding the building of social institutions for the protection of society against the implications of unbridled market competition and what he described as the commodity fiction of labour power. Without those institutions, he presciently argued, the fabric of society would be destroyed because it would be 'subordinated to the laws of the market' (ibid.: 74–75). Michael Schwalbe makes a kindred point when he argues that moral hazard is not restricted to dubious financial-sector practices, but is endemic to capitalism:

> Every form of exploitive economy, including capitalism, is built on a condition of moral hazard. This condition exists as soon as human beings are reduced to mere means to ends. . . . What this condition invites is the treating of people as manipulable, disposable, things, treatment that would readily be recognized as dehumanizing, were it not so normalized. (Schwalbe 2015)

In Central America, conditions of moral hazard are endemic. Neoliberal hostility to regulation means that social institutions protecting society are weak and ineffectual, efforts to mount Polanyian countermovements are repressed and regional free markets are increasingly integrated. Evidence can certainly be offered that social fabrics are being destroyed, as the poor are increasingly made disposable and vulnerable, a process that is both mirrored and intensified in the shadow economy of organized crime.

Rooted in marginalization and exclusion, and sustained by systemic corruption, criminal economies share neoliberalism's indifference to moral hazard and participate in the same logic. As Wendy Brown argues in a discussion of Foucault,

> neoliberal rationality, which exceeds the economic sphere and permeates the political and the social with market values, has a corrosive effect on the rule of law as this rationality molds both individual and state activity to entrepreneurial criteria. These criteria displace the supremacy of the rule of law and every other supervenient moral authority. (Brown 2010: 96)

The imperatives of risk, profit and efficiency become the measure of states and individuals alike, and 'supplant law and other principles normatively binding conduct', a process that blurs the distinction between legal and illegal activity, introduces intense moral ambiguity into economic practices and makes crime 'just another' market (ibid.: 97).

As the drug economy expanded in the region, with increasing profits, corruption and violence, this rationality has become evident among those economic and political elites with links to organized crime and the drug economy through, for example, political funding, drug importation and money laundering (Perry 2012; CICIG 2015; Lohmuller 2015), while corruption has intensified at all political levels. At the same time, strident government rhetoric about commitments to combat crime and win the War on Drugs means that, at the street end of the drug economy in particular, *mano dura* (zero-tolerance) militarized policing of gangs has resulted in the suspension of rights and criminalization of poor neighbourhoods, while prompting the gangs that control them to increase their 'level of organization, technological sophistication and international links' (Pérez 2013: 219). States are thus at once complicit with and opposed to criminal economies, while poor populations are left with few economic options and considerable risk.

One way that the poor respond to this situation is 'perverse integration' (Koonings and Kruijt 2007: 16) into criminal economies.

Poor young men in particular may be drawn into joining gangs by the prospect of earning a living, by a sense of belonging and brotherhood that gang membership might afford, by the attractions of gangster glamour, by anger emerging from marginalization or, in some cases, because they are coerced into doing so. But while criminal gangs in some respects defy the marginalizing structural violence of the state, their predatory and unforgiving practices of extortion and control towards ordinary people shadow aspects of neoliberal policy in the region, not least in their repudiation of formal rules and values, their authoritarian power relations, their ruthless exploitation of unprotected labour and their intolerance of dissent.

More common responses of the poor to their situation include work in the informal economy or undocumented migration to the United States, increasingly fuelled by gang violence as well as by economic marginality. Among the unenviable choices of assembly-plant cheap labour, informality and precarity within violent environments, it is unsurprising that undocumented migration continues to be confirmed as the solution to social-reproductive challenges. As Daniel Reichman (2011: 171) points out, however, for neoliberal governments, 'practices such as undocumented migration and sweatshop labor [are viewed] as beneficial economic resources rather than social problems'. Moral hazard again leads to economic advantage. At the same time, migration has become a great deal more dangerous, as migrant transience and the vulnerability contingent on illegal status have created expanded opportunities for criminal markets in people smuggling and a range of forms of violent extortion that track and beleaguer migrants on their journeys north – markets in which migrants become abundant and disposable commodities (Vogt 2013).

Thus, when people decide to migrate they expose themselves to very high risk in order to escape their immediate economic and physical precarity and to build a better future. These decisions also involve the elaboration of moral positions and rationales that are rooted in social and familial responsibility, and in a belief in the inherent value of work. These positions are presented in opposition to the moral hazards generated by governments, which promise, but fail to provide, dignified work and security. They are also presented in opposition to the moral refusals of organized crime, as gang membership is routinely portrayed, and rejected, by migrants as the only alternative to migration for those hoping to escape persistent poverty.

Decisions to Leave: The Moral Economy of Migrants

'We migrants,' explained Daniel, 'we're a brilliant business'. He had arrived the previous evening at the migrant refuge in San Luis Potosí.[1] The city is in north-central Mexico, so when migrants arrive they have completed the larger part of their journey, and pause there before embarking on the last stretch. Shortly before Daniel arrived he had been assaulted on the freight train he was riding – not that he had anything left to steal by then. He said that since leaving Honduras he had been obliged to pay bribes and extortion thirteen times.

With his assertion that migrants are a brilliant business, he was not referring only to the opportunities for extortion and robbery that they present: he did not differentiate between legal and illegal exploitation. In fact, his enumeration of the ways in which people who migrate represent a lucrative 'deal' for others began with rates of pay back home:

> They only pay 100 lempiras [about $US 4.70 at the time] a day, less, about 80 [about $US 3.75] if you work in the countryside, if you can get work. And then, in the US, we get low pay to do the jobs nobody else wants to do. Even the companies that wire the money we send home, they make a fortune – and the government at home, they benefit from that too. Migrants send a huge amount of money home.[2] The government is very happy that migrants send money back to the country, but does nothing to improve the situation for people. Everything they do benefits the rich – you know they're planning to sell bits of the country to private business [as special economic development zones], right? Meanwhile we have to risk all of this.

Although he offered this assessment with remarkable humour, he was outlining what he perceived as the aggregate injustices of exploitation and disregard that migrants such as him experience. These accumulated grievances are rooted in neoliberal environments of business practices that render people surplus, and in the withdrawal of public goods that make it hard for people to put together a livelihood, take care of their families and look to their own future and that of their children.

Talking about their decisions to leave, virtually all of the migrants referred to the enormous frustrations of the labour market back home: the impossible arithmetic of wages in relation to the cost of living, the scarcity of jobs, the insecure and intermittent nature of work, the prevalence of cronyism and the need for a 'recommendation' to get more desirable jobs. As Abel, another migrant, put it:

> You'll see in Honduras, often there's maybe eight people in a family, and only one working. There's families there surviving on a dollar a day. There's no work, the cost of the *canasta básica* [basic household supplies] is really high, and crime's terrible as well. It's difficult, it's really hard. That's why 50 per cent, more, of the migrants you see passing through here are Honduran.

He was hazarding a guess: in fact, Hondurans were well over 80 per cent of those passing through the refuge.

The discrepancy between what one can hope to earn and the costs of social reproduction is increased by neoliberal reduction of the social functions of the state or the transfer of them to NGOs (Reichman 2011), resulting in inadequate provision for poor communities, especially in education and healthcare. Most of the migrants I spoke to had started work after or even during primary school, in order to help support large and poor families. This meant that an ethic and an expectation of helping family was deep seated, and many sought to earn enough in the United States to provide their own children with an education beyond that offered by the neglected state schools.

Medical costs present another worry. Workers in the informal sector in Honduras have no health insurance, so sick family members can present a huge economic challenge and often prompt migration north. In the formal sector, workers have enjoyed reasonable health cover, but corruption uncovered in 2014 revealed the theft of several hundred million dollars from the Honduran Institute of Social Security. The fraud revolved around sham private medical supply companies and caused the death of an estimated three thousand patients, left without appropriate medicine (Isla 2015). Unsurprisingly, Honduran workers saw this as a graphic illustration of structural violence, corruption and indifference.[3]

Survival was made more difficult because, as Abel noted, militarized policing tactics and lack of 'citizen security' (Koonings and Kruijt 2007: 12–13) have encouraged gang activity and organized crime. Migrants told of injuries that they sustained from violent assaults and of the death or disappearance of family and friends, the effects of which ripple out as familiar neighbourhoods become unsafe places and people deal with trauma, anxiety and grief. In these circumstances, migration seems the only way to break the downward spiral, yet the decision is not an easy one. The length, cost, danger and uncertain outcome of migration has to be weighed against the economic position of migrants' families and migrants' responsibilities to their family and kin, and the decision to migrate may remain under the worried scrutiny of family and migrant alike for the length of the journey.

The difficulties that propel people north are frequently associated with violence, but the link between violence and the decision to migrate is often fairly direct. Gang extortion of 'rent' or 'protection' from those in their territory impoverishes people further and is viewed as parasitic, but gangs do not brook refusals. The extortion of wages from formal and informal sector workers, and of the proceeds of small businesses that people have established, leaves them unable to get by and at greater risk of gang violence when they can no longer pay, once their businesses have been bled dry and collapsed.[4] Migrants reported that they were escaping death threats for seeking to defend their businesses, for refusing to pay or no longer being able to pay what gangs demand, for refusing to work for gangs, perhaps as drug sellers or informants, and for attempting to report gang activities to the authorities. Women and children are equally vulnerable to such 'invitations', and women to sexual violence. Gangs, too, operate zero-tolerance policing within their territory.

In important senses, both migrants and many of the gang members they seek to avoid or escape are products of the same neoliberal environment, responding in different ways to economic marginalization and exclusion. Migrants' perception that their only real alternatives are joining a gang or migrating reflects this commonality, as well as reflecting the extent to which the expanding drug economy offers one of the few options open to marginal populations in many regions (Bourgois 1995; Koonings and Kruijt 2007). As mentioned above, there are a raft of reason why people join gangs, and research has made a significant contribution to understanding gang social and political logic, culture, territoriality and the sense of belonging that forms part of gang cohesion (see, e.g., Zilberg 2007; McIlwaine and Moser 2007; Campbell 2009; Gutiérrez Rivera 2010; Pérez 2013; Bruneau 2014). However, people who are not members are highly likely to experience gangs as controlling, oppressive and threatening, rather than as protectors of the community against the aggressions of the police. This is increasingly the case, since what analysts have identified as neighbourhood youth and street gangs have become affiliated to dominant organized crime groups and subject to their discipline.

The Mara Salvatrucha (MS-13) and Barrio 18 gangs, active throughout the Northern Triangle and Mexico, are most relevant in this regard and are the gangs most often complained about by migrants, who describe them as implacable and predatory. Those two gangs have become transnational criminal organizations with complex structures and have links with transnational drug traffickers; they specialize in homicide, kidnapping and money laundering as well as extortion (Pérez 2013: 225–26). Migrants experience their extortion of *la renta* as blunt coercion that further impoverishes people and spreads fear. Their occupation of neighbourhoods, extortion and forms of rule on the street exploit and reinforce the marginalization produced by state neglect. It is in this sense that organized criminal gangs mirror both authoritarian political power and an unforgiving economic regime that views the poor as exploitable and expendable.

Migrants certainly understand the social and economic forces that make gang activity and membership appealing. They see youths they have known since they were children, peers and sometimes their own family members get caught up in it, and so are sad about it as well as frustrated and angry. But while they share the marginality that feeds gang activity and rationales, migrants respond differently by trying to reposition themselves within the broader regional economy, as undocumented labour in the United States. This reflects a belief in the inherent moral value of working for what one has, however little that may be. Distancing themselves from crime and violence, migrant narratives counter the low value attributed to their labour and themselves as humans that is evident in deprived and neglected environments. Instead, they express dignified attachment to (dreams of) the transformative power of their own physical effort, and a sense of self rooted in their capacity to work, their pleasure in working and the moderate nature of their goals.

Migrants invariably summarized their goals and the solution to their dilemmas in the way Alex did: 'I just need a job. I can work, I know how to work, I can do any job you want, I can work all the hours. I can save'. Talk of 'the job' often sounded like a mantra, loaded with anticipation. It was framed as an uncomplicated, decent desire that could not be too much to ask for, and with a palpable yearning for a physical sense of taking some control of their lives and future, through receiving a reward for work that does not humiliate them. This was just as invariably followed with the qualification, 'I don't want to be a millionaire. Just to be able to live a bit better back home'. The modesty of their aspirations reflected a dim view of grandiose ambition and those motivated by greed, including migrants who had settled in the United States and turned their backs on their family and home country (for similar judgements of greedy vs needy migrants in rural Honduras, see Reichman 2011: 40). The ideal plan is to spend two or three years in the United States and save enough to invest in something like a small shop or a fishing boat, in order to live that bit better back home.

The presentation of a wholesome future affirms good intentions, but also provides a framework of meaning as a counterweight to the complex and ugly perils of the journey and to the anxieties left behind. Migrants do not attempt to present themselves as models of virtue in their focus on work. Rather, they elaborate principles of moral economy and of moral codes that provide guiding ideas and values about how one should shape oneself and relate to others, and that make sense of their journey, even if the circumstances of that journey mean that deviation from those ideals might become a necessity or a temptation. Here, the core referents of family support and obligation come under particular strain, and relations are tested and sometimes broken in both directions. Those obligations can be broken by family members in the United States who promise to help to pay for a *coyote* (a common term for people smugglers), only to withdraw the offer when the migrant is close to the border. This leaves the migrant stranded and facing the hard question of whether the relative is unable or only unwilling to help. Conversely, several migrants reached the north of Mexico before contacting relatives for help, strategically intensifying the obligation to do so with accounts of hardship endured, having come so far.

The micro-economy of the migrant trail involves many small gestures of solidarity and mutual support, but also includes occasional theft from other migrants, passing on information to kidnappers, hoarding the items of clothing distributed by the shelter to trade en route, or using a currency of victimhood to try to secure extra help from shelter workers. Such activities rarely go unnoticed by other migrants, who condemn them, but they do not undermine the guiding ideas of the moral economy. On the contrary, they help to discursively reinforce its value, even though it is impossible for migrants to realize it in their present position. In the roots of that position, migrants perceive a double wrong.

They are wronged firstly by self-serving governments that have not protected people from the moral hazards arising from the imposition of market fundamentalism and that oppress them when they protest. Borrowing again from Polanyi ([1944] 2001: 82), this can be seen as a disavowal of what he called the 'right to live' – a concept central to efforts in England in the eighteenth century to protect the poor from the encroaching vicissitudes of the expanding market economy. It finds its echo in the right to a decent life that migrants envisage, entailing social justice and dignity in work, indignant opposition to the adverse effects of neoliberal policies deepened by repression, and a sense of wrong deepened by corruption. Central American migrants as much as Polanyi's English labourers sought protection from the commodity fiction of labour power and, under neoliberalism, from the decoupling of wages from the costs of social reproduction and from the selective production of residual labour (Smith 2011).

Secondly, migrants feel wronged by those *delincuentes* who counter this state-led discarding of populations by embracing and valorizing criminal modes of reproduction that imitate it, and then exploit and oppress people, while fuelling the association of marginality and wrongdoing that affects everyone in poor communities. Limited in their ability to right these wrongs, migrants head north, invoking 'the American dream' but doing so with irony and a certain self-mockery, recognizing that the best they can hope for is to live under the radar as undocumented labour in circumstances that are a 'bit less impossible'. Hardly a dream, the prospect of work in the relative security of the United States would help to restore migrants' pride in their capacity for hard work and their faith that this can change things, and would offer hope that they might recover some sense of the dignity of their labour.

On their journeys north, however, they share routes with dense criminal economies that intensify the awareness that they are exploitable and disposable. They also enter political spaces in which the attribution of wrong and moral blame is reversed, for their efforts to compensate for the brutal relationship between economy and society in their countries of origin are treated as threats to the economic and social order in the United States.

Dangerous Journeys and Hostile Borders: The Migrant Business

What Daniel described as the 'brilliant business' of migrant exploitation takes on threatening forms along routes across Mexico, where migrants are plagued with the very real possibility of violent assault, robbery, extortion and kidnap by organized criminal gangs and corrupt state agents. Undocumented migrants face considerable risk on their journeys, which ultimately derive from the illegality of their undertaking.

As Daniel's comments also implied, Central American (and Mexican) governments have long ignored the implications of the illegal nature of much migration north, benefiting as they have from the high levels of remittances migrants send home, which provide some of the social safety net that neoliberalism repudiates. In the United States, on the other hand, the rise of neoliberalism has been associated with the increasing condemnation of undocumented migration, even as regional free markets have continued to integrate (see Heyman, this volume). In addition, migration has increasingly been seen as a security issue (since 2003 under the Department of Homeland Security, formed in the wake of 9/11) and immigration policy has increasingly focused on deterrence, border militarization and surveillance, and deportation. At the same time, Mexico was enjoined to support US deterrence efforts by strengthening the security of its own southern border and more recently, under the Plan Frontera Sur launched in 2014, significantly increased deportations from its own soil.

The incremental criminalization of undocumented migration has had significant consequences. It has affected migrants' chances of reaching the United States, finding work and remaining undetected. It has also affected the ways in which they are perceived there; and, most immediately, it has increased their exposure to violent criminal economies that target them. Moving through Mexico, undocumented migrants have to evade police and immigration officials, who will deport them or demand money to allow them to continue on their way. They also have to circumvent strengthened immigration checkpoints and surveillance, which means crossing remote areas on foot, which is both physically demanding and dangerous. Migrants' illegal status obliges them to use routes dominated by organized gangs and drug-trafficking organizations, where their lack of protection makes them at once a valuable resource and very low-hanging fruit.

The conditions that enable the large-scale exploitation of migrants along these transit corridors have much in common with the conditions that propelled them north. Neoliberal reform in Mexico increased its own poor, insecure surplus population, variously drawn to, repelled and persecuted by criminal economies. The regional power of drug-trafficking organizations reflects the Mexican state's baleful response to the expansion of the drug economy and the corruption and violent power struggles that expansion entailed (Serrano 2012). Like the zero-tolerance policing of gangs in Central America (and equally consistent with regional security initiatives),[5] Mexico's militarized confrontation with drug cartels since 2006 has been staggeringly counterproductive. It produced unprecedented numbers of deaths and caused cartels to fragment, multiply, reorganize and fight back (Campbell and Hansen 2014: 159). Some also moved parts of their operations south to the Northern Triangle, forming alliances with Central American drug-trafficking organizations and transnational gangs (Reineke and Martínez 2014), thus further integrating their own regional shadow economy. This makes many areas that migrants traverse exceptionally dangerous, where cartels fight within and amongst themselves and with the government, or else ally with local governments, allowing them to exercise de facto political control and operate in zones of impunity (Campbell and Hansen 2014).

That impunity and migrants' lack of protection allow economies of migrant exploitation to flourish. The fees migrants pay to *coyotes* rose substantially from the 1990s, as evading detection while crossing the border became more of a challenge in the face of increased border militarization (Massey, Durand and Malone 2003; Theodore 2007). It rose even more as drug-trafficking organizations began in turn to charge *coyotes* for moving people over the stretch of the border that the organizations controlled. And, of course, it is very risky for migrants to attempt to cross independently, without paying. Yet undocumented migrants have little option but to navigate clandestine trails where violent crimes are rarely investigated and where migrants themselves constitute a market in extortion and organized kidnapping, often carried out with the complicity of the Mexican authorities (Izcara Palacios 2012: 45). If neoliberalism in their countries of origin produces migrants as surplus population, when they travel they become expendable commodities in the trade in *Cachucos* (a derogatory term for Central Americans) (Vogt 2013).

For Central Americans, crossing Mexico has never been free of danger or exploitation, but the current conditions are particularly toxic. One reason is that neoliberal indifference to the moral hazard of profit seeking has pervaded criminal economies, wherein treating people as disposable things is a premise rather than a consequence of criminal activities, often with fatal effect. And there is a steady supply of those who are surplus, the already-disposable residual populations who are most susceptible to criminal forms of accumulation as they make their slow and uncertain journey across Mexico, as the figures for Central Americans dead or missing in Mexico testify.[6]

Economies of migrant exploitation are diverse and innovative. Along migrant routes, criminal gangs scrutinize migrant activity for new opportunities, responding to the core neoliberal imperative by creating markets within the informal world of migrant transit. For example, they take control of stretches of track and charge people to get on the freight trains that many migrants ride on their way north, generically referred to as *La Bestia*; however, fewer are riding the trains since the Mexican government stepped up deterrence.

Large numbers of people riding precariously atop freight trains offer opportunities not only for extortion, but also for organized assault and robbery, either while the train is moving or, in collusion with drivers and guards, while the train is stopped in selected, isolated spots. This also facilitates organized kidnapping of fairly large numbers of people all at once. Impoverished migrants do not generate large ransoms, but they are numerous, and even the poor embody the values of affective family ties that can be exploited for ransom (Vogt 2013: 774) – and if no ransom is paid, they may be released arbitrarily or just disappear. Organized kidnapping is a low-cost and fairly low-risk business, so much so that it attracts freelance kidnappers not linked to organized gangs. Those migrants who pay *coyotes* to guide them the length of the journey are vulnerable to bogus *coyotes* who lead them some way into Mexico before robbing and abandoning them. Near the US border there is the risk of being picked up by the criminal organization called Los Zetas and coerced into carrying drugs across. If such migrants are caught by the US authorities they risk a hefty prison sentence. Rumours circulate that those who carry the drugs across successfully may be killed by Los Zetas anyway.

The common incidence of migrant deaths suggests that extreme violence is not some sort of collateral damage produced by the criminal migrant business, but is its predicate. Violence against migrants appears intentionally brutal. The beating, rape, throwing people off moving trains and random homicide serve to guarantee obedience and seal fearful reputations. That violence is a condition of accumulation in the predatory and competitive market in migrant bodies – an example of what Sayak Valencia (2010) elaborates as 'gore capitalism'. The overinvestment in violence not only guarantees profit but also produces terror as an instrument of power and as a strategy of expansion (Campbell and Hansen 2014). Hence, what migrants confront and witness is their radical disposability, generated by neoliberal policies in their home countries and confirmed on their journeys by their emergence as a 'gore precariat' (Valencia 2010). They are effectively being denied a right to live.

Beyond these multiple risks from organized crime, migrants fear being apprehended by immigration authorities, which is all the more dispiriting if they have made it as far as the US border. If they are caught, everything that induced them to leave their homes and all that they have experienced on the journey is erased by an exclusive focus on their illegality, setting in motion deportation processes that are legal but, from their perspective, are not just. Moreover, even if they are caught and deported, so long as conditions back home remain the same, migrants feel compelled to repeat the journey. Immigration policies that focus on securing the border while ignoring what leads people to migrate have thus only boosted the militarized policing, surveillance technology, construction of fencing and detention facilities, NGO activity, media interest and the like that Ruben Andersson (2014) calls the 'illegality industry'. The fixation on the illegality of undocumented migration also cuts across and organizes spaces in ways that designate migrants as criminal while increasing their vulnerability. In doing so they abet the organized predation of migrants, putting those migrants both at risk and in the wrong.

Defining migrants exclusively by their illegality is profoundly stigmatizing, as it conflates them with drug traffickers and other border menaces. It also makes a crime of their efforts to counteract the violent disintegration of their livelihoods and to restore their right to live. This attribution is acutely felt by migrants, as it associates them with a criminality that they have repudiated and that oppresses them, as it denies the moral reasoning of their undertaking. That reasoning recognizes that undocumented migration is not legal, but does appeal to a sense of fairness by insisting that the desire to work and live is far from criminal, certainly is not wrong, and that it is unjust to treat it as such.

None of this, however, reduces anti-immigrant sentiment in the United States, or public demand for border reinforcement. Instead, strident discourses are generated about the economic and social resources that the country offers as a destination, and about how migrants covet them and seek to abuse the system, thereby putting those resources at risk for those who are entitled to them. The focus on illegality and border control thus repeats and strengthens a racialized narrative of the migrant as a dangerous, non-White interloper with low morals and criminal intent. Anti-immigrant nativism thus also invokes its own arguments about economic fairness and economic wrong, framed in terms of the entitlement to decent jobs and prospects that attaches to citizenship (Dohan 2003) and belongs to the national community. Neoliberal restructuring of the US labour market has threatened those entitlements and, for many workers, created a gap between their expectations and what the labour market actually has to offer – namely, degrading jobs with little pay; nonetheless, this still generally presents better prospects for migrants than what is available for them at home. The debate about what is wrong with the relationship between economy and society in the United States, which reflects a sense of betrayed entitlement, thus misrecognizes migrants themselves as the carriers of moral hazard.

If neoliberal thought champions self-reliance and the responsibility of individuals to improve their position with respect to market opportunity, it could be argued that no one takes those injunctions more seriously than migrants; yet their efforts to improve their position are punished. In globalized markets where everything circulates freely except the poor, the ordinary meaningful economic aspirations of migrants are converted into crime and subversion, and their moral arguments become void. The demonization of illegal migrants and, indeed, of their criminal exploiters, rules out scrutiny of the conditions that lead people into crime or out of their countries of origin, and of the ways in which global neoliberal 'economic imperatives frequently *produce* what are [subsequently] characterized as security concerns' (Brown 2010: 95) – especially so when they turn up at the border. Migrants' attempts to respond to a home turned hostile by neoliberal reform expose them to markets in human vulnerability, and to the potent censure of nativist indictments.

Conclusion

Across the region, neoliberal economic imperatives render the poor surplus, both producing migrants and rationalizing the option of organized crime, while the security framework that protects those imperatives itself exacerbates the dangers migrants seek to escape and those they are exposed to during their journeys. Central American and Mexican governments facilitate neoliberal projects that lead to poverty wages and the displacement of people while being indifferent to the risk of causing harm and to the moral implications of those policies. Indeed, the moral-economy arguments of the poor are viewed with hostility as they articulate the vision of a relationship between economy and society that challenges elite economic power and invokes Cold War ghosts that will not lie down. Residual, surplus populations head north or integrate into growing and complex criminal economies that simulate both unrestrained market logic and oppressive state power in their extortion of poor communities and their violent exploitation of migrants along their trails.

For its part, US border policy has increasingly combined immigration with threats to security and transferred blame onto the figure of the economic migrant. The increased deportation and deterrence associated with this policy has made the need for, and cost of, smugglers much higher, as well as inflating corrupt extortions by Mexican authorities. As people continue to be compelled to attempt to travel north and enter the United States, albeit in reducing numbers, these policies have the effect of confining migrants within brutal geographies, guaranteeing their exposure to predation by shadow economies predicated upon violence and thus abetting the generation of economies of human vulnerability.

In this circumstance, migrants circulate precariously between connected worlds of moral hazard in which it is acutely problematic for them to either stay where they are or arrive anywhere else. For anti-immigrant nativism, inflamed by the Trump administration, the illegality of their enterprise, misrecognized as a threat to economy and society, denies them the pursuit of ordinary human goals and even their common humanity, while neoliberal rationality integrates zones of market economy and security, simultaneously dismantling the right of surplus populations to live. This leaves migrants with no safe ground on which to try to build a moral economy of work and worth.

Kathy Powell is a Lecturer at the School of Political Science and Sociology at the National University of Ireland, Galway. Her long-standing research interests are in political anthropology, focusing on socio-economic change, politics and violence in western Mexico: 'Political Practice, Everyday Political Violence and Electoral Processes during the Neoliberal Period in Mexico', in Wil G. Pansters (ed.), *Violence, Coercion, and State-Making in Twentieth-Century Mexico* (Stanford University Press, 2012). She has also worked on the effects of neoliberalism on political ideology: 'The Mexican Revolution 100 Years On: Is It Over?', in William Richardson and Lorraine Kelly (eds), *Power, Place and Representation* (Peter Lang, 2012). She is currently working on authoritarian neoliberalism and the reshaping of relations between capital and labour, looking in particular at the status of migrant labour.

Notes

1. During periods in 2014 and 2015, I conducted fieldwork in a migrant refuge in San Luis Potosí, Mexico, run by the Catholic charity Cáritas.
2. In 2012, the proportion of GDP made up by remittances was 15.7 per cent for Honduras, 16.5 per cent for El Salvador and 10.0 per cent for Guatemala (Cohn, González-Barrera and Cuddington 2013: Table 1).
3. One of the companies involved had contributed to President Hernández's election campaign. The scandal led to repeated calls for the president to resign, and prompted the formation of the *oposición indignada*, the 'indignant opposition'.
4. Displaced Mexican families in similar situations also passed through the shelter.
5. Mexico's War on Drugs was endorsed and supported by the 2008 Mérida Initiative. Ostensibly that was an 'unprecedented partnership between the United States and Mexico to fight organised crime and associated violence, while furthering respect for human rights and the rule of law', but in practice seems to be 'NAFTA-land Security – essentially a Homeland Security vision for the NAFTA space' (Ashby 2015).
6. There are obvious difficulties in estimating the number of migrant deaths, but in Mexico between 2007 and 2013 it ranges from 47,000 to 70,000 (Reineke and Martínez 2014: 69).

References

Andersson, Ruben. 2014. *Illegality, Inc. Clandestine Migration and the Business of Bordering Europe*. Oakland: University of California Press.

Arias, Enrique Desmond, and Daniel M. Goldstein (eds). 2010. *Violent Democracies in Latin America*. Durham, NC: Duke University Press.

Ashby, Paul. 2015. 'Is the Merida Initiative Working?' Mexico City: Americas Program. www.cipamericas.org/archives/15568 (accessed 23 July 2015).

Beachy, Ben. 2015. 'CAFTA's Decade of Empty Promises Haunts the TPP'. Mexico City: Americas Program. www.cipamericas.org/archives/15725 (accessed 14 August 2015).

Block, Fred. 2001. 'Introduction', in Karl Polanyi, *The Great Transformation*. Boston, MA: Beacon Press, pp. xviii–xxxviii.

Bourgois, Phillipe. 1995. *In Search of Respect: Selling Crack in El Barrio*. Cambridge: Cambridge University Press.

Brown, Wendy. 2010. *Walled States, Waning Sovereignty*. New York: Zone Books.

Bruneau, Thomas C. 2014. 'Pandillas and Security in Central America', *Latin American Research Review* 49(2): 152–72.

Campbell, Howard. 2009. *Drug War Zone: Frontline Despatches from the Streets of El Paso and Juárez*. Austin: University of Texas Press.

Campbell, Howard, and Tobin Hansen. 2014. 'Is Narco-violence in Mexico Terrorism?' *Bulletin of Latin American Research* 33(2): 158–73.

Centeno, Miguel Angel, and Alejandro Portes. 2006. 'The Informal Economy in the Shadow of the State', in Patricia Fernández-Kelly and Jon Schefner (eds), *Out of the Shadows: Political Action and the Informal Economy in Latin America*. University Park: Penn State University Press, pp. 23–48.

CICIG (Comisión Internacional contra la Impunidad en Guatemala). 2015. 'Informe: el financiamiento de la política en Guatemala'. Guatemala City: Comisión Internacional contra la Impunidad en Guatemala. www.cicig.org/index.php?mact=News,cntnt01,detail,0&cntnt01articleid=616&cntnt01returnid=67 (accessed 4 January 2016).

Cohn, D'Vera, Ana González-Barrera and Danielle Cuddington. 2013. 'Remittances to Latin America Recover – But Not to Mexico'. Washington, DC: Pew Research Center. www.pewhispanic.org/2013/11/15/remittances-to-latin-america-recover-but-not-to-mexico (accessed 6 April 2014).

Davis, Patricia. 2014. 'Guatemala Suppressing Dissent at Home and Abroad'. Mexico City: Americas Program. www.cipamericas.org/archives/11961 (accessed 21 May 2014).

Dohan, Daniel. 2003. *The Price of Poverty: Money, Work and Culture in the Mexican American Barrio*. Berkeley: University of California Press.

Garcia Soto, Jovanna. 2014. 'Honduran Garifuna Communities Evicted by Tourism Interests'. Boston: Grassroots International. www.grassrootsonline.org/news/blog/honduran-garifuna-communities-evicted-tourism-interests (accessed 4 April 2015).

Gledhill, John. 2015. *The New War on the Poor: The Production of Insecurity in Latin America*. London: Zed Books.

Gutiérrez Rivera, Lirio. 2010. 'Discipline and Punish? Youth Gangs' Response to "Zero-Tolerance" Policies in Honduras', *Bulletin of Latin American Research* 29(4): 492–504.

Isla, Jessica. 2015. 'The Scorching Summer of Honduras' "Indignant Opposition"'. Mexico City: Americas Program. www.cipamericas.org/archives/15675 (accessed 14 August 2015).

Izcara Palacios, Simón Pedro. 2012. 'Coyotaje y grupos delictivos en Tamaulipas', *Latin American Research Review* 47(3): 41–61.

Koonings, Kees, and Dirk Kruijt (eds). 2007. *Fractured Cities: Social Exclusion, Urban Violence and Contested Spaces in Latin America*. London: Zed Books.

Lievesley, Geraldine. 2011. 'Unearthing the Real Subversives: The US State, Right-Wing Think Tanks and Political Intervention in Contemporary Latin America', in Francisco Dominguez, Geraldin Lievesley and Steve Ludlam (eds), *Right-Wing Politics in the New Latin America: Reaction and Revolt*. London: Zed Books, pp. 44–59.

Lohmuller, Michael. 2015. 'Honduras Closes Bank as Elite Money Laundering Case Hits Savers'. Washington, DC: InSight Crime. www. insightcrime.org/news-briefs/honduras-closes-bank-as-elite-money-laundering-case-hits-savers (accessed 4 January 2016).

Lukes, Steven. 1997. 'Social Justice: The Hayekian Challenge', *Critical Review* 11(1): 65–80.

Mackey, Danielle Marie. 2014. 'I've Seen All Sorts of Horrific Things in My Time, But None as Detrimental to the Country as This', *New Republic* (15 December). www.newrepublic.com/article/120559/honduras-charter-cities-spearheaded-us-conservatives-libertarians (accessed 8 January 2015).

Main, Alexander. 2014. 'The U.S. Re-militarization of Central America and Mexico'. New York: North American Congress on Latin America. https://nacla.org/news/2014/7/3/us-re-militarization-central-america-and-mexico-0 (accessed 16 July 2014).

Martin, Patricia. 2007. 'Mexico's Neoliberal Transition: Authoritarian Shadows in an Era of Neoliberalism', in Helga Leitner, Jamie Peck and Eric S. Sheppard (eds), *Contesting Neoliberalism: Urban Frontiers*. London: Guilford Press, pp. 51–70.

Massey, Douglas S., Jorge Durand and Nolan J. Malone. 2003. *Beyond Smoke and Mirrors: Mexican Immigration in an Era of Economic Integration*. New York: Russell Sage Foundation.

McCain, Greg. 2015. 'Honduras: The Failings of Neoliberalism'. *Counterpunch* (21 January). www.counterpunch.org/2015/01/21/honduras-the-failings-of-neoliberalism (accessed 22 January 2015).

McIlwaine, Cathy, and Caroline O.N. Moser. 2007. 'Living in Fear: How the Urban Poor Perceive Violence, Fear and Insecurity', in Kees Koonings and Dirk Kruijt (eds), *Fractured Cities: Social Exclusion, Urban Violence and Contested Spaces in Latin America*. London: Zed Books, pp. 117–37.

Moodie, Ellen. 2010. *El Salvador in the Aftermath of Peace: Crime, Uncertainty and the Transition to Democracy*. Philadelphia: University of Pennsylvania Press.

Nash, June (ed.). 2005. *Social Movements: An Anthropological Reader*. Oxford: Blackwell Publishing.

Peralta, Adriana. 2014. 'Honduras Wants ZEDEs by 2016, Calls on Neighbors to Follow its Lead', *PanAm Post* (9 June). http://panampost.com/adriana-peralta/2014/06/09/honduras-wants-zedes-by-2016-calls-on-neighbors-to-follow-its-lead (accessed 8 February 2015).

Pérez, Orlando J. 2013. 'Gang Violence and Insecurity in Contemporary Central America', in Eric A. Johnson, Ricardo D. Salvatore and Pieter Spierenburg (eds), *Murder and Violence in Modern Latin America*. Oxford: Wiley-Blackwell, pp. 217–34.

Perry, John. 2012. 'Honduras – Three Years after the Coup', *OpenDemocracy* (27 June). www.opendemocracy.net/john-perry/honduras-three-years-after-coup (accessed 18 May 2014).

Polanyi, Karl. (1944) 2001. *The Great Transformation: The Political and Economic Origins of Our Time*. Boston, MA: Beacon Press.

Portes, Alejandro, and Kelly Hoffman. 2003. 'Latin American Class Structures: Their Composition and Change during the Neoliberal Era', *Latin American Research Review* 38(1): 41–82.

Reichman, Daniel R. 2011. *The Broken Village: Coffee, Migration, and Globalization in Honduras*. Ithaca, NY: ILR Press.

Reineke, Robin, and Daniel E. Martínez. 2014. 'Migrant Deaths in the Americas (United States and Mexico)', in Tara Brian and Frank Laczko (eds), *Fatal Journeys: Tracking Lives Lost during Migration*. Geneva: International Organization for Migration, pp. 45–83.

Robinson, William I. 2008. *Latin America and Global Capitalism: A Critical Globalization Perspective*. Baltimore, MD: The Johns Hopkins University Press.

Salomón, Leticia. 2014. 'Honduras: A History that Repeats Itself'. New York: North American Congress on Latin America. https://nacla.org/article/honduras-history-repeats-itself (accessed 5 April 2015).

Schwalbe, Michael. 2015. 'The Moral Hazards of Capitalism', *Counterpunch* (1 September). www.counterpunch.org/2015/09/01/the-moral-hazards-of-capitalism (accessed 2 September 2015).

Serrano, Monica. 2012. 'States of Violence: State–Crime Relations in Mexico', in Wil G. Pansters (ed.), *Violence, Coercion and State-Making in Twentieth-Century Mexico: The Other Half of the Centaur*. Stanford, CA: Stanford University Press, pp. 135–58.

Smith, Gavin. 2011. 'Selective Hegemony and Beyond – Populations with "No Productive Function": A Framework for Enquiry', *Identities* 18(1): 2–38.

Theodore, Nik. 2007. 'Closed Borders, Open Markets: Immigrant Day Laborers' Struggle for Economic Rights', in Helga Leitner, Jamie Peck and Eric S. Sheppard (eds), *Contesting Neoliberalism: Urban Frontiers*. London: Guilford Press, pp. 250–65.

Valencia, Sayak. 2010. *Capitalismo gore*. Barcelona: Editorial Melusina.

Vogt, Wendy A. 2013. 'Crossing Mexico: Structural Violence and the Commodification of Undocumented Central American Migrants', *American Ethnologist* 40(4): 764–80.

Zilberg, Elana. 2007. 'Refugee Gang Youth: Zero Tolerance and the Security State in Contemporary U.S.–Salvadoran Relations', in Sudhir Venkatech and Ron Kassimir (eds), *Youth, Globalization, and the Law*. Stanford, CA: Stanford University Press, pp. 61–89.

8

How Does Neoliberalism Relate to Unauthorized Migration?

The US–Mexico Case

Josiah McC. Heyman

Unauthorized migration of Mexicans to the United States and the unauthorized or legally ambiguous employment of such migrants has a long history and has shaped societies on both sides of the border. The subsequent extension of this Mexican pattern to Central America, touched on periodically in this chapter, is explored more fully in Kathy Powell's chapter. Unauthorized migration, whether it be unauthorized entry or the violation of the terms of a visa, certainly is legally wrong. Some migrants enter the United States looking for work in order to earn money; and even those who enter for other reasons (e.g. fleeing violence or persecution) need money in order to survive, and so are also likely to look for work. Some of them obtain work authorization in the asylum application process, but others become unauthorized workers. Only in 1986 was the employment of unauthorized migrant workers by businesses and households forbidden, so since that date, those employers have violated the law. Even when it was permitted, such employment was often treated as a semi-deviant end run around legal migration.

This book asks how neoliberalism relates to dubious economic activity and its assessment. The vast flow of migrants to the United States and the range of places where they work offer a compelling case to examine that question. Neoliberalism in sending regions also provides intriguing material. The answer, however, is not simple. Changes in rural Mexico and in US policies concerning employing migrants were shaping migration long before the rise of neoliberalism, and continued to do so at the height of state-regulated capitalism on both sides of the border. While the quintessential formations of such capitalism did not support unauthorized migration or employment, important secondary formations did. Neoliberalism certainly exacerbated the processes pushing unauthorized labour migrants out of sending areas, and the xenophobia that accompanied neoliberalism in the United States made employing them illegal and hence more obviously wrong, while the parts of the US economy where such migrants are employed have grown and spread geographically with the rise of neoliberalism. But neoliberalism was by no means the origin of these patterns. Rather than being a distinctly neoliberal phenomenon, treating Mexican migrants as wrongdoers and thus stigmatized, vulnerable, and in some ways unfree labour proves to be a persistent theme cutting across changing legal statuses and several periods of capitalism.

To approach the question of the relationship of neoliberalism to this form of economic activity, it is useful to delineate the various meanings attached to 'neoliberalism'. One of these is the freeing of individuals to make voluntary economic decisions, with government activity reduced to the minimum necessary for things like public safety. The policies of the US government and common public opinion do not approach Mexican migration in neoliberal terms. It is true that key policy measures since the 1970s have been neoliberal. These have included structural adjustment (privatization), beginning gradually in the United States in the late 1970s, and drastically in Mexico in 1982, as well as the North American Free Trade Agreement (NAFTA) in 1994 and the Central American Free Trade Agreement (CAFTA) in 2004. These indeed increased the unregulated spatial mobility and market operations of investment capital and commodities, and of small numbers of managerial and ownership elites, but they did not provide market freedom to labouring people. The free movement and employment of labour is restricted, and an impressive enforcement system is arrayed against it: in Fiscal Year 2014 the US Border Patrol arrested 486,651 people attempting to enter the United States freely for labour, family and refuge reasons; almost all of them were either from Mexico or Central America (USCBP 2014: 3). A philosophically neoliberal government would seek to free this flow rather than resist it.

There are substantial non-professional guest-worker programmes that allow legal, temporary migrant labour; in 2014, unskilled non-agricultural occupations got 89,274 visas, and unskilled agricultural occupations got 68,102 (United States Department of State 2015; this does not break down visas by country of origin, but Mexico and

Central America are important). Guest-worker programmes serve the labour needs of some segments of capital, but workers' movements and their place in the labour market are strictly managed by both government and employers, and so can hardly be said to be neoliberal in the free-market sense. This suggests that policies and practices that might be called neoliberal encourage market liberalization in some instances (e.g. commodities, investment capital, profit repatriation), but market regulation and partial repression in others (e.g. labour). Unauthorized labour migration and unauthorized employment, then, are activities that evade limitations on market processes within incomplete neoliberalism. The outcome, however, is not simply the expression of market forces just like any other, but rather a form of illegal and partly unfree labour not fitting the market ideal, though also not fitting the regulatory state ideal.

Another common use of 'neoliberalism' is to refer to the bundle of characteristics of a historical era, perhaps beginning with the elections of Margaret Thatcher in 1979 and Ronald Reagan in 1980. As a simple historical periodization, this fails to encompass unauthorized Mexican migration (extensive Central American migration did begin in the 1980s, driven by civil wars and US intervention). As we will see, the northward flows from Mexico began in the late nineteenth century and their illegalization or restriction (i.e. guest-worker programmes) date to the period 1917–29, with mutating continuity to the present. Examining this history, I find useful the idea that neoliberalism is not a singular or unified arrangement implemented in a particular historical period. Rather, elements that have recently grown in prominence began as secondary socio-economic arrangements that existed alongside the dominant socio-economic systems in the United States and Mexico.

In this analysis, I follow an important argument of George Baca (2004), that historically Fordism did not characterize the American South, and that post-Fordism is, in some ways, an expansion of the labour regime of the South to the entire country. In this perspective, what neoliberalism replaced, Keynesian capitalism, was not uniform in the United States, and the growth of neoliberalism was the spread of existing secondary formations. That growth nationalized the existing economic formation that was Southern capitalism, with roots in unfree labour, and also it spread an existing labour formation more widely, one that had roots in the Southwest: unauthorized Mexican migration. Put simply, unfree labour regimes had long existed, having a distinctive history well before 1980, but they have expanded and deepened since then.

Neoliberalism, in both its free-market and historical senses, is often used as a covering term for global capitalist processes that displace peasants. This is often seen to connect neoliberalism with unauthorized migration. Again, in the case that I will examine here, the capitalist transformation of rural Mexico that freed and forced peasants to become labour migrants long predates key neoliberal markers such as NAFTA, and even long predates 1982, the beginning of structural adjustment in Mexico that removed public subsidies and market restraints in the countryside. To understand Mexican and, latterly, Central American labour migration we need to move beyond neoliberalism to examine a broader phenomenon: the crushing bias against primary producers in capitalism (Hornborg 2001) that pushes peasants into capitalist labour as peasant workers. Unquestionably, structural adjustment and free-trade agreements without labour freedom have worsened the situation in rural Mexico but, again, the pertinent processes have a broader and deeper history. In making this argument, I draw particularly on the labour-centred synoptic history of the two countries by Gilbert González and Raul Fernández (González 2006; González and Fernández 2003).

In overview, then, I argue that unauthorized and guest-worker migrants from Mexico and Central America, and their employment in the United States, were reinforced by neoliberalism but were not a product of it. Rather, they existed before the rise of neoliberalism and contributed to its rise. I propose, based on this argument, that neoliberalism is best seen as an attack on labour bargaining power and societal redistribution mechanisms of the sort that have been called social democracy, Keynesianism and Fordism. In some instances, these attacks do have a free-market orientation, but in others they do not; equally, they do not necessarily occur in the historical period associated with neoliberalism. In the present case, these attacks utilize various arrangements of partially unfree labour that lurked as a pre-existing possibility in the historical relationship between the United States and Mexico. Drawing on the arguments of Ruth Gomberg-Muñoz (2012, 2017), what I will describe may best be understood as an unfree labour arrangement reflecting race or national origin. This unfree system has varied in significance over time, but it has coexisted with the dominant free labour regimes in US and Mexican capitalism since the 1880s. As such, racialized unfree labour is distinct from, but articulated with, several different capitalist regimes – the classically liberal, the Fordist, and the neoliberal. So, while it may appear deviant from the perspective of the dominant regime, it actually is part of the wider system.

I have referred both to guest workers and to unauthorized workers, even though guest-worker programmes do not entail legal wrongdoing in terms of border entry, presence in the country or employment. However, guest workers and unauthorized workers should be considered together for two reasons. One is the patterned alternation between the two modes of migration in US–Mexican history. The other is that, like unauthorized workers, guest workers are not free labour, for they are bound to specific contracts and employers, and can be deported if they step outside those bounds. Indeed, unauthorized workers may be freer, as they can look for work without contractual limitations, although they are subject to arrest and deportation if the authorities find out about them. Comparable to guest workers are asylum applicants, who are in a legal limbo during the (often extended) adjudication of their applications, during which time they are authorized to work, but that authorization can easily be removed; this particularly applies to recently increasing Central American flows. In addition, recipients of Deferred Action for Childhood Arrivals permits, other deferred enforcement statuses and temporary protected status have tentative legal status but are still constrained by the possibility of loss of residence and work rights and deportation from the country (see USCIS n.d.a, n.d.b). Hence, migrant legal wrongdoing arising from economic motivations is part of the analysis in this chapter, but it is secondary to the central theme of partially unfree labour (Gomberg-Muñoz 2012).

This history informs us about the intersection of specific kinds of class exploitation with racial and national inequality, which together produce the social fiction 'commodity Mexican'. That fiction is a unit of obtainable and disposable labour that is seen as less than fully human and as inferior to citizens, who are held to be White and to belong to the dominant society (Vélez-Ibáñez 1996: 70–87). It also helps to illuminate emerging patterns of the use of partially unfree labour, such as new waves of guest workers, prisoners and so forth, which may emerge as an important component of future capitalism in North America and elsewhere.

Of course, that fiction is a fiction. Despite their social placement, such workers are not passive commodities, but instead often struggle for rights and material goods. Furthermore, the stereotype of Mexicans as illegal immigrants is misleading. In fact, the majority of people of Mexican origin in the United States are citizens by birth or naturalization. As well, over half of all foreign-born Mexicans resident in the United States are legal permanent residents or were such residents and became naturalized citizens (Gonzalez-Barrera and

Lopez 2013). Similarly, the stereotype that the illegal migrant entered by covertly crossing the border is, at best, only half true. A recent estimate is that around 58 per cent of unauthorized immigrants in 2014 entered legally but then violated the terms of their visas, for example by overstaying the time period or working without authorization (my calculation, based on data in Warren and Kerwin 2015: 92). Finally, unauthorized migrants are not solely Mexican. In 2006 the long-standing pattern of Mexicans making up the large majority of unauthorized arrivals ended, and by 2012 non-Mexicans, especially Central Americans, accounted for twice as many unauthorized arrivals as Mexicans (ibid.: 90). I devote most of my attention to Mexican migrants because I want to focus on their specific and distinctive history of unauthorized and guest-worker migration.

The Introduction to this volume presents good reason for abandoning the conventional view that economic wrongdoing occurs because people with an inadequate moral compass violate clear rules. The migration at issue in this chapter certainly supports the point that, despite the claims of its supporters, neoliberalism does not necessarily lead to following the rules or being transparent. Rather, it includes, and in some ways encourages, violation of formal rules both from above, as a means of maximizing capital accumulation, and from below, as a means of survival. As the Introduction noted, non-standard economic activities and their assessment as deviant or wrong need to be understood in terms of the political-economic context that shapes them. In this chapter, I take note of a long historical pattern in labour flows from Mexico and Central America to the United States that mixed guest workers, unauthorized workers, asylum seekers and others. This is a deeper and more comprehensive view of this relationship than the recent emphasis on illegality. Compared with open, formal capitalist relations of labour recruitment, these arrangements are best communicated with three phrases: alternative, subordinate, racially stigmatized. They have existed side by side with several different periods of what have commonly been considered standard capitalist labour relations. They thus appear to deviate from standards at each moment in history, but in fact articulate with them.

This chapter tells its story from two sides: the ways that Mexican and Central American peasant workers break US immigration laws in order to cope with the effects of uneven development and the ways that US employers break laws or evade official programmes to employ such workers. The history that I present shows that employers and the state shifted back and forth between legal programmes that deprive workers of freedoms and rights, and the surreptitious employment of illegalized labour. (A third part of the historical narrative, the racist politics motivating immigration enforcement at the Mexican border and in the interior, is something that I have addressed elsewhere; e.g. Heyman 2012a.) My extended historical timeline and analytical precautions about neoliberalism bolster and deepen a point made in this volume's Introduction about the underside of pure-market ideologies: partially unfree labour is an important part of the historical stream that flows into and exists within contemporary capitalism – precisely the opposite of its ideology of legality, transparency and individual rights and responsibilities. I thus conclude by pointing to the continuing, if subordinate, role of hidden and unfree labour arrangements in capitalism, building on the arguments of Gomberg-Muñoz (2012).

Migration History

Mass northward Mexican labour migration began in the 1880s and, as noted above, it was in the years from 1917 to 1929 that it began to be relatively unfree through the imposition of legal obstacles, border enforcement and the first guest-worker programmes (a reliable and compact summary of the vast literature on the history of Mexican migration to the United States is Massey, Durand and Malone 2002; the earlier periods are intelligently synthesized in Ngai 2004).[1]

The initiation of this migration was encouraged by extensive rule violation by employers north of the border. In 1885, the Alien Contract Labor Law, aimed at the Chinese but applying to all nationalities, forbade the assistance or encouragement of migrant labour into the United States, although uninduced migration, with a few exceptions, remained free. There is considerable evidence of employers inducing Mexicans to migrate in decades before 1929 (Spener 2009), while the spread of rail lines linking Mexico and the United States facilitated this development. The foundation of migrant networks was laid at a time when classic-liberal policy prescriptions began to drive Mexican peasants off the land. The Ley Lerdo, passed in 1856 but implemented only in the 1870s, allowed the forced sale of the church estates, rural community commons and state and local holdings that constituted the property base of the Mexican peasantry. The dictator Porfirio Díaz (1876–1910) opened Mexico to international and domestic capital engaged in primitive accumulation of property and capitalist investment in novel or reorganized production (the 'Porfiriato'). US capital and the US state, historically deeply capitalist and with few domestic peasants, followed the prescriptions of classic liberalism by being open to domestic and international labour mobility, although the South was, as I noted, a partial exception. Certainly, then, liberalism, the conceptual ancestor of neoliberalism, formed the context of the beginning of Mexican labour migration to the United States. The question is, why and in what ways did this pattern continue, even as classic liberalism ended or was modified and limited from 1920 to 1980?

The Mexican Revolution began in 1910, with the end of the Díaz regime, and lasted until 1920. It displaced vast numbers of Mexicans, mainly internally but also in considerable but poorly documented numbers to the United States. As is always the case, refugees also sought incomes, mostly in wage work. This reinforced the previous decades' momentum towards self-reproducing migration networks. In 1917, during a period of xenophobia in the United States, things began to change: the head tax on arriving migrants was raised from 50 cents to $8, a substantial sum at the time; the rules against previously contracted and recruited migrants were strengthened; and a literacy requirement was imposed on all migrants over the age of sixteen. The measures were fairly easily implemented at seaports, but Mexicans could travel across land borders and thus easily avoid official crossing points. This, however, made them unauthorized immigrants.

There had been some mobile Immigration Inspectors along the Mexican border, but in 1924 the US Border Patrol was founded. Although initially deployed to stop Chinese migrants seeking to enter via Mexico, they quickly added Mexicans to their duties. From the beginning, the Border Patrol and Inspectors operated in a flexible manner, allowing migrants into the United States when needed by powerful employers and expelling them when unneeded or resistant. While this direct functional service to employers eventually mostly ended, the particular social role of illegal and disposable Mexican migrant labour has continued to the present.

The 1917 measures intended to restrict migration were complemented by an interesting experiment with a guest-worker programme that lasted until 1921. Guest workers were excused from the head tax, literacy test and, most importantly, the bar on contract labour; they were largely hired by agricultural producers in the Southwest. The programme was a fiasco, with many more workers contracted by employers than there was work available, resulting in large numbers of homeless and hungry migrants, who were then forcibly expelled from the country. The programme is worth mention especially because it shows the early pattern of alternating options for unfree labour: managed legal migration or illegal but otherwise independently mobile migrants.

This botched programme aside, the 1920s was a period in which Mexican labour migration to the United States flourished. A number of factors brought this about: the bubble economy in the United States attracted labour; the devastation in Mexico following the revolution drove peasants away, exacerbated by the counter-revolutionary Cristero revolt in the most important migrant sending zone, west-central Mexico; and labour recruiters were active and autonomous migration networks were getting stronger. Modest land reform in Mexico restored some communal property to peasants, but in the main the great privatization, the enclosure of common land, of the Porfiriato continued in place. Also in the 1920s, the United States largely halted immigration from Southern and Eastern Europe (Asian migration had already been blocked). Capitalists interested in Latin American and Caribbean labour obtained exemption of the Western Hemisphere from these restrictive measures; but even so, many people entered without authorization. The 1920s, then, marked the shift in US labour flows from authorized Europeans and a short burst of Asians to substantially unauthorized or temporary Mexicans plus other, smaller flows. The contemporary pattern was beginning to emerge.

In the Great Depression, mostly in the early years, at least half a million and possibly a million people of Mexican descent were driven out of the United States. They held a wide variety of legal statuses, from US citizen to unauthorized immigrant. What they had in common was their ancestry in Mexico. Some left voluntarily, taking advantage of modest assistance in moving to Mexico during a period of massive job losses, but mainly they were coerced, with people being persecuted and physically driven out of the country. These events, and particularly the coercive removal of US citizens of Mexican ancestry, clearly show that the United States treated Mexicans as disposable labour that could be sent home when not needed.

Meanwhile, in the 1930s, the Mexican government broke sharply from the previous liberal policies. Under President Lázaro Cárdenas (1934–40), and then on a diminished scale until 1982, a significant number of large rural estates were distributed to individual peasants and collective peasant groups. Also, increasingly during this period the Mexican government intervened in agriculture, offering credits and agricultural inputs to producers, including peasants, and supporting prices for agricultural products. As well, large government projects such as irrigation schemes provided resources to peasants and capitalist farmers of various scales. These more social-democratic policies would appear to make autonomous and guest-worker migration less likely. That was not the case, however, and the reason why is analytically important: Mexico's place in the world capitalist economy. The land distribution was incomplete, and often the best land was retained by capitalist farmers or appropriated by post-revolutionary politicians. The country produced a wide variety of commodities sold on the global market, such as cotton, produced mainly by capitalist farmers but also by some peasants. The overall pattern of development from 1940 onwards had a strong urban bias, both in relative product prices (e.g. corn vs consumer goods) and in government investments and services (e.g. schools).

In a detailed study of the Bajío region, Juan Vicente Palerm and José Ignacio Urquiola (1993) examined how extensive peasant labour migration to the United States occurred during this period. Land distribution was incomplete, and capitalist farmers retained the most productive land, the locus of the introduction of high-technology agriculture in Mexico. That was the Green Revolution that replaced labour-intensive farming methods with high-input, high-productivity crops (Hewitt de Alcántara 1976), and that led to the renewal of northward labour migration. The remaining peasant farms were labour intensive and often utilized ancient cultivars that had significant subsistence value but also ancient cultivation techniques that had low productivity. In this situation, cash income levels were quite low, while there was growing demand for consumer goods that could only be had for cash. Patriarchal peasant households allocated labour in diverse ways, including sending out junior men and, ultimately, women to earn incomes as temporary proletarians. The combination of people obtaining a modicum of land and subsistence food, gradually improving health conditions, and a high demand for children, produced a rapid demographic expansion that reinforced the other developments.

Over time, the Mexican government did provide some support for peasant agriculture, but these social-democratic policies were over-whelmed by the increased population and the fragmentation of the original land distributions with the passing of the generations. Also, social-democratic redistributions such as healthcare and schooling were concentrated in politically powerful cities, with fewer benefits reaching peasant zones. One response to this urban bias was migration to cities within Mexico. Another was seeking to supplement household incomes, but the mechanization of capitalist farms and farms in a few peasant communities reduced the local demand for labour. Fortuitously, the United States had a growing demand for manual labour in the large-scale cultivation of fruits and vegetables, and later in construction, services and light manufacturing. In 1942 the Bracero guest-worker programme, described below, started to draw in Mexican labour to help to meet that demand, and after the programme ended in 1964 unauthorized circular migration also helped in this respect.

Based on their analysis, which I have summarized briefly, Palerm and Urquiola (1993) identify what they call a 'binational' system, centred on unfree peasant-worker labour in the core period of social democracy in Mexico and the United States, 1930 to 1982. Part of the reason that Mexican migration after 1982 looks like a response to neoliberalism is that international emigration has spread to new areas of the country, such as Oaxaca and Chiapas, and also to Central America, while the use of such migrants in the US has expanded geographically and diversified across labour sectors. However, the historical depth of this system suggests that we look beyond neoliberalism to what Palerm and Urquiola describe – the place of peasants in uneven capitalist development.

Roots of the Current Pattern

The Bracero programme brought legal temporary migrant labour to the United States from Mexico between 1942 and 1964. At its peak, from 1955 to 1959, over four hundred thousand workers a year entered the country. This programme, then, existed during the period of Fordist, social-democratic policies in the US. However, it entailed labour relations that were not at all social-democratic, including the repression of unionization, the binding of workers to specific employers, limiting free movement and little enforcement of labour regulations. This apparent paradox can be understood by seeing the Bracero programme as a concession to the sectoral and regional interests of large-scale capitalist agriculture in the West, and to a small degree in the South (see Mitchell 2012). What was acceptable labour relations and what was not, then, reflected intricate negotiations of particular economic and state interests (Calavita 1992).

Although the Bracero programme provided a legal framework, both for employers and workers, before 1954 it was often bypassed, with the law broken on both sides. Employers who did not want to deal with programme regulations and processes, minimal as they were, hired unauthorized migrant workers outside the programme, as did employers in Texas, which was boycotted by the Mexican government for a period because of outrageous racism. Likewise, workers bypassed the programme hiring offices in Mexico because of favouritism and corruption there, and also because there were more workers seeking contracts than there were contracts available. In 1954, however, US officials decided to put an end to this parallel system. They did so not by identifying and punishing employers (indeed, the laws at the time did not largely hold them accountable), but instead by identifying and punishing the Mexican workers, a pattern repeated throughout history.

Immigration authorities conducted mass raids throughout Mexican settlement areas in the United States (Operation Wetback), arresting and deporting upward of a million people (García 1980). A significant proportion of those people were US citizens and legal residents, but remember that Mexicans generally were thought of as disposable foreigners, regardless of legal status. In the politics of punishment, rules are specific to social positions, so that evading the Bracero programme was defined in Operation Wetback as pertaining to racially Mexican people, many of them workers, and not as pertaining to their employers, who were mostly Anglo-American. Operation Wetback achieved its goal, for until the Bracero programme ended in 1964, labour flows and hiring largely adhered to the legal, albeit low-rights, guest-worker regime (Calavita 1992).

There are debates about why Congress ended the Bracero programme, but an important factor was a brief moment of successful social-democratic, union-based political pressure before the emergence of neoliberalism in the 1970s. This triumph, however, consisted of illegalizing worker–employer connections that the Bracero programme had created, rather than bringing them into conformity with social-democratic standards. Unsurprisingly, then, the underlying binational labour system persisted for both ends: the peasant-worker areas of Mexico and the employers in the United States. This persistence was demonstrated in impressive fashion by Massey et al. (1990), who traced individual braceros, their close male relatives and their US employers as they moved directly into unauthorized labour migration arrangements. As I noted in my introduction, smaller legal temporary labour programmes also continued after the end of the Bracero programme.

The current phase of the binational unauthorized-labour system began with networks emanating from previous migrants. In Mexico those networks extended geographically, from a few traditional northern and western sending regions to areas more towards the centre and south of the country; they extended racially, from the mestizos who culturally are Euro-Mexicans to indigenous Mexicans; and they extended in class terms, as working- and middle-class urban Mexicans began to migrate (though peasants remain the mainstay of labour migration). In the United States they diffused geographically, from the Southwest to the entire nation, and sectorally, from agriculture to diverse low-wage occupations. Recently, Mexican migration appears to have slowed considerably, possibly because urbanization has led to the decline of the peasantry, while Central American peasants and urban dwellers, who began to migrate in the early 1980s as a result of US-sponsored civil wars and repressive violence, have supplanted the Mexican flow. The overall contours of the unauthorized migrant labour system, however, have remained in place from 1965 to the present.

Limited social-democratic policies continued in rural sending regions of Mexico until 1982, including sporadic additional land redistribution and the expansion of production credits and regulated markets. The latter mainly benefited capitalist farmers, sharpening disparities in the countryside, but they did benefit some peasant producers. In 1982, however, the century-long pattern of uneven development that displaced peasants accelerated sharply, resulting in the deepening and widening of the binational, and ultimately multinational, unfree labour linkages. In that year, accumulating debt led to a repayment crisis.[2] In emerging neoliberal fashion, of which Mexico was an important test case, bank repayment was ensured by structural adjustment – the restructuring of the political economy. Massive inflation and job losses ensued, except in the export-assembly economy, and redistribution to the rural economy largely ended. Together, these encouraged what I described above: migration from regions of the country and classes of people that had not previously been noteworthy sources of migrants.

In 1986, Mexico entered the General Agreement on Trade and Tariffs, subsequently renamed the World Trade Organization, and became one of the most import-open economies in the world. In 1989, the International Coffee Agreement, which supported and stabilized coffee prices, was allowed to lapse as a neoliberal policy measure. Prices plunged, and many peasant households in Mexico and Central America suffered. In 1994, Mexico went through another debt repayment crisis, due to outrageous elite behaviour (crony capitalism, bad borrowing, and capital flight), reinforcing emigration, and NAFTA was enacted, followed later by the parallel CAFTA. These agreements encouraged capital-intensive agricultural production of things like fresh vegetables for export, while opening Mexico and Central America to imports of inexpensive basic grains and legumes from the north. This severely weakened commercial and peasant grain producers, especially those who grew corn, the fundamental crop throughout the region, though some traditional corn production continues. Looked at from the viewpoint of Mexico and Central America, certainly there is a case to be made that neoliberalism amplified the survival-oriented activities of the masses, which often involved unauthorized migration to flee violence or to gain income, even in the face of an increasingly restrictive legal regime in the United States, which I turn to now.

Changing US Policy

As noted, the end of the Bracero programme in 1964 led to an increase in unauthorized migration. At first, the US government responded slowly, with limited border and interior enforcement and informal local policies of letting unauthorized workers in and out to serve agriculture in the border region. However, border enforcement expanded from the late 1970s, reflecting renewed anti-immigrant sentiment in the United States. The history of anti-immigrant and border-enforcement politics has been narrated elsewhere (Nevins 2002; Heyman 2012a); here it suffices to point out that these changes in laws and, more importantly, in law enforcement practices turned a marginalized or secondary migration flow into an illegal flow. In this situation, we need to understand unauthorized migration from two, somewhat different perspectives simultaneously: as a form of economic wrongdoing by migrants, smugglers and employers; and as the continuation of a patterned, entrenched and often accepted secondary economy, sometimes legal and sometimes not, that is systemic rather than deviant.

In 1986, several million unauthorized immigrants were given legal status, the Border Patrol was given amplified legal powers, and employing an unauthorized migrant was made illegal. It was at this point, then, that the overall unauthorized-migrant labour system became illegal from above as well as from below. Yet the reality was different from those formal terms. Not surprisingly, given the political and ideological power of business, penalties on employers (employer sanctions) have been sparse and fragmented. This gap between formal codes and enforcement practices brings into question the ideologies of the impartial state and law-abiding and above-board capitalism, as discussed in this volume's Introduction.

The 1986 law makes it illegal to employ an unauthorized migrant, but in fact employers face relatively little risk of prosecution. For one thing, employers comply with the law if workers produce the appropriate documents attesting to their status, even though coun- terfeit versions of those documents are pervasive. Moreover, many workers are employed indirectly, via subcontractors, which means that the main employer is free from prosecution. Finally, enforce- ment itself has been sporadic and is usually only applied to employ- ers who are distinctly abusive, such as those who not only employ unauthorized migrants but also do not pay for all the hours worked. It should be noted that centralized electronic verification systems are being introduced, but these are still uncommon in sectors where unauthorized migrants actually work. In recent years, those who employ such migrants have faced fairly light sanctions, often little more than a review of the employer's records and the demand that any unauthorized employees be fired. In comparison, the employee loses his or her job. In other words, the price of policing employers is borne overwhelmingly by the unauthorized migrants.

Following the 1986 measures, immigration enforcement stabilized until 1993, when a new cycle of intensification began, which has lasted to the present (Nevins 2002; Dunn 2009; Heyman 2014). This cycle coincided with the introduction of NAFTA, an archetypal neoliberal measure that was supposed to weaken borders and allow freer trade. A number of efforts were made to tighten the US–Mexico border, including walling portions of the border and increasing the size of the Border Patrol more than fivefold. Tightening the border meant that an illegal crossing became more risky, sometimes even fatal; it also became more expensive, as smugglers charged more, which affected not just those seeking to cross but also those linked to them (Heyman 1998, 2012b, 2014; see Powell this volume). While enforcement has been concentrated near the border, it has grown substantially through- out the US interior. A notable aspect of this is stopping motorists for minor traffic violations, the perception of which is notoriously sub- jective, and checking the motorist's immigration status. Those who cannot produce the appropriate documents are brought to local jails, from whence they are turned over to national immigration police.

This set of enforcement activities has demonstrable effects on labour relations, although these are uneven and complicated.[3] They are also often resisted by migrants in various ways. Extending an established line of research (Heyman 1998; Zlolniski 2003; De Genova 2005), Sarah Horton (2015) has documented the effects of workers borrow- ing documents and identities in order to skirt employer sanctions.

Their actions involve complex webs of collaborative but unequal arrangements among workers, relatives and friends, supervisors, contractors and employers. These arrangements and relations extend back into Mexico, and now Central America, consistent with the binational system described above. Among the effects are incentives to work at high intensity and to put up with personal suffering, bad work conditions and low pay, as well as the absence of health services, retirement earnings and the record of work and residence that would help migrants to achieve a more secure status in future immigration proceedings. An entire unfree lifeway is constituted by these sub-market, off-the-books labour relations. Not only are there specific exploitative advantages gained by a variety of actors, but the United States as a whole benefits from what amounts to stolen retirement earnings and reduced use of public health services. The result is that illegal activity by unauthorized workers and employers reproduces and intensifies the historical pattern of subordinated Mexican and Central American labour seen in a variety of periods and arrangements.

The current situation is one of failure of political resolution at the national level in the United States, including failure of legalization initiatives, failure of additional permanent legal immigration visa allocations, xenophobic resistance to widening access to citizenship, and a vast border enforcement that deters some, but not most, unauthorized entrants. Weighing against this, demand for subordinate labour has returned since the end of the Great Recession. One resolution to these contradictions is to avoid confronting racism and xenophobia head on, while responding to labour demand by expanding current Bracero-like temporary labour migration programmes, 'managed migration' programmes or, as the leading expert (Griffith 2014) terms them, 'mismanaging migration' due to the way that government agents defer to business interests. Likewise, refugees (legally admitted) and asylum applicants (authorized to work while their cases are adjudicated) have some resemblance to managed-labour migrants in terms of the way official organizations regulate their lives. This is, for example, the fate of many Central Americans now arriving at the border. Refugees and asylees from many countries form an increasingly important part of the US immigrant workforce.

Conclusion

Across the history of migration from Mexico and Central America to the United States, people have largely entered exploitative and stigmatized labour relations with few rights. This has occurred across a wide variety of policy periods in sending and receiving countries, including classic liberalism, redistributive revolutions, repressive counter-revolutions, tepid social democracy and neoliberal capitalism. It has also occurred across a variety of legal migration regimes, including legal permanent migration, non-migrant contract labour, asylum and unauthorized migration, some of them occurring side by side. Routinely, however, this migration has been shaped by and fed into a subordinate labour regime in capitalist North America. This is the principal point of this chapter.

At times, this subordinate labour regime has involved illegal activity in the form of unauthorized border-crossing, unauthorized work and unauthorized employment of those workers. Most of the time such activity was undertaken by working people with few options, since the laws banning the employment of unauthorized workers were not enacted until 1986, and even then they were weakly enforced. The legal violation matters, because being unauthorized has put migrants in the most vulnerable position in labour relations and in the policing of public spaces. However, the overall pattern of subordinated labour relations covers the whole of the history of this migration and it captures the full set of shared characteristics better than do concepts like unauthorized, deviant or autonomous migration. It might be most insightful to shift the conceptual orientation away from the legality implicit in the idea of unauthorized migration and instead to think in terms of the wider pattern of social inequalities that separates these workers and their communities from primary labour markets and rights in liberal capitalist society, inequalities that are often justified by pointing to legal wrongdoing.

The proposition that neoliberalism, which ostensibly promotes transparency and the rule of law, actually produces illegal activity from above and below, has some truth to it, but as I have shown in this chapter, it needs considerable modification. Only at the very beginning, in the era of classic liberalism, did state policy allow open labour markets across North America. Since 1917 the movement of labour from Latin America has been restricted through a changing mixture of barriers to entry, expulsion of migrants and state management of labour. These sorts of restriction have increased since the advent of North American neoliberalism around 1980, and have become more obviously hypocritical since the rise of the dogma of free trade. Restrictions on free labour markets clearly are xenophobic political impositions within the otherwise capitalist history. Also, while it was the dispossession associated with classic liberal policies in Mexico that led to the onset of significant migration, that migration continued under the subsequent political-economic systems of subsidized and managed markets, populist resource redistribution and, since 1982, neoliberal policies, as described in Powell's chapter. Unauthorized border-crossing may be a response to capitalist transformations, but its history and persistence suggest that what is pertinent is a broader pattern of capitalist devaluation of the peasantry. The idea of neoliberalism, whether as a political-economic philosophy or as a period of history, provides some insights, but misses much that is important in this history.

Following George Baca's (2004) analysis of the American South discussed in the introduction to this chapter, what we may well be seeing from the rise of neoliberalism is the spread of various repressive labour systems that have lurked in particular historical and geographic reserves and that deviate from both free markets and social-democratic arrangements. This suggests that we might envision neoliberalism as a political attack on the Fordism and social-democratic versions of capitalism that were dominant in the mid twentieth century. Partially unfree labour arrangements, such as the continuum between managed temporary labour migration and unauthorized migration, have presented a useful alternative to Fordism in certain sectors and for certain employers. Those partially unfree arrangements do not conform to the social-democratic standards of Fordism but they cannot be categorized as the neoliberal freeing of market forces because labour in these arrangements is either managed by state–business alliances or is unauthorized and heavily policed.

Recognizing the coexistence of a variety of systems of labour helps to provide a more realistic and complex notion of capitalist history. Unfree labour arrangements are not only found at the beginning of capitalism (Mintz 1985) but also have persisted as subordinate but significant elements across several subsequent capitalist periods. As Gomberg-Muñoz (2012) points out, today we see in the same labour markets a number of different labour sources, including unauthorized migrants, legal temporary migrants (who know that they can lose their legal status for any real or imagined violation of the rules), refugees and asylum applicants (who also fear deviating from the rules), guest workers and prisoners. Employers set these vulnerable groups against each other, alternating among them with two goals: to defeat worker struggles for wages and rights, and to deflect government regulations intended to detect the employment of unauthorized migrants. From the point of view of workers, this is a race to the bottom. It is hard to know if this pattern is spreading or if it will remain a small, secondary pattern, but low-rights, temporary legal migration is the direction in which other advanced capitalist countries are also moving (e.g. Canada; Sharma 2006). If so, it is important to understand these phenomena, past and present.

Acknowledgements

I owe special thanks to Ruth Gomberg-Muñoz for conversations about our converging ideas on immigration and stigmatized, constrained and unfree labour.

Josiah McC. Heyman is Professor of Anthropology, Endowed Professor of Border Trade Issues and Director of the Center for Inter-American and Border Studies at the University of Texas at El Paso. His work focuses on borders, states, power, migration and engaged social sciences. He is the author or editor of four books and over 140 articles, book chapters and essays. A notable recent publication is *The U.S.–Mexico Transborder Region: Cultural Dynamics and Historical Interactions* (Arizona, 2017, ed. with C. Vélez-Ibáñez). He also participates in community initiatives addressing public policy and human rights at the US–Mexico border.

Notes

1. Other, more lateral elements of the history will be bypassed here, for simplicity's sake. These include the military and legal primitive accumulation of resources from Mexicans and Native Americans after the Texas rebellion (1835–36) and Mexican–American War (1845–48), as well as the use of non-Mexican labour forces in similar roles (Chinese, Japanese, Filipino, Native American, African American, poor White, Puerto Rican, etc.).
2. The debt accumulation occurred in part because of Mexican elite activities such as massive corruption and capital flight, in collaboration with international banks, as well as the fiscal contradictions of state-managed development within semi-peripheral capitalism, including these rural programmes, and tactical misestimations of new oil revenues.
3. An important question is if these labour effects loop around to shape the causes of enforcement policies, border and workplace practices, and everyday life, constituting a capitalist-functionalist system, or if there is more of a complex intersection between the economic effects of enforce-

ment and the relatively autonomous politics of racism and xenophobia. I have argued for the latter (Heyman 1998, 2012a, 2012b, 2014), but this is not relevant to the present analysis, since the various causal paths end up with the same unfree-labour outcomes.

References

Baca, George. 2004. 'Legends of Fordism: Between Myth, History, and Foregone Conclusions', *Social Analysis* 48(3): 169–78.

Calavita, Kitty. 1992. *Inside the State: The Bracero Program, Immigration, and the I.N.S.* New York: Routledge.

De Genova, Nicholas. 2005. *Working the Boundaries: Race, Space, and 'Illegality' in Mexican Chicago.* Durham, NC: Duke University Press.

Dunn, Timothy J. 2009. *Blockading the Border and Human Rights: The El Paso Operation that Remade Immigration Enforcement.* Austin: University of Texas Press.

García, Juan Ramon. 1980. *Operation Wetback: The Mass Deportation of Mexican Undocumented Workers in 1954.* Westport, CT: Greenwood Press.

Gomberg-Muñoz, Ruth. 2012. 'Inequality in a "Postracial" Era: Race, Immigration, and Criminalization of Low-Wage Labor', *Du Bois Review* 9(2): 339–53.

———. 2017. 'Beyond Il/legality: Persistent Inequality and Racialized Borders of US Citizenship', in Carlos G. Vélez-Ibáñez and Josiah Heyman (eds), *The U.S.–Mexico Border Region: Cultural Dynamics and Historical Interactions.* Tucson: University of Arizona Press, pp. 228–43.

González, Gilbert G. 2006. *Guest Workers or Colonized Labor? Mexican Labor Migration to the United States.* Boulder, CO: Paradigm Publishers.

González, Gilbert G., and Raúl A. Fernández. 2003. *A Century of Chicano History: Empire, Nations, and Migration.* New York: Routledge.

Gonzalez-Barrera, Ana, and Mark Hugo Lopez. 2013. *A Demographic Portrait of Mexican-Origin Hispanics in the United States.* Washington, DC: Pew Hispanic Center, Pew Research Center.

Griffith, David (ed.). 2014. *(Mis)managing Migration: Guestworkers' Experiences with North American Labor Markets.* Santa Fe, NM: School for Advanced Research Press.

Hewitt de Alcántara, Cynthia. 1976. *Modernizing Mexican Agriculture: Socioeconomic Implications of Technological Change, 1940–1970.* Geneva: United Nations Research Institute for Social Development.

Heyman, Josiah McC. 1998. 'State Effects on Labor Exploitation: The INS and Undocumented Immigrants at the Mexico–United States Border', *Critique of Anthropology* 18(2): 157–80.

———. 2012a. 'Constructing a "Perfect" Wall: Race, Class, and Citizenship in US–Mexico Border Policing', in Pauline Gardiner Barber and Winnie Lem (eds), *Migration in the 21st Century: Political Economy and Ethnography*. New York: Routledge, pp. 153–74.

———. 2012b. 'Capitalism and US Policy at the Mexican Border', *Dialectical Anthropology* 36(3): 263–77.

———. 2014. '"Illegality" and the U.S.–Mexico Border: How It Is Produced and Resisted', in Cecilia Menjívar and Daniel Kanstroom (eds), *Constructing Illegality in America: Immigrant Experiences, Critiques, and Responses*. New York: Cambridge University Press, pp. 111–35.

Hornborg, Alf. 2001. *The Power of the Machine: Global Inequalities of Economy, Technology, and Environment*. Walnut Creek, CA: AltaMira Press.

Horton, Sarah. 2015. 'Identity Loan: The Moral Economy of Migrant Document Exchange in California's Central Valley', *American Ethnologist* 42(1): 55–67.

Massey, Douglas S., Rafael Alarcon, Jorge Durand and Humberto González. 1990. *Return to Aztlán: The Social Process of International Migration from Western Mexico*. Berkeley: University of California Press.

Massey, Douglas S., Jorge Durand and Nolan J. Malone. 2002. *Beyond Smoke and Mirrors: Mexican Immigration in an Era of Economic Integration*. New York: Russell Sage Foundation.

Mintz, Sidney W. 1985. *Sweetness and Power: The Place of Sugar in Modern History*. New York: Viking.

Mitchell, Don. 2012. *They Saved the Crops: Labor, Landscape, and the Struggle over Industrial Farming in Bracero-Era California*. Athens: University of Georgia Press.

Nevins, Joseph. 2002. *Operation Gatekeeper: The Rise of the 'Illegal Alien' and the Making of the U.S.–Mexico Boundary*. New York: Routledge.

Ngai, Mae M. 2004. *Impossible Subjects: Illegal Aliens and the Making of Modern America*. Princeton, NJ: Princeton University Press.

Palerm, Juan-Vicente, and José Ignacio Urquiola. 1993. 'A Binational System of Agricultural Production: The Case of the Mexican Bajío and California', in Daniel G. Aldrich Jr and Lorenzo Meyer (eds), *Mexico and the United States: Neighbors in Crisis*. San Bernardino, CA: The Borgo Press, pp. 311–67.

Sharma, Nandita Rani. 2006. *Home Economics: Nationalism and the Making of 'Migrant Workers' in Canada*. Toronto: University of Toronto Press.

Spener, David. 2009. *Clandestine Crossings: Migrants and Coyotes on the Texas–Mexico Border*. Ithaca, NY: Cornell University Press.

USCBP (United States Customs and Border Protection). 2014. 'CBP Border Security Report Fiscal Year 2014'. Washington, DC: United States Customs and Border Protection. www.cbp.gov/sites/default/files/

documents/FINAL%20Draft%20CBP%20FY14%20Report_20141218.
pdf (accessed 17 February 2016).

USCIS (United States Citizenship and Immigration Services). n.d.a.
Consideration of Deferred Action for Childhood Arrivals (DACA).
Washington, DC: United States Citizenship and Immigration Services.
https://www.uscis.gov/humanitarian/consideration-deferred-action-
childhood-arrivals-daca (accessed 17 February 2016).

——— n.d.b. 'Temporary Protected Status'. Washington, DC: United
States Citizenship and Immigration Services. https://www.uscis.gov/
humanitarian/temporary-protected-status (accessed 17 February 2016).

United States Department of State. 2015. 'Worldwide H1B, H2A, and
H2B Visa Issuances Fiscal Years 2009–2014'. Washington, DC: United
States Department of State. http://travel.state.gov/content/dam/visas/
Statistics/Graphs/H%20VisasWorldwide.pdf (accessed 17 February
2016).

Vélez-Ibañez, Carlos G. 1996. *Border Visions: Mexican Cultures of the
Southwest United States*. Tucson: University of Arizona Press.

Warren, Robert, and Donald Kerwin. 2015. 'Beyond DAPA and DACA:
Revisiting Legislative Reform in Light of Long-Term Trends in
Unauthorized Immigration to the United States'. *Journal of Migration
and Human Security* 3(1): 80–108.

Zlolniski, Christian. 2003. 'Labor Control and Resistance of Mexican
Immigrant Janitors in Silicon Valley', *Human Organization* 62(1):
39–49.

Conclusion

All That Is Normal Melts into Air
Rethinking Neoliberal Rules and Deviance

Steven Sampson

Social scientists have generally occupied themselves with one of two domains of study: that which is routine and that which is extraordinary. Those who study the routine focus on everyday life in institutions, organizations, small groups or interpersonal relations, hoping to discover how this daily life is reproduced. Those who study the extraordinary focus on the deviant, the fantastic or the violent, on the crises or social movements that punctuate social life. Some of these deviant phenomena, the most horrific, are studied to discover how to prevent them from happening again, while others, such as laudable social movements or coping practices, are studied to discover how they could be supported or strengthened.

In our research interests, most of us oscillate between these two domains. We map out the routine and rule-based behaviour in order to understand rule violation and the deviant. In doing so, regrettably, we often reproduce an artificial distinction between these two kinds of phenomena.

The chapters in this volume seek to break out of the trap of the separation of the routine and the deviant. They problematize deviance in such a way that we are compelled to re-evaluate what it means to be normal, legal and conventional, what 'the rules' really are. In various ways, across different ethnographic and institutional fields, the chapters demonstrate how the institutional and the extraordinary, the routine and the deviant, the legal and the illegal may dissolve into each other in the context of neoliberalism. The underlying argument of these chapters is that something special is happening in the relationship between the institutions of economics, politics and law on the one hand, and people's actual practices on the other, and that this dissolution of the normal and the deviant is a noteworthy feature of the neoliberal era.

What is it about neoliberalism that has led to the near dissolution of the distinction between what is normal and legal and what is deviant and even wrongful? How is the reconstitution of normality and deviance manifested? What are its consequences for societal development and for a possible anthropology of neoliberalism? Should we approach neoliberalism as a distinct set of practices that may appear and then disappear, or as a historical epoch of capitalism? It is these kinds of questions that the authors approach in their various ways.

While the theme of this volume is the relation between neoliberalism and deviance, an overriding message in these chapters is that we need to rethink not just deviance, but normality. To turn a phrase, 'Deviance is the new normal'. We need to rethink the relationship between normality and deviance in the same way that scholars rethink relationships between structure and agency, emergence and reproduction, or social integration and social conflict. The economic processes described in this book, analysed under the rubrics of neoliberalism and deviance, offer us an opportunity to rethink the normal and to reassess what the deviant is, how it emerges and what being deviant means to various actors in specific contexts. The examination of the intermingling of normality and deviance in practices as diverse as the market clientelism of pharmaceutical researchers, bribery in Romanian hospitals, taxation in the EU, key performance indicators in public management, migration regimes and marijuana growing compels us to search out an alternative framework for understanding what are rules, whether they are formal and written or the informal rules of everyday life, and what is deviant. The dichotomy of the rule-bound versus the deviant, which exists in everyday thought and among social scientists, seems to be getting in our way. It is just too simplistic.

The inadequacies of the rules–deviance dichotomy can be illustrated by two examples from contemporary economic life: the Panama Papers and the Wells Fargo Bank scandal. The Panama Papers are eleven million documents from a law firm specializing in helping firms and individuals to hide their assets, typically to avoid creditors or taxes. The scale of this activity is much bigger than we thought. Luke Harding, who has studied the Panama Papers, concludes: 'Previously, we thought that the offshore world was a shadowy, but minor, part of our economic system. What we learned from the Panama Papers is that it *is* the economic system' (Rusbridger 2016: 22). Wells Fargo Bank was caught up in a major scandal in September 2016, when it was revealed that over a five-year period the bank had 5,300 employees setting up 1.5 million bogus accounts and an additional half a million hidden credit cards and then billing customers for fees. In one case, a homeless woman was set up with six checking (UK: 'current') and savings accounts (Reckard 2013). Wells Fargo was fined a total of $185 million by the US Consumer Financial Protection Bureau, and Wells Fargo executives were brought before Congressional committees to explain themselves. Wells Fargo's CEO insisted that the problem was caused by overzealous employees who 'misinterpreted' the bank's 'product sales goals' (CNBC 2016). However, several Wells Fargo employees insist that they reported these irregularities to their managers or to the company hotline and ended up being fired. Soon after the scandal broke, the head of Wells Fargo's retail banking department suddenly retired with a $125 million severance package, as did the CEO, with stock plus $24 million (Chappell 2016; Egan 2016a, 2016b; Gandel 2016; Sorkin 2016).

In both the Panama Papers and the Wells Fargo scandals, there is a hazy line between what the implicated actors (on all sides) see as expected or acceptable and what they see as deviant or wrong. In fact, the deviance seems to be regarded as business as usual. As most analysts of the Panama Papers have explained, setting up off-shore accounts is legal, even if it may be ethically questionable; the problem comes in reporting those accounts to the relevant authorities. In the Wells Fargo case, the size of the fine was small in relation to the bank's assets and income. In the company's view, they did not swindle millions of people when they used their social security numbers to set up accounts without letting them know. For Wells Fargo's CEO, it was just a case of overzealous staff misinterpreting the bank's sales incentives. Yet the 'bad apples' defence is belied by the numbers: two million false accounts set up over a five-year period by 5,300 staff.

With examples like these and the cases described in this volume, we need to rethink the nature of economic deviance in our neoliberal era. How do people deviate from the rules? How do they justify crime? How do they articulate what they are doing as something that is not deviance at all, but rather is expected behaviour? More generally, we need to ask: What are rules anyway? What are rules when the people enforcing them often do not seem to care who breaks them, when the people who violate them actually helped to write them through lobbying or state capture, when rules redefine deviance as incentives that are misinterpreted or, as Daniel Seabra Lopes describes in his chapter, as 'creative innovations' (at least when they work)?

The chapters in this volume address these questions. Here I will try to draw together some common themes, expanding on James Carrier's Introduction, and also try to draw out some implications regarding how we should define and investigate concepts such as neoliberalism, rules, regulation, normality and deviance. The reader should be aware that as I write these lines, the new US president, with a Cabinet from the highest echelons of American business, is also rewriting a few rules about how government should operate and how the American economy should work. He has already relaxed a host of regulations aimed at business, he has reduced taxes especially for corporations, he is in the process of revoking treaty agreements, watering down banking regulations and erecting tariff and immigration walls.

Neoliberalism generally connotes the increasing encroachment of market rationality into spheres of social life formerly governed by non-market logics. A common academic rendering of neoliberalism contains a package of ideas and practices: distrust of state regulation, confidence in the efficiency of markets, outsourcing and privatization of public services, and rational cost–benefit calculations of inputs and outputs using performance measures, indicators and transparency. Associated with this is a denigration of practices that cannot be put into this kind of market-calculation framework. Such practices are viewed benignly as 'traditional' or more critically as 'a brake on progress' or even as a political threat.

This package of ideas and practices, generally assumed to have flowered first under President Reagan in the United States and Prime Minister Thatcher in the United Kingdom, has been exported to the rest of the world through aid programmes, trade agreements and transnational agreements that bring together state, multilateral and non-state actors such as NGOs, as well as through the growth of international credit and financialization. The result is a neoliberal global regime, such that what is called globalization is sometimes seen as synonymous with neoliberal expansion.

Neoliberalism as Disembedding

The impact of the spread of neoliberal ideas and practices has been described using many terms, the most common being disembedding

(Polanyi 1944) and the successor to Marx's concept of primitive accumulation, dispossession (Harvey 2004). Disembedding entails the undercutting of the social by market rationality or, to use Zygmunt Bauman's metaphor, liquidity in various forms (Bauman 1998, 2000). From a modernist and capitalist perspective, adopted by many economists, disembedding is desirable, in so far as it is a liberation from the traditional and its attendant hierarchical obligations that hinder economic growth.

Most social scientists, especially if they are not economists and have been influenced by the work of Marx and Polanyi, see disembedding more negatively. It is the loss of the commons, and more generally the loss of social resources that can help people and communities to reproduce themselves and their relationships, especially in times of crisis. Disembedding is thus associated with the polemical description of the bourgeois project of capitalist accumulation in the *Manifesto* as 'all that is solid melts into air' (Marx and Engels 1848: Chap. 1). In this sense, disembedding is viewed as undesirable, destructive of the social life presumed to characterize pre-capitalist societies, in which economic activity is somehow governed by, or at least contained within, social relations. Pre- and non-capitalist societies are presumed to be more integrated than the disembedded because deviance, and especially economic deviance, is constrained by a moral economy (Thompson 1971; Scott 1976). From such a perspective, disembedding encourages, or even creates, the deviance that is described and problematized by the chapters in this volume. Deviance in this sense can be a means of restoring the moral economy that has been undermined by disembedding.

Accordingly, most social scientists, including the contributors to this volume, have focused on the negative consequences of disembedding for society as a whole, and especially for vulnerable groups such as minorities, migrants, rural villagers and disenfranchised citizens. The anthropological project is to describe how people who are affected by disembedding (or the imminent threat of it) find ways to cope with, transform or resist it. From this perspective, disembedding has caused people to become increasingly vulnerable, while their efforts to reassert the value of the social realm, their everyday practice, is defined as deviance by the neoliberal powers that be.

An Anthropology of Neoliberalism

In describing disembedding, anthropologists have focused on neoliberalism as an active, driving force and explanatory concept, in much the same way as we have used globalization, underdevelopment and resistance. Such broad concepts, with their many connotations of agency, have their benefits: neoliberalism helps us to elucidate how market ideology, market relations and market logic penetrate into realms of social life previously shielded from those things – realms such as kinship obligations, communal solidarity, sharing of resources, social trust and welfare services.

As several of the papers in this volume point out, neoliberal penetration tends to bring with it certain technologies, such as market calculation, objectification, standardization and statistical measurement schemes. While these technologies predate the neoliberal era, they have increasingly come to dominate how we work, how we deal with each other and even who we are. In our own world of academia, for example, our scholarly performance is now measured in terms of articles published, number of downloads and impact factor; our value to the university in terms of the amount of external grant money procured; and our teaching in terms of student satisfaction with how we 'provide content' (e.g. Carrier 2016: Chap. 1). These technologies and statistical indicators, as several of the chapters attest, are contested during regulatory conflicts between public authorities and various interested parties subject to regulation or measurement; even marijuana confiscations, as Michael Polson points out in his chapter, can be seen as part of a give and take between authorities and growers. Hence, it is not just financial actors who are deploying neoliberal technologies; states are doing so as well. Neoliberalism is thus both market regulation and state bureaucracy, the two being mirror images of each other (Graeber 2015).

The very seductiveness of neoliberalism as an explanatory device, the connotation that it only destroys and disrupts, means that it is likely to be overused and misused. It is not enough to view it as some kind of encroachment of market logic on the social sphere, as if market logic were an independent, ahistorical actor. A more nuanced approach is needed. Here we might distinguish three aspects of neoliberalism: as an ideological construct about free choice in human activity; as a historical era, which like any historical era will draw to a close and be replaced by something else; and as a set of specific market-related practices that, as Josiah Heyman observes for migrant

Mexican labour, could have existed before the rise of present-day neoliberalism (in effect, neoliberal tools prior to the neoliberal era). These different approaches to neoliberalism are likely to generate different research questions, different views of its force and durability, and different ways in which we view deviance.

The chapters in this volume generally approach neoliberalism in terms of the third aspect mentioned above, as practice. They describe what the neoliberal toolbox contains and how it works. In showing who does what to whom with what tool, the chapters also reveal the kinds of deviant activities that can emerge as people engage with neoliberal practices. The chapters thus investigate the nature of rules and rule breaking under neoliberal conditions. In so far as deviance is related to actors' expectations (as described by James Carrier in his Introduction), the chapters tell us how neoliberal conditions create, reinforce and at times undermine actors' expectations about what is ordinary and what is deviant.

Let us imagine a typical neoliberal moment in which market rationality, 'market logic' in the current jargon, encroaches on a social sphere formerly shielded from that logic, such as a community of peasant households with common lands and shared social obligations. We know that people in such a community can attempt to reassert their control over market encroachment with practices like barter and smuggling, migration and other non-violent weapons of the weak, or in more violent ways, like banditry, riot and rebellion. The research task, therefore, is to do more than point to instances of resistance. The chapters in this book do just that, detailing the many strategies and tactics that people and communities use when faced with neoliberal encroachment into their lives.

One example of such resistance is that of the Romanians, who, as Sabina Stan describes, give bribes to doctors in order to assert their claims to healthcare, claims that have been undermined by privatization. Other examples are the Mexican and Central American migrants who for decades have been crossing the southern US border seeking work, or the California marijuana growers who skirt drug laws to produce and sell a popular drug. As several chapters in this volume point out, whether these practices are in fact illegal or even deviant is not the sole issue, not even for law enforcement officials. For those pursuing these informal strategies, avoiding police is a practical necessity, but the need to obtain medical treatment in Romania or to make enough to live on by finding a job or selling marijuana in California, takes priority. Calling such practices deviant activities or 'reactions to neoliberalism' underplays the complexity of the process, and the chapters in this volume bring out just this complexity. Neoliberalism can be resisted, subverted or even temporarily embraced and manipulated. The operating term here might be that of 'engagement': actors 'engage' with neoliberalism.

One additional value of these chapters is that they show what it is like not only for those who have been disembedded or disenfranchised by neoliberalism (anthropology's 'suffering subjects'), but also for those able to deploy the neoliberal toolkit to their own advantage, those on the winning side. Over a century ago, primitive accumulation gave us a triumphant bourgeoisie. Today, neoliberal disembedding benefits global corporations, agricultural employers, tax evaders and their financial advisors. These beneficiaries of disembedding can renegotiate or evade regulations, as they can exploit employees or state subsidies for their own benefit. In doing so, they may re-embed the economic activities of others so as to lock them into a distinctly subordinate position. This is re-embedding with a vengeance. Josiah Heyman and Kathy Powell, for example, point out how migrants who find jobs in the US economy are nevertheless unable to assert their rights to receive a legal wage or ensure proper working conditions.

Those neoliberal winners who are able to carry out the disembedding must also look over their shoulders at social movements or at aggressive social-democratic state regulatory bodies. The winners therefore deploy their own technologies to stay ahead of the regulators, redefining what is meant by adequate performance, efficiency, quality, innovation, legality and ethics, even something as concrete as 'fair taxation'. This helps to account for the fetishization of statistics and measurement, as pointed out by Kalman Applbaum for pharmaceuticals, by Thomas Cantens for taxation, by Emil Røyrvik for performance indicators and by Daniel Seabra Lopes for regulatory compromise.

With the interaction between the winners and losers in the disembedding struggle, we observe a blurring of lines between what is acceptable and what is deviant, what is moral and what is immoral, what is legal and what is illegal. In so far as regulators cannot readily enforce rules and regulations, what we once understood as enforcement turns into some kind of negotiation. Deviance, or evidence of deviance, becomes not so much a grey zone somewhere between the routine, the unusual and the grossly illegitimate; it becomes instead a matter of interpretation, or simply dissolves altogether. With deviance as normal, the concept of normal melts into air.

Rethinking Regulation

The contributors to this volume describe examples of the evisceration or perversion of government regulations by the activities of powerful economic actors. Regulation is the most visible way in which economic actors are embedded in society, others being voluntary standards, corporate ethics (Sampson 2016) and compliance programmes. It follows that when the contributors describe that evisceration and perversion, they describe a form of disembedding that combines both positive and negative aspects, both liberation from norms and dispossession from resources. With this variation in reactions comes the necessary variation in what constitutes deviance.

The disembedding process goes beyond a simple tug of war between private actors seeking to maximize profits and state regulators. As mentioned in the Introduction, the neoliberal project includes private actors who rewrite the rules, firms or sectors that capture the state or some of its parts by ensuring that special laws are enacted or bloated contracts concluded, or where these actors escape social responsibility by imposing social or environmental costs on the state (Hellman et al. 2000; Wedel 2003; Fazekas and Tóth 2014). Hence, it is not just disembedding or the shrinking state but also state capture that characterizes the neoliberal era. These processes reveal how neoliberalization is a dynamic combination of the evasion or subversion of rules by economic actors, and regulatory evisceration and state capture through lobbying, patronage and corruption. This complex neoliberalization is reflected in Polson's observation that modern forms of deviance require a state to do some of the dirty work, as well as in the fact that the watering down of some federal regulations under the Trump administration is accompanied by the strengthening of other organs of control and surveillance. As most social scientists have now realized, neoliberalism does not mean the disappearance or even the significant reduction of the state. Rather, the state acts as a guarantor of certain neoliberal projects while it attempts to repress those social actors or groups who might contest further neoliberalization; hence the Romanians described in Stan's chapter who object to further privatization of healthcare are described by the state as corrupt.

These reflections on the nature of regulation raise the question of rules and deviance, of what ought to be and what is. This question has long interested anthropologists: recall the discussion in the 1950s about preferential and prescriptive marriage rules. People like Keith

Hart (1973, 2012) have been instrumental in helping us to understand the informal underside of developing economies. Stuart Henry (1987), Louis Ferman, Stuart Henry and Michele Hoyman (1987), Dick Hobbs (1989) and Gerald Mars (1982), studying the informal economy in the United Kingdom, and Alina Ledeneva (1998, 2001) doing the same in socialist and post-socialist Russia, have helped us to understand formal and informal relationships, where informality can range from everyday social survival to organized crime (see also Morris and Polese 2014).

These scholars point out what any interested ethnographer will discover, and what anyone working in any kind of organization knows: social groups operate with a gap between rules and actual practices. There are ideas, even norms, about how rules should be bent, ignored or broken. This gap between rules and practices is not necessarily harmful to organized social life; such gaps may help organizations to function more smoothly. This is indicated by the fact that a standard way for workers to express grievances (short of going on strike) is the work-to-rule – doing what the rules specify, which invariably causes the organization to stop working.

It seems, however, that the rise of neoliberalism has meant a change in how actors understand what it means to follow rules and to deviate from them. This is not simply because neoliberal practices lead to a greater propensity or willingness to bend or ignore the rules. Rather, it is also because neoliberalization involves a new way of writing and rewriting rules. We watch this happening in Stan's chapter on the Romanian health sector, where people's survival strategy of paying bribes to get what they in fact deserve from the healthcare system is now condemned by the regime as a corrupt practice that only further privatization can eliminate. We also see it in Lopes's chapter on EU financial regulation, where regulators seem helpless against innovative actors, and in Røyrvik's description of key performance indicators, where statistics and measures do not simply index practices but actually reformulate rules, however informal they may be. We seem to have a situation in which it is deviance that sets the rules rather than rules marking out what is deviant. If anything, the rules seem to be an artefact of deviance.

I noted earlier that state bodies may be captured by powerful economic actors. One should not assume, however, that those actors always manage to hold the state hostage to their projects. State regulatory bodies have their own resources and agendas as well, as do the politicians who run them. As several of the contributors to this volume point out, state bodies may formulate rules that compel some actors to break them if they are to realize their goals, whether they are Central American migrants to the United States, or Romanian patients. In this sense, regulation induces illegality. In other cases, rules are so vague or cumbersome that they are difficult to enforce, which effectively gives people carte blanche to pursue their interests as they see fit, as is apparent in Heyman's description of labour regimes for migrants, Cantens's analysis of taxation systems and Polson's description of marijuana growers. Finally, state authorities can set up rules that they enforce only selectively, as shown in the chapters on migration control and drug enforcement, and as described in the Introduction. In these areas, we could speak of symbolic enforcement, what is often called 'sending a signal'.

What Is Normal?

The chapters in this volume consider the idea that neoliberalism has led to new forms of deviance. Since deviance can only be understood in the context of legal and administrative rules, moral precepts and actors' expectations, any assessment of what constitutes deviance under neoliberalism entails an assessment of normality. One is tempted to say that neoliberalism has altered our concepts of normality to the point that anything goes, though this would be an exaggeration. Nevertheless, the chapters of this book, in observing the machinery of neoliberalism in EU regulation, in financial calculation, in tax collection and in performance indicators, reveal how the very rules themselves are constantly rewritten or even dissolve altogether. In the name of transparency and regulation, the rules have become so complex that many of those actors to which these rules are directed cannot understand them, while other actors can manipulate them. In practice, we find rules that have become so cumbersome as to be unenforceable, partly because people's expectations of deviance have become so high.

Neoliberalism is creating new grey zones by dissolving the very distinction between normative rules, deviant practices and people's expectations of what is or is not deviant. Cantens describes the consequences of this dissolution when he discusses the loss of faith in the ability of tax authorities to compute tax liability. For Lopes, it is a cat-and-mouse game of financial actors masking their deviance under the slogan of innovation, creative financial devices with which regulators are unable to keep up. Røyrvik describes the cult of amoral routinization and calculability as a kind of performance of transparency. Applbaum describes the dissolution of scientific ethics as medical researchers and drug companies shape testing to enhance a drug's market potential. In Romania, Stan describes how people's effort to obtain scarce services by paying doctors a bit extra now becomes deviant, while the neoliberal privatization of the system, which marginalizes even more citizens, becomes the norm. In the same way, Heyman and Powell point out how migration across the Mexican border to the United States is part of a regime that creates its own illegality. In all these cases, the line between the legal or normal and the deviant dissolves. Deviance is expected. Deviance is the norm.

I said that anthropology has always been good at investigating the grey zones between rules and practice. These chapters reveal the complexity of those zones, but what they describe suggests that the idea of the grey zone itself needs rethinking. This is because it assumes some kind of black and white on either side of the zone. What if the clearly rule-bound and the clearly deviant are just not there anymore? What if they are irrelevant? In significant sectors of economic and social life, neoliberal practices may have led us to this point, where the white–grey–black continuum itself melts into air.

Take Cantens's description of taxation, where the negotiation of taxes replaces the legality or morality of collecting them. The wealthy and their financial advisors can complicate the authorities' task of calculating their taxes, and the more difficult it is to calculate taxes the more leeway the wealthy have to negotiate how much of their income they elect to pay. For Heyman and Powell, neoliberal-ism operates in two ways: migrants break immigration laws in order to cope with the effects of uneven development, while employers evade labour regulations in order to employ these workers. The result of this dual deviance, argues Heyman, is that neoliberalism, despite its rhetoric, embeds undocumented migrants in unfree labour regimes that are far from the free-market liberal ideal. For Røyrvik, techniques of measurement and calculation produce what would otherwise be called deviance, so that here again we have a merging of the routine and the deviant. This merging is also visible in Romania: Stan describes how the government asserts that further privatization of healthcare will prevent the bribes, but these measures only further disenfranchise citizens.

What makes a rule a rule? Is it in its formulation, its intent or its enforcement? For Lopes and Cantens, we end up with rules that are opaque or unenforceable, rules that can be endlessly renegotiated or manipulated so that a dubious activity is turned into an innovation. Innovation becomes a deviance that is sanctioned because it is successful. For Heyman and Powell, the rules to control migration create the dual deviance of migrants' illegal movement and employers' illegal employment of migrants. If the power differential were not so great, we might even term this collusion. In other chapters, the rules are a tool for state capture by the winners in the disembedding struggle. And for Polson, marijuana production, drug enforcement and its partial legalization create such a confusing set of rules themselves that deviance is pretty much inevitable.

Conclusion: Deviance as the New Normal

Let me conclude by reiterating the main lessons learned from this volume. Of particular importance are the relations between rules and deviance, the dynamic nature of neoliberalization and the understudied field of regulation.

First, our effort to rethink the concept of deviance should begin with a rethinking of what is normal, legal and routine: we need to rethink the concept of rules. Further insight and understanding of normalization, legalization and routinization are needed in order to understand the genesis and reproduction of the deviant, the wrong and the criminal. The conditions and practices of neoliberalism lead to new, distinct kinds of normalization, legalization and routinization, most notably in the use of techniques of measurement and objectification. More generally, we can identify a new discursive hegemony about what is human nature, what is rational, what is freedom-to and freedom-from. In addition, we find new definitions and expectations of deviance. Studying normalization under neoliberalism helps us to see how definitions of the normal and the deviant, and attacks on the deviant, take hold. We need a better understanding of what rules are about and how we should approach them. This is not a simple task, for rules can be invoked as guidelines for practice, as justifications of practice and performative scripts, as well as weapons for determining who and what is deviant, just as deviance can suddenly bring us to question rules. We need an anthropology of rules.

Second, as Carrier noted in his Introduction to this volume, we need to rethink how we invoke neoliberalism: as an explanatory device, as a scientific concept, as a set of practices or as a historical era. Within academia, neoliberalism tends to be an epithet. Raising the 'neoliberalism' red flag may make us feel good, but it is a poor tool for understanding how people and institutions act in changing situations. For some, neoliberalism is a historical era that begins with

Thatcher and Reagan. For others it is a set of practices and discourses about market efficiency, restricting of social obligations, reducing the public sector, and subordinating social solidarity to means–ends rationality. These practices and discourses come in waves, and like waves they inundate and then recede, leaving people to pick up the now-disembedded pieces. Picking up those pieces may entail some sort of re-embedding. Some of the social movements we have seen in the last decade are clearly aimed at re-embedding, by freeing communities or countries from the strictures of market logic through, for example, debt cancellation movements, and then by instituting a new kind of sociality. These movements, both their failures and successes, are certainly worthy of study, since they portend new forms of the normal and the deviant.

Third, our preoccupation with financial actors and their deviance, understandable as it is, has led us to overlook the nature of regulation. This is regrettable, since several of these chapters describe regulatory failure and inefficiency, as well as the subversion of regulation by the powerful. We need, therefore, a research agenda that includes an anthropology of regulation. I do not mean just governance. I mean a fuller investigation of regulatory instruments and how they are constructed and deployed. Some anthropologists of policy have begun to do this, and in their descriptions of taxation, performance indicators, drug policies and marijuana prohibitions, several of the chapters in this volume illustrate the need to understand the nature of this thing called 'regulation', and the regulatory as a sphere of activity.

By regulation, we need to understand not just law and its violation, not just the diffusion of ethical norms, industry standards, governance and soft law, and not just the tug of war between state actors and private firms, but also the way in which regulatory regimes create the deviant. There are echoes of Foucault here, obviously, but we need more reflection on why regulation, as these chapters show, can be as slippery a concept as deviance. Neoliberal regimes certainly have regulations, sometimes as weapons of disembedding, but these same regimes are also accused of having needless regulations and bureaucracy that presumably inhibit entrepreneurial freedom and public sector efficiency. Regulatory regimes are thus rather slippery, and it is precisely their slippery character that makes it imperative to focus on regulation as an object of study.

Fourth, there is a long tradition in social science that certain key concepts are criticized, rejected and then brought back in new form. In our own field, we have seen what has happened with concepts such as identity, kinship and gender, which have become cast in more dynamic terms, with identity replaced by identification, kinship by kinning, gender by gendering and, within my own field of NGO studies, we have terms like 'ngo-ing' and 'transparenting'. What if we were to apply this technique to the concepts of neoliberalism and deviance? In this book, we have seen innumerable examples of what may clumsily be called 'neoliberalization' and 'deviantization'. We have also seen initiatives to create, reproduce and reassemble various practices and give them new content and new ideological valences, what we might call a kind of re-embedding. The task is to reassess our concepts of neoliberalism and economic deviance by looking at everyday practices, retaining the dynamism that is lost when we think instead in terms of stable concepts. Rather than viewing them as entities or states of being, we could view them as processes with degrees of intensity, as vectors. In this way, we can begin to understand how neoliberal regimes and neoliberal deviance might fit together.

As I write this, we see an American administration attempting to dismantle regulations on commerce and to allow more energy exploitation on formerly protected lands. It is now attempting to redefine, exclude or deport various suspect (deviant) groups that it classifies as terrorist threats, social undesirables or illegal aliens. The techniques used range from intensified scrutiny of personal biographies ('extreme vetting') to traffic stops and surprise raids on your local convenience store. We are watching a new phase of neoliberalization, and with it a redefining of the relationship between rules and deviance.

New forms of socio-economic life will invariably create new practices, some of which will be labelled deviant while others will lead to new understandings of what is normal, legal and conventional. New forms of deviance will, strangely enough, generate new rules. The field for an anthropology of the neoliberal, of disembedding, of rules, of regulation, is wide open. Let's get to work.

Steven Sampson is emeritus professor of social anthropology at Lund University. He has done research on bureaucracy and planning in socialist Romania, democracy export and NGOs in post-socialism, the global anti-corruption industry and business ethics. Recent publications include: 'The Anti-corruption Industry: From Movement to Institution' (*Global Crime*, 2010); 'The Anti-corruption Package' (*Ephemera*, 2015); 'The Audit Juggernaut' (*Social Anthropology*, 2015); and 'The "Right Way": Moral Capitalism and the Emergence of the Corporate Ethics and Compliance Officer' (*Journal of Business Anthropology*, 2016). As well, he is co-editor of *Cultures of Doing*

Good: Anthropology and NGOs (Alabama, 2017, ed. with Amanda Lashaw and Christian Vannier).

References

Bauman, Zygmunt. 1998. *Globalization: The Human Consequences.* Cambridge: Polity Press.
———. 2000. *Liquid Modernity*. Cambridge: Polity Press.
Carrier, James G. (ed.). 2016. *After the Crisis: Anthropological Thought, Neoliberalism and the Aftermath*. London: Routledge.
Chappell, Bill. 2016. 'Wells Fargo Unit's Leader Departs with $125M after Bank Incurs Record Fine'. National Public Radio (13 September). www.npr.org/sections/thetwo-way/2016/09/13/493791920/wells-fargo-units-leader-departs-with-125-million-after-group-incurs-record-fine (accessed 1 April 2017).
CNBC. 2016. 'Wells Fargo CEO John Stumpf Talks with CNBC's Cramer: "I'm accountable"' CNBC (18 September) (accessed 12 March 2018).
Egan, Matt. 2016a. '$124 Million Payday for Wells Fargo Exec Who Led Fake Accounts Unit', *CNN Money* (13 September). http://money.cnn.com/2016/09/12/investing/wells-fargo-fake-accounts-exec-payday/ (accessed 1 April 2017).
———. 2016b. 'I Called the Wells Fargo Ethics Line and was Fired', *CNN Money* (21 September). http://money.cnn.com/2016/09/21/investing/wells-fargo-fired-workers-retaliation-fake-accounts/ (accessed 1 April 2017).
Fazekas, M., and I.J. Tóth. 2014. 'From Corruption to State Capture: A New Analytical Framework with Empirical Applications from Hungary'. Working Paper CRCB-WP/2014:01. Budapest: Corruption Research Center. www.crcb.eu/?p=718 (accessed 1 April 2017).
Ferman, Louis A., Stuart Henry and Michele Hoyman. 1987. *The Informal Economy*. Newbury Park, CA: Sage Publications.
Gandel, Stephen. 2016. 'Wells Fargo Exec Who Headed Phony Accounts Unit Collected $125 Million', *Fortune* (12 September). http://fortune.com/2016/09/12/wells-fargo-cfpb-carrie-tolstedt/ (accessed 1 April 2017).
Graeber, David. 2015. *The Utopia of Rules: On Technology, Stupidity, and the Secret Joys of Bureaucracy*. Brooklyn, NY: Melville House Publishing.
Hart, Keith. 1973. 'Informal Income Opportunities and Urban Employment in Ghana', *Journal of Modern African Studies* 11(1): 61–89.
———. 2012. 'How the Informal Economy Took Over the World', *The Memory Bank*. http://thememorybank.co.uk/2012/10/17/the-informalization-of-the-world-economy/ (accessed 1 April 2017).

Harvey, David. 2004. 'The "New" Imperialism: Accumulation by Dispossession', *Socialist Register* 40: 63–87.

Hellman, Joel S., Geraint Jones, Daniel Kaufmann and Mark Schankerman. 2000. 'Measuring Governance, Corruption, and State Capture: How Firms and Bureaucrats Shape the Business Environment in Transition Economies'. Policy Research Working Papers 2312. Washington, DC: The World Bank.

Henry, Stuart. 1987. 'The Political Economy of Informal Economies', *The Annals of the American Academy of Political and Social Science* 493(1): 137–53.

Hobbs, Dick. 1989. *Doing the Business: Entrepreneurship, the Working Class, and Detectives in the East End of London*. Oxford: Oxford University Press.

Ledeneva, Alena V. 1998. *Russia's Economy of Favours:* Blat, *Networking and Informal Exchange*. Cambridge: Cambridge University Press.

———. 2001. *Unwritten Rules: How Russia Really Works*. London: Centre for European Reform.

Mars, Gerald. 1982. *Cheats at Work: An Anthropology of Workplace Crime*. London: Allen and Unwin.

Marx, Karl, and Friedrich Engels. 1848. *Manifesto of the Communist Party*. Numerous editions.

Morris, Jeremy, and Abel Polese. 2014. *The Informal Post-socialist Economy: Embedded Practices and Livelihoods*. London: Routledge.

Polanyi, Karl. 1944. *The Great Transformation: The Political and Economic Origins of Our Time*. Boston, MA: Beacon Press.

Reckard, E. Scott. 2013. 'Wells Fargo's Pressure-Cooker Sales Culture Comes at a Cost', *Los Angeles Times* (13 December). www.latimes.com/business/la-fi-wells-fargo-sale-pressure-20131222-story.html (accessed 16 March 2018).

Rusbridger, Alan. 2016. 'Panama: The Hidden Trillions', *The New York Review of Books* (27 October): 22–24.

Sampson, Steven. 2016. 'The "Right Way": Moral Capitalism and the Emergence of the Corporate Ethics and Compliance Officer', *Journal of Business Anthropology* 3 (special issue): 65–86.

Scott, James. 1976. *The Moral Economy of the Peasant: Rebellion and Subsistence in Southeast Asia*. New Haven, CT: Yale University Press.

Sorkin, Andrew Ross. 2016. 'Pervasive Sham Deals at Wells Fargo, and No One Noticed?' *The New York Times* (12 September).

Thompson, E.P. 1971. 'The Moral Economy of the English Crowd in the Eighteenth Century', *Past and Present* 50: 76–136.

Wedel, Janine R. 2003. 'Clans, Cliques and Captured States: Rethinking "Transition" in Central and Eastern Europe and the Former Soviet Union', *Journal of International Development* 15(4): 427–40.

Index

randomized controlled trials (RCTs).
    See clinical drug trials
rational market assumption, 23
Reed, Michael, 82
regulation
    inducing illegality, 249–50
    nature of, 253
regulatory arbitrage, 93, 94, 101, 103
revolving door, 15–16
right to live, 206–07
Risperdal, 45
    marketing plan, 49–50
    sales, 47–48
Romania
    austerity policy, 181–83
    peripheral neoliberal development,
        179–80
Romanian law on healthcare reform
    (2006), 180–181
Romanian law on healthcare reform
    (2011), 182
    linked to informal exchange, 183–84
    protest against, 187–188
Romanian law on social health
    insurance (1997), 178–79
Rousseau, Jean-Jacques, 69, 120, 125,
    127–28, 135n5
rule of law, 11, 12, 13
    vs legal practice, 144, 231–32
    See also legal procedure
rules
    concept of, 252
    vs practices, 249

San Francisco's Buyer's Cooperative,
    158–59
San Luis Potosí (site of migrant
    refuge), 202
Schneider, Jane, 172–73
Schneider, Peter, 172–73
Schroeder, Stephen (of Robert Wood
    Johnson Foundation), 58–59
scientific value vs marketing value,
    44–45, 47
Scottish Enlightenment, 17
second generation antipsychotic
    medicines. *See* SGA

secondary labour formation in US,
    233–34. *See also* Southern
    capitalism
Securities and Exchange Commission,
    12, 13
See Change Strategy LLC, 162–63
segmentation of taxpayers, 129–31
Senate Bill 420 (California). *See*
    Proposition 215
Seventeenth Amendment to the US
    Constitution, 14
SGA
    clinical trials of, 54
    sales in the US, 47
    side effects, 54, 56
Sherman Antitrust Act, 14
Shon, Steven (involved with Johnson
    & Johnson), 52, 57–58, 59, 60
Smith, Adam, 10, 69, 149–50
    individualism, 17–18
social realm, 9–10
    denial of, 19–20
sociality, 69
Southern capitalism, 220, 235
şpaga. *See* informal exchange in
    Romanian healthcare
The Spine Journal, 42–43
state capture. *See* neoliberalism: and
    state capture
Statoil (Norwegian oil and gas
    company), 71, 78–79
stereotype of Mexican as illegal
    migrant, 222–23
Struyk, Bill (of Johnson & Johnson),
    58
Suicide (book), 7–8
Sutton, Willie (bank robber), 6, 11
system. *See* economic realm: systemtic
    orientation
systemic risk, 106–07

tax authorities
    differing relationships with,
        128–30
    distinctive nature of, 127
    and high net worth individuals,
        129–30

EASA Series

Published in association with the European Association of Social Anthropologists (EASA)

Series Editor: Aleksandar Bošković, University of Belgrade

Social anthropology in Europe is growing, and the variety of work being done is expanding. This series is intended to present the best of the work produced by members of the EASA, both in monographs and in edited collections. The studies in this series describe societies, processes and institutions around the world, and are intended for both scholarly and student readership.